The Many and the One

The Many and the One

Creation as Participation in Augustine and Aquinas

Yonghua Ge

LEXINGTON BOOKS
Lanham • Boulder • New York • London

Published by Lexington Books
An imprint of The Rowman & Littlefield Publishing Group, Inc.
4501 Forbes Boulevard, Suite 200, Lanham, Maryland 20706
www.rowman.com

6 Tinworth Street, London SE11 5AL, United Kingdom

British Library Cataloguing in Publication Information Available

Library of Congress Cataloging-in-Publication Data Available

ISBN 9781793629104 (cloth) | ISBN 9781793629111 (epub)

♾™ The paper used in this publication meets the minimum requirements of American
National Standard for Information Sciences—Permanence of Paper for Printed Library
Materials, ANSI/NISO Z39.48-1992.

Contents

Table of Abbreviations

CG	*City of God against the Pagans*
DT	*De Trinitate*
RO	Radical Orthodoxy
RONT	*Radical Orthodoxy: A New Theology*
RORT	*Radical Orthodoxy and the Reformed Tradition: Creation, Covenant and Participation*
ST	*Summa theologiae*
SCG	*Summa contra Gentiles*
TST	*Theology and Social Theory*

Introduction

GOD AND THE WORLD IN MODERN DEBATES

How God relates to the world lies at the heart of modern philosophical and theological debates. The tremendous success of Newtonian physics in the seventeenth century gradually gave rise to a mechanistic worldview and deistic conceptions of God in Western thought. According to this view, apart from being the initial cause, God is not involved with the operation of the world but lets it run itself according to natural laws. God is distant and removed, if not completely absent, from the world.[1] At the other end of the spectrum, pantheistic concepts of God, as represented by the Dutch philosopher Baruch Spinoza (1632–1677), became another strong current in modern philosophy and theology. In contrast to deism, which sees God as entirely detached from the world, pantheism identifies God with nature and removes the distinction between the two.[2] Less extreme and yet related to this was occasionalism, as promoted by Nicolas Malebranche (1638–1715), who argued that all movements in the world, whether of nature or of the mind, are immediately caused by God. Nature is not God, but since natural operations are direct actions of God, the distinction between God and nature is not always clear. As such, Malebranche's occasionalism ran considerably close to Spinoza's pantheism, the only difference being that "Malebranche drew the conclusion that God was the only agent in the universe; Spinoza went further and claimed that he was the only substance."[3]

Debates on God's relation with the world became only intensified in more recent times. Major theological developments such as *nouvelle théologie*, the revival of Trinitarian theology, process theology, open theism, panentheism, Radical Orthodoxy, and postmodern continental theology all seek to reconstruct the God-and-the-world relation. For instance, in reaction to the sharp

1

division between the natural, which is seen as neutral and autonomous, and the supernatural (the realm of grace) in the scholastic Thomism of Vatican I, Henri de Lubac and others in the *nouvelle théologie* camp maintained that nature is never autonomous but already graced. By going back to patristic theology (*ressourcement*), these theologians sought to recover a much more intimate relationship between God and all created domains,[4] which, as we will see, is also the key concern of the Radical Orthodoxy Movement.[5] Dissatisfied with classical accounts of God's relationship with the world, theologians with a panentheistic bent also push for a radically close relation between God and the universe,[6] which they argue is not only more biblically grounded but more consistent with modern science.[7] Likewise, discontent with the transcendent, unchanging, and all-knowing God of classical theism, process and open theologians contend for a more immanent God that is intimately associated with the changing world.[8] Similar criticisms of the classical account of God's relation to the world are echoed in the modern renaissance of Trinitarian theology initiated by Karl Barth and Karl Rahner and championed by Robert Jenson, Colin Gunton, Jürgen Moltmann, and others.[9] This suspicion of classical theism is shared by postmodern anti-metaphysical thinkers who argue that classical theism is a type of onto-theology that reduces the biblical God, who freely engages with the world, into a frozen idol of being, to whom we cannot pray.[10]

In the midst of these debates, the most significant recent development in Christian theology is arguably the Radical Orthodoxy Movement,[11] which appropriates the Platonic idea of participation as a fundamental tool for critiquing modernity. For Radical Orthodox (RO) thinkers, at the heart of the malaise of modernity (i.e., pervasive secularism and the exclusion of Christianity from public life) is a deeply distorted view of God's relation to the world. A universal assumption of modernity is that, with the help of reason, life and society can function without recourse to God and as such the world has become increasingly autonomous and secularized. However, without being grounded in God, RO contends, "the world is so flattened that all we have is immanent" and "the immanent implodes upon itself," which ultimately results in nihilism.[12] To counter nihilism, we need a participatory ontology that refuses any territory independent of God and insists that all of creation depends on God. For RO, participatory ontology is *the* antidote to the crisis of modernity.

While RO turns participation into an influential theme in British academy, Hans Boersma is presenting a similar proposal in North America. Like RO, Boersma is deeply concerned about the excessive secularism and fragmentation of modernity and is convinced that participatory ontology is the only way out of the modern predicaments.[13] But unlike RO, who takes an offensive approach to domains outside Christian theology, Boersma is more interested in theological issues within the Christian circle. If RO is more philosophical,

Boersma is more theological. His diagnosis of the problem is also slightly different. While sharing RO's criticism of modernity, Boersma locates the root of the dilemma in the "worldliness" of modernity, in which "bodily goods, cultural endeavors and political achievements have become matters of ultimate concern."[14] Such exclusive focus on here and now is the result of moving away from the premodern participatory view of reality, which emphasizes that temporary goods have meaning only because they participate in and point toward the eternal goodness of God. Accordingly, Boersma's proposed solution to the modern crisis is to restore the participatory ontology in the Christian-Platonist synthesis.

What do RO and Boersma exactly mean by "participation"? Is it legitimate to use a Platonic concept as a foundation for Christian theology? With these questions in mind, we will look at RO and Boersma's theologies of participation more closely.

PARTICIPATION IN RADICAL ORTHODOXY AND BOERSMA

RO on Participation

In their manifesto, *Radical Orthodoxy: A New Theology*, leaders of the RO movement claim:

> The central theological framework of radical orthodoxy is 'participation' as developed by Plato and reworked by Christianity, because any alternative configuration perforce reserves a territory independent of God. The latter can lead only to nihilism (though in different guises).[15]

Although participation is foundational to the RO project, it is difficult to find a concentrated discussion on the meaning of "participation" as such in their writings.[16] Rather, RO theologians use the idea of participation primarily to counter the ontology that underlies secular modernity. So in order to understand what RO means by "participation," we must first examine what participatory ontology opposes. As RO thinkers understand it, the ontological framework of modern secularism is "grounded in the univocity of being that grants an autonomy to things such that it is supposed that the world can be understood in itself—that is, without reference to its transcendent origin, the Creator."[17] Thus for RO, the antithesis of participation is the ontology of immanence grounded in Duns Scotus's teaching. In place of the analogy of being, which maintains that God's being differs fundamentally from that of a creature, Scotus claims that "to be" can be predicated of God and of creatures in the same way. As Philip Blond puts it, "Duns Scotus, when considering the universal science of metaphysics, elevated being (*ens*) to a higher station over God, so that being could be distributed to both God and His creatures."[18] As such, being became an abstract, neutral category that is separable from God and the creation became flattened, devoid of theological depth. "Scotist univocity," Pickstock argues, "separates the creation from God" and produces autonomous realms independent of God, which is at the root of secularism.[19]

While RO's interpretation of Duns Scotus is contestable, from what they said about Scotus we can have a sense of the opposite of participatory ontology. As we have seen, their main complaint about Scotus's ontology is that it cuts off creatures' link to God and thereby turns the world into a purely immanent realm without a transcendent anchor. If participation is the direct opposite of this ontology, then central to the RO's concept of participation is the creation's *connectedness* to God and its *transcendent* dimension. So in RO's view, participatory ontology maintains that the world is anchored in God and can only be understood in the light of its ecstatic relation to its transcendent origin.[20] RO describes the concept of participation as a "suspension of the material," since "only transcendence, which 'suspends' things in the sense of interrupting them, 'suspends' them also in the other sense of upholding their relative worth over-against the void."[21] Although ontologies of immanence seek to protect the integrity of "language, knowledge, the body, aesthetic experience, political community, friendship, etc.," by separating them from God, such ontologies only end up in making "this worldliness dissolve."[22] Immanent materialism results in the destruction of matter.

> By contrast, the theological perspective of participation actually saves the appearances by exceeding them. . . . Hence, by appealing to an eternal source for bodies, art, language, sexual and political union, one is not ethereally taking leave of their density. On the contrary, one is insisting that behind this density resides an even greater density—beyond all contrasts of density and lightness (as beyond all contrasts of definition and limitlessness). This is to say that all there is *only* because it is more than it is.[23]

Hence, according to RO, by grounding the material world in its transcendent origin, not only does participatory ontology not compromise the integrity of matter; it in fact secures its goodness. Far from denigrating matter, participatory ontology at its root affirms the goodness of matter and creation.[24] Transcendence by no means destroys immanence; on the contrary, "only transcendence can make immanence as such."[25] As Milbank puts it, "The theological appeal alone sustains a non-reductive materialism and is the very reverse of any notion of idealism."[26] Thus, the central aspects of RO's concept of participation include the world's close connection with God,[27] transcendence, and the goodness of material creation.

Boersma on Participation

While RO has turned participation into one of the most discussed topics in European academic theology, Boersma has made it accessible to a wider evangelical audience in North America. Like RO, Boersma laments that modernity is an era in which theology is trivialized and marginalized, because earthly things instead of God have become the exclusive focus of modern life. Obsession with created goods, however, does not encourage people to respect the value of creation but fosters the "denigration and commodification of the created order."[28] Likewise, Boersma argues that when the world is cut off from God, it becomes fragmentary and drifts "on the flux of nihilistic waves."[29] The solution to the modern crisis, he contends, is to return to the sacramental or participatory ontology, which had been "the broad consensus of the Church Fathers and medieval theologians," or "the Great Tradition," as he calls it.[30] In comparison to RO theologians, Boersma offers more explicit explanations of the meaning of participation.

First, he explains the concept of mystery, arguing that until late Middle Ages "people looked at the world as a mystery":

Mystery referred to realities behind the appearances that one could observe by means of senses. That is to say, though our hands, eyes, ears, nose, and tongue are able to access reality, they cannot *fully* grasp this reality. They cannot *comprehend* it. The reason for this basic incomprehensibility of the universe was that the world was, as the poet Gerard Manley Hopkins famously put it, 'charged with the grandeur of God.' Even the most basic created realities that we observe as human beings carry an extra dimension, as it were.[31]

Next, Boersma explains the idea of sacrament. He suggests that "the *sign* of a mystery," while "present in the created order," transcends human comprehension. To illustrate, he compares a sacrament with a symbol. While both a sacrament and a symbol point to something else, there is a fundamental distinction between them: where the reality that a symbol points to is external, the reality that a sacrament points to is *present* in the sacrament. In other words, a sacrament captures both the transcendence and immanence of the reality it reflects. For this reason, the idea of sacrament or participation was extensively used by traditional theologians to describe the creation's relationship to God. "The reason for the mysterious character of the world—on the understanding of the Great Tradition, at least—is that it *participates* in some greater reality, from which it derives its being and its value."[32] For Boersma, sacramental ontology and participatory ontology are interchangeable.

According to Boersma, at the heart of participatory ontology is the emphasis that God is *really present* in the world and that the created order is not
autonomous but points toward God. Such was the consensus of the Great
Tradition, which maintained a balance between affirming the goodness of
creation and avoiding the idolatry of making created goods our ultimate
concern. This balance, however, was disrupted by historical developments
such as the univocity of being and nominalism in late medieval ages. Like
RO, Boersma blames Scotus for turning "being" into a neutral category that
both God and creatures share. The univocity of being not only undermined
the transcendence of God but turned the created order into an independent
realm from God. Likewise, nominalism, in rejecting universals, cut the link
between the natural and the supernatural. Together, these ideas paved the way
for modernity:

> The scissors of modernity—leading from analogy to univocity and from real-
> ism to nominalism—cut the sacramental tapestry into two and thus caused the
> decline and ultimately the near-collapse of the Platonist-Christian synthesis in
> the modern Western world. . . . The outcome was the desacralized culture of
> modernity, in which the natural order had been cut from its sacramental partici-
> pation in the life of God.[33]

Modernity is thus an era in which participatory ontology is abandoned.
But without participation, created things are disconnected from God, their
transcendent source of being and unity, and become groundless. "The only
faithful way forward," Boersma concludes, "—not only theologically but also
ecumenically—is by way of a sacramental ontology."[34]

Critiques of Participatory Ontology

While participation has become a hugely influential topic in contemporary
theology, it has attracted criticism on many grounds. Those who are allergic
to metaphysics are critical of the idea of participation in that it is unasham-
edly metaphysical.[35] Others complain that RO's concept of participation is
abstract, speculative, and fails to affirm the particularity of Christ's redemption.[36] The most substantial criticisms of RO's participatory ontology, however, are voiced by Reformed theologians whose key concern is that RO's
unwarranted reliance on Platonism contains the danger of undermining the
goodness and integrity of creation.

It is evident that RO's concept of participation has deep Platonic roots.
In his ground-breaking work, *Theology and Social Theory*, Milbank already
evoked the Platonic notion of participation to support his undertaking.[37] The
editors of *RONT* claim to articulate "a more participatory . . . even 'more

Platonic' Christianity."[38] According to Pickstock, it is not just the Platonic tradition, but the thought of Plato, that RO seeks to recover. She contends that Plato's concept of participation does not denigrate but affirms the goodness of materiality: "The strong positive view of *methexis* (participation) in *Phaedrus* frees [Plato] from the charge of otherworldliness and total withdrawal from physicality."[39] This interpretation challenges dualist readings of Plato. For "Plato portrays the transcendence of the good, its beyond presence-and-absence, as a kind of a *contagion*, for its plenitude spills over into immanence, in such a way that the good is revealed in the beauty of the physical particulars."[40] For Pickstock, Plato with his participatory ontology is a staunch defender of material creation and thereby a legitimate ally for the RO movement.

Such a positive reading of Plato, however, is called into question by Reformed thinkers. James K. A. Smith, for instance, suggests that Pickstock fails to account for aspects of the Platonic corpus that contradict her interpretation.[41] While he admits that there are some passages in *Phaedrus* that speak positively of matter, Smith points out that these accounts attribute at best "an *instrumental* goodness to the physical," since "the body and time are indeed ladders that are kicked away once the ascent has been completed." For instance, he suggests that in *Phaedo* the body is descried as an "evil" and "contamination" from which the soul seeks purification (*Phaedo* 66a-67b). As such, the body is a "prison" from which the soul is released upon death (*Phaedo* 79a-81d). Likewise, in *Republic*, the philosopher-kings, detached from their bodies as a practice for death, rule over the lower classes that are too attached to their bodies (*Republic* 414b-415c). Such disdain of the body is finally evident in Plato's teaching of the immortal, disembodied soul as the *telos* of humanity, which is diametrically opposed to the Christian doctrine of bodily resurrection. These accounts in Plato's corpus make it difficult to say that for Plato embodiment is a good thing.[42] For Reformed thinkers, therefore, RO's interpretation of Plato is historically questionable and their appropriation of Platonism a threat to the goodness of creation.

In addition, the Reformed thinkers are wary about the fact that participatory ontology tends to deny the *integrity* of creation. RO authors have spoken of creation as nothing-in-itself, which gives one an impression that creation has nothing intrinsic to itself. For instance, one of RO theologians, Graham Ward, asserts that the potential of things "is not contained within the material but 'in and around' it."[43] In response this statement, Smith writes:

> So there is a sense in which the being of things seems to be extrinsic to them rather than inhering in them. As a result, RO's participatory ontology can slide toward an occasionalism that requires the incessant activity of the Creator to uphold what would seem to a deficient creation—a tendency to emphasize the

creature's participation in the divine to the extent that it seems the divine does everything.[44]

While sympathetic to RO's rejection of the modern idea of an autonomous nature, Smith suggests that RO goes too far: emphases on creation's nothing-in-itself-ness and continuous dependence on God seem to imply that creatures have no inherent reality to themselves. To be fair to RO, Smith's complaint that RO's emphasis on creation's continuous dependence on God deprives its integrity is unwarranted.[45] The key issue, however, is whether creatures have their *own* being or reality. In this respect, Smith's criticism has certain validity. RO's claim that creation has no reality intrinsic to itself does seem to suggest that a creature is not *real* in itself. However, as we will see later in the book, Aquinas argues that a creature, while participating in God's goodness, must have its *own* goodness and that participation by no means abrogates its integrity. Unfortunately, RO's version of participation is not as subtle as Aquinas's. Relying too heavily on Platonism, their participatory ontology indeed gives one an impression that the intrinsic goodness and integrity of creation is not unequivocally affirmed. For this reason, while admitting that some kind of participatory ontology is needed, Smith is skeptical of RO's version:

> Milbank and Pickstock's Plato scholarship has not convinced me that we need Plato for such a project, nor even that Plato offers a properly incarnational ontology of participation. In this respect, then, I think the Reformed tradition's allergy to Platonism remains warranted. But for just that reason, we ought seriously to engage with Radical Orthodoxy in the articulation of an incarnational participatory ontology that unpacks the goodness of creation.[46]

To a certain extent, such reservation can also be applied to Boersma's participatory ontology. Like RO, Boersma, in his effort to recover a theocentric worldview, is extremely critical of the modern mindset that treats created goods as ultimate. Following Augustine, he contends that created goodness cannot be "enjoyed" for its own sake, but may only be "used":

> Accordingly, while we may *use* this good created order, only the triune God—Father, Son, and Holy Spirit—is to be *enjoyed*. . . . The temporal, created order may only be used with an eye to the eternal purpose of the enjoyment of God.[47]

While it is understandable that Boersma is anxious to rebuke the idolatrous nature of modern culture, his argument does give one an impression that creation has no intrinsic value or goodness of its own. The emphasis on creation's participation in God seems to suggest that we cannot gaze at the beauty and goodness of creation but must look *past* them to the source—divine beauty and goodness. Such a view of creation is evident when he asserts that "the recognition of the goodness of the created order is always predicated on its participatory status: that is, *its goodness is not its own.*"[48] To emphasize creatures' complete dependence on God, Boersma may have overacted and his rhetoric suggests that creatures have no intrinsic goodness of their own. To say that the creation does not have its own goodness does tend to downplay its integrity and substantiality.

The Proposal

As we can see, both RO and Boersma's accounts of participatory ontology are subject to the critique that they tend to deprive creation of its intrinsic goodness and integrity. This vulnerability, I propose, comes from the fact that their concepts of participation depend too heavily on Platonism and underestimate the foundational Christian teaching of *creatio ex nihilo*.[49] Participatory ontology in its Platonic origin indeed contains an inherent mistrust for materiality. To become a core concept in Christian theology, I argue, participatory ontology must be more substantially Christianized—especially, it must be more thoroughly transformed by the doctrine of creation. In this process of Christianization of participation, as we will see, Augustine and Aquinas played particularly crucial roles. Foundational to both theologians' thought is the doctrine of *creatio ex nihilo*, which enables them to profoundly transform the concept of participation in the light of this doctrine. In Augustine and Aquinas, as the book will argue, we find a more distinctively Christian concept of participation which avoids the weaknesses of RO and Boersma's accounts. An advance on RO and Boersma can therefore be made by retrieving the concepts of participation in Augustine and Aquinas. It is true that RO is indebted to both Augustine and Aquinas, but they have not sufficiently examined the exact meaning of participation in these two classical theologians, especially the significance of *creatio ex nihilo* in their participatory ontology. Likewise, although Boersma draws heavily from Augustine, yet unlike Augustine, whose notion of participation is intrinsically linked to *creatio ex nihilo*, Boersma pays little attention to the doctrine of creation when developing his participatory ontology. As a way forward from RO and Boersma, this book will examine how Augustine and Aquinas Christianized participatory ontology in the light of *creatio ex nihilo*.

At its origin, participation was a notion employed by Plato to explain the way in which many things can warrant the same name.[50] Participation was therefore essentially a theory to account for the relationship between the Many and the One.[51] In the Christian context, while the meaning of participation has been transformed and used to describe the relation between God and creation, the Many-and-One structure remains.[52] God as the sole Creator of all things is the unifying One, while the Many refers to created plurality. It is in this sense that Colin Gunton in his Bampton Lectures at Oxford University re-invoked the ancient paradigm of the One and the Many to discuss modern issues in the God-and-creation relation.[53] Influenced by the Platonic priority of unity over plurality, he argues, the God of traditional Western theology had been seen as a suppressive One, which was evetually rejected by modernity in its revolt against the One. In particular, Gunton argues that Augustine and Aquinas are to blame for perpetuating the Platonic defect of elevating the One at the cost of the Many.[54] Following Gunton, in this book, I will use the framework of the One and the Many to examine the concepts of participation in Augustine and Aquinas. In critical response to Gunton, however, I will argue that in developing participatory ontology, Augustine and Aquinas were not slavish to Plato or Platonism but profoundly transformed the originally Platonic concept of participation in the light of *creatio ex nihilo*. In this reformulated concept of participation, God is no longer the repressive One, but the One that sustains creaturely plurality. A retrieval of the participatory ontology in Augustine and Aquinas will thus prove crucial for modern theological discussions—it will help contemporary theologies of participation, as found in RO and Boersma, be anchored in more distinctively Christian and less Platonic grounds. This participatory ontology, which is a metaphysical expression of *creatio ex nihilo*, will also prove essential for establishing a coherent worldview—a unity that embraces plurality—in the postmodern world. This worldview, I will argue, is superior to alternative systems and has profound implications for dialogues between science and religion.

OUTLINE OF THE CHAPTERS

The structure of the book will be as follows. In chapter 1, I will examine Augustine's theory of participation, emphasizing how *creatio ex nihilo* helps him refigure the (neo)Platonic concept of participation. One of the significant changes he makes is to identify the One with Being, which has profound consequences, not the least of which is that the One is not exclusive of the Many but embraces it. Subsequently, Augustine's notion of divine simplicity also differs from the Plotinian Simplex. Elevation of the One does not automatically suppress the Many and participation in the One (God) by no means compromises the integrity of the Many (creation).

Chapter 2 examines Augustine's understanding of multiplicity. The main argument of this chapter is that in Augustine's mature thought, multiplicity is not the negation of unity; in fact, the opposite of unity is division, not multiplicity. As such, unity and multiplicity are not in opposition. Unlike

Plotinus, who sees plurality as an imperfection, Augustine views multiplicity as essentially good. It is for this reason that he engages in the debate with "the Platonists" over the goodness of the body. *Contra* the Platonists, Augustine argues persistently that it is the will, not the body, that is the cause of evil, and that the nature of the body is intrinsically good.

Since the heart of participation is relationality, in chapter 3 I discuss Augustine's view of the relationship between the One (God) and the Many (creation). One of the main contributions Augustine makes to the theory of participation is to have resolved the dialectic of transcendence and immanence, which had been otherwise insolvable in Greek philosophy. With the implications of *creatio ex nihilo*, Augustine shows that only the truly transcendent God can be truly immanent to creatures. One of the implications of *creatio ex nihilo*—God's radical immanence—has, however, not been fully fleshed out in Augustine, and for a more thorough Christianization of participatory ontology, we need to look at his medieval successor—Aquinas.

In chapter 4, I will show that there is an even tighter connection between the metaphysics of participation and *creatio ex nihilo* in Aquinas, thanks to his rigorous metaphysics of creation. In his treatment of the One, Aquinas furthers Augustine's insight on the convertibility of unity and being, which leads to the concept of divine simplicity. Against modern critics of divine simplicity, I argue that the concept must be understood in connection to the doctrine of creation. For Aquinas, divine simplicity highlights the fact that God is the Creator and to start with divine simplicity is to start with the truth of creation.

In chapter 5, I examine Aquinas's treatment of multiplicity. Here, Aquinas makes explicit what was still relatively implicit in Augustine—the opposite of unity is not plurality but division. He develops a sophisticated account of the relationship between unity, division, and multiplicity. By distinguishing between different types of multiplicity, Aquinas makes it clear that multiplicity is not univocal and hence does not necessarily negate unity. For this reason, it is possible to claim a thing as one and many at the same time.

Finally, we will examine relationality in Aquinas's participatory ontology. With his creative exposition of *creatio ex nihilo*, Aquinas is emphatic that creation is not a change but a relation and that the existence of all creatures is anchored in their relation to God. Furthering Augustine's insight, he makes it more explicit that God is immanent to creatures because he is truly transcendent. More significantly, Aquinas is able to extend the implications of God's transcendence and immanence further into his vision of reality, finally overcoming the deficiencies in Augustine's thought. For Aquinas, God's radical transcendence means that creatures have their own substantial goodness, and that participation does not diminish the integrity of creatures. God's profound immanence also ensures that empirical reality is a stable and reliable source for our knowledge of God. In Aquinas, then, we find a thorough transformation of participatory ontology in the light of *creatio ex nihilo*, which offers a promising resolution to the problem of the One and the Many.

In the Conclusion, I will discuss how Augustine and Aquinas can provide RO and Boersma's participatory ontology with a more solid Christian foundation. This participatory ontology not only unifies all things in God but also respects the integrity of created plurality. As a worldview, I argue, this Christianized participatory ontology is superior to pluralism and physicalism and as such has also important implications for contemporary dialogues between science and religion.

NOTES

1. For a historical survey of deism and the mechanistic worldview, see Alister E. McGrath, *The Science of God: An Introduction to Scientific Theology* (London: T&T Clarke, 2004), 53–6.

2. See Michael P. Levine, *Pantheism: A Non-theistic Concept of Deity* (London: Routledge, 1994). Needless to say, pantheism was not a modern invention. However, through Spinoza, pantheism found a new, sophisticated expression which made its way into the mainstream of Western thought, especially in Romanticism. Poets such as Wordsworth and Coleridge tended to worship Nature as divine.

3. Anthony Kenny, *A New History of Western Philosophy* (Oxford: Clarendon Press, 2010), 552.

4. For a detailed discussion of *nouvelle théologie*, see Hans Boersma, *Nouvelle Théologie and Sacramental Ontology: A Return to Mystery* (Oxford: Oxford University Press, 2009).

5. Further discussions on Radical Orthodoxy will be offered later in the chapter.

6. Panentheism is not to be confused with pantheism. Unlike pantheism which identifies God with nature, panentheism claims that the whole cosmos exists *in* God.

7. See, for instance, Philip D. Clayton, *God and Contemporary Science*, Edinburgh Studies in Constructive Theology (Edinburgh: Edinburgh University Press, 1997).

8. For a survey of process theology, see Bruce G. Epperly, *Process Theology: A Guide for the Perplexed* (NY: T&T Clark, 2011). Open theism is a relatively recent theological development. The term "open theism" was introduced by Richard Rice, *The Openness of God: The Relationship of Divine Foreknowledge and Human Free Will* (Hagerstown, MD: Review and Herald Pub. Association, 1980). The movement became influential in 1994 when five evangelical scholars published essays in Clark H. Pinnock et al., *The Openness of God: A Biblical Challenge to the Traditional Understanding of God* (Downers Grove, IL: IVP, 1994).

9. See Colin E. Gunton, *The One, the Three and the Many: God, Creation and the Culture of Modernity* (Cambridge: Cambridge University Press, 1993). Gunton argues that the single, simple, and unchanging God of classical theism has been seen as a suppressive One that leaves no room for created diversity. He thus calls for a return to a more Trinitarian picture of God in relation to creation.

10. Merold Westphal, *Overcoming Onto-theology: Toward a Postmodern Christian Faith* (Washington, DC: Fordham University Press, 2011); Jean-Luc Marion, *God without Being*, hors-texte, second edition, trans. Thomas A. Carlson (Chicago, IL: The University of Chicago Press, 1995).

11. James Smith compares Milbank's *Theology and Social Theology: Beyond Secular Reason* (hereafter *TST*, Oxford: Blackwell, 1990) to Barth's bombshell-like *The Epistle to Romans* and acknowledges the considerable impact Radical Orthodoxy has made on contemporary theology. See James K. A. Smith, *Introducing Radical Orthodoxy: Mapping a Post-secular Theology* (Grand Rapids, MI: Baker Academic, 2012), 33. In his endorsement of Smith's book, Fergus Kerr writes, "Radical Orthodoxy, like it or hate it (and many do!), is the only interesting phenomenon on the British theological scene." Radical Orthodoxy is a movement that involves many authors and this book will primarily deal with the thought of the two main leaders, namely John Milbank and Catherine Pickstock, as a representative of RO. So in the rest of the book, when RO is mentioned, it is assumed that we are not dealing with all the authors associated with the movement but only Milbank and Pickstock.

12. Smith, *Introducing Radical Orthodoxy*, 75.

13. Hans Boersma, *Heavenly Participation: The Weaving of a Sacramental Tapestry* (Grand Rapids, MI: Eerdmans, 2011), 189.

14. Ibid., 3.

15. John Milbank, Catherine Pickstock and Graham Ward, eds., *Radical Orthodoxy: A New Theology* (hereafter, *RONT*) (London: Routledge, 1999), 3.

16. It has to be noted that, Andrew P. Davison, who considers himself one of the members of *RO* (a fact not known to me until now),has most recently published a very extensive treatment of the concept of participation: *Participating in God: A Study in Christian Doctrine and Metaphysics* (Cambridge: Cambridge University Press, 2019).

17. Smith, *Introducing Radical Orthodoxy*, 185.

18. Philip Blond, "Introduction: Theology before Philosophy," in *Post-secular Philosophy: Between Philosophy and Theology*, ed. Philip Blond (London: Routledge, 1998), 6.

19. Catherine Pickstock, *After Writing: On the Liturgical Consummation of Philosophy* (Oxford: Blackwell, 1998), 132.

20. Smith, *Introducing Radical Orthodoxy*, 188.

21. *RONT*, 3.

22. *RONT*, 3.

23. *RONT*, 4, italic original.

24. John Milbank and Catherine Pickstock, *Truth in Aquinas*, Radical Orthodoxy Series (London: Routledge, 2001), 41.

25. Smith, *Introducing Radical Orthodoxy*, 190.

26. John Milbank, "Materialism and Transcendence," in *Theology and the Political: The New Debate*, ed. Creston Davis, John Milbank and Slavoj Žižek (Durham, NC: Duke University Press, 2005), 396.

27. Justin S. Holcomb summarizes this relation well with the phrase "being bound to God." "Being bound to God," he writes, "means that all that exists is the creation of God and suspends from God and that all creation is perpetually being bound to God. . . .

For Radical Orthodoxy, the language that articulates this reality is that of *participation*."
Justin S. Holcomb, "Being Bound to God," in *Radical Orthodoxy and the Reformed
Tradition: Creation, Covenant and Participation* (hereafter *RORT*), ed. James K. A.
Smith and James H. Olthuis (Grand Rapids, MI: Baker Academic, 2005), 243.

28. Boersma, *Heavenly Participation*, 29.

29. Ibid., 2.

30. Ibid., xi.

31. Ibid., 21.

32. Ibid., 22–4.

33. Ibid., 81–2.

34. Ibid., 189.

35. See, for instance, Michael S. Horton, "Participation and Covenant," in *RORT*:
107-132. Horton accuses RO's project as a type of *onto-theology*.

36. "Radical Orthodoxy strongly emphasizes what is universal, general, and
speculative at the expense of affirming and defending the particularity of divine
redemption in Christ." Holcomb, "Being Bound to God," 250; see also R. R. Reno,
"Review of *Radical Orthodoxy: A New Theology*," *Modern Theology* 15 (1999): 530;
N. Vorster, "A Critical Assessment of John Milbank's Christology," *Acta Theologica*
32, no. 2 (2012): 277–98.

37. *TST*, 290.

38. *RONT*, 3.

39. Pickstock, *After Writing*, 14.

40. Ibid., 12.

41. James K. A. Smith, "Will the Real Plato Please Stand Up?" in *RORT*, 71.

42. Ibid.

43. Graham Ward, *Cities of God*, Radical Orthodoxy Series (London: Routledge,
2001), 88.

44. Smith, *Introducing Radical Orthodoxy*, 204.

45. Ibid. Smith himself admits that it is possible to simultaneously affirm creation's radical dependence on God and its intrinsic goodness.

46. Ibid., 72.

47. Boersma, *Heavenly Participation*, 30, emphases added.

48. Ibid., 30–1, emphases added.

49. Again, we note that this observation is based on the writings of Milbank and
Pickstock only.

50. *Republic* X, 596a6–7.

51. Plato uses the idea of participation to refute Zeno's monism, proposing that
both the many and the one are real and that the many in the sensible world participate
in the one in the ideal world. See Plato, *Parmenides* (Leob Classical Library), 207.

52. For the historical development of participation, see M. Annice, "A Historical
Sketch of the Theory of Participation," *The New Scholasticism* 26 (1952): 49–79. See
also W. Norris Clarke, "The Meaning of Participation in St. Thomas," *Proceedings
of the American Catholic Philosophical Association* 26 (1952): 147–57.

53. Gunton, *The One, the Three and the Many*.

54. Robert Jenson, "A Decision Tree of Colin Gunton's Thinking," in *The
Theology of Colin Gunton*, ed. Lincoln Harvey (London: T&T Clark, 2010), 9.

Part I

AUGUSTINE'S PARTICIPATORY ONTOLOGY

Chapter 1

Augustine's Participatory Ontology and the Question of Unity

In many ways, both RO and Boersma look to Augustine as a major source of inspiration, and yet they have not carefully examined what the Bishop of Hippo actually said about "participation." Part of the reason is that "very little attention has been paid to this theme in his thought" by modern scholars.[1] Although participation appears frequently in Augustine's writings and is one of the three principles which form "the essential nucleus of his philosophy,"[2] only a few articles have touched upon this topic and none of them has systematically investigated how he understands and uses this term.[3] To my knowledge, no monograph has been written on Augustine's concept of participation, especially its metaphysical aspect.[4] However, if participation is indeed central to Augustine, it is essential to delineate what he really means by "participation" and how his idea of participation is in continuity with and differs from the Platonic tradition. In this chapter, we will first examine Augustine's metaphysical thought of participation and then discuss how *creatio ex nihilo* reshapes his concept of participation, particularly his notion of unity. It needs to be noted from the outset that this book does not aim to provide a comprehensive account or treatment of Augustine's theory of participation in relation to Platonism. How Augustine's concept of participation depends upon Plato and Platonism is a complicated topic, on which I will only offer a few broad sketches. While acknowledging Augustine's indebtedness to the Platonic tradition, this book will nonetheless focus on how he moves *beyond* the latter—particularly how the doctrine of creation helps him to reshape the concept of participation in order to describe the God-creation relationship. It must also be admitted that the Christianization of participation did not began with Augustine—Christian thinkers before him had already initiated the process and laid a foundation on which he could build. So discussing Augustine's advance over Platonism by no means downplays the

17

contribution of Christian thinkers before him nor his indebtedness to them. I will introduce some pre-Augustinian theologians' work in Christianizing participatory ontology, but will not provide a detailed account of how Augustine draws from them, for the book is not a survey of the historical development of participatory ontology.[5] Rather, I will particularly focus on how the doctrine of creation *ex nihilo* plays a foundational role in the Christianization of participation in Augustine.

AUGUSTINE'S METAPHYSICAL CONCEPT OF PARTICIPATION

The notion of participation (*methexis*) goes back at least to Plato, who used the term to explain how multiple particular things can be predicated of the same name.[6] For instance, in reality we see many individual human beings, but how can all the individuals be called "human"? According to Plato, all the different individuals can be called human, because they participate in or share the Form of humanity. Because participation involves both unity and plurality, it is essentially a theory about the relation between the One and the Many. In technical terms, "'participation' signifies the fundamental relationship of both structure and dependence in the dialectic of the many in relation to the One and of the different in relation to the Identical."[7]

In Christian contexts, participation describes the way in which creatures relate to the Creator and the way in which human beings share the divine life. The two kinds of participation have been recognized by the Church Fathers as "weak participation" and "strong participation," which is also called "deification."[8] Appropriating from Platonism, the Church Fathers employed the notion of participation extensively in their theological writings. For instance, it has been recognized that participation was central to Athanasius' thought.[9] To express the profound truth that all of creation participates in Christ, through whom all things were made (John 1:1-3), Athanasius writes:

> That what came into being might not only be, but be good, it pleased God that his own Wisdom should condescend to the creatures, so as to introduce an impress and semblance of its image on all in common and on each, that what was made might be manifestly wise works and worthy of God.[10]

The idea of participation also played a crucial role in Irenaeus's thought, especially in his refutation of Gnosticism.[11] On the one hand, participation rooted in the doctrine of creation enabled him to maintain the ontological distinction between God and creatures, refuting the Gnostic claim that human souls were divine.[12] On the other hand, participation makes it possible for human beings to have a relationship with God, because "the very orientation and goal of our creaturehood is towards participating more and more in God."[13] For Irenaeus, the truths of both creation and deification were captured by the concept of participation.

Like the Church Fathers before him, Augustine used the notion of participation extensively in his writings.[14] There are three kinds of participation in his thought, namely ontological participation, epistemological participation, and deification.[15] The first kind, namely ontological participation, describes how creatures depend on God for their existence and perfection. The second type has to do with how the human mind is illumined by the light of God. The third kind is deification, through which humanity receives eternal qualities from God. In distinction from deification, the first two kinds of participation, namely ontological and epistemological, can be grouped under the category of metaphysical participation, which will be the focus of this book.[16] Particularly, we will examine how Augustine's metaphysical concept of participation develops over time and especially how it differs from that of Plato.[17]

Early Thought

Augustine's early idea of participation is heavily indebted to Plato. In *Phaedo*, Plato offers a theory of participation that involves three factors.[18] To answer the question of what makes a thing beautiful, Socrates suggests that "nothing else makes it beautiful but the presence or communion of absolute beauty, however it may have been gained."[19] Socrates's answer contains three factors: the first is the transcendent Form of beauty, a perfect, underived essence; the second, the immanent form of beauty in the sensible thing; and the third, the thing that receives the immanent form of beauty. In a similar fashion, Augustine uses the three-factor theory of participation to describe the relation between creatures and God in *De Moribus Manichaeorum*, one of his earliest works. For him, the most fundamental difference between God and a creature is that God is the perfect Good, which is good by itself, whereas a creature is good only by participation in the perfect Good. In this case, the first factor in the participatory relation is God, the transcendent Form of Good, while the second factor is the immanent form of good in a creature. The third factor is the creature that has received the immanent form of good from God. This three-factor structure of participation allows Augustine to articulate with precision the unique God-creation relation: God, the transcendent source of all goodness, remains unchanged, while he imparts limited goodness to a creature. While God *is* the Good, a creature has goodness by participation in God. For Augustine, participation at once secures God's radical transcendence and equally radical intimacy to creation.[20]

Apart from *De Moribus Manichaeorum*, another early work of Augustine which substantially uses the idea of participation is *Miscellany of Eighty-Three Questions* (collected between 388 and 395 AD). The principle of participation undergirds the very first sentence of the book: "Everything that is true is true by reason of the truth."[21] There, he distinguishes between what is true (*verum*) and the truth itself (*veritas*): while *verum* cannot be true on its own but becomes true only by reason of *veritas* and thus depends on *veritas*, *veritas* is true in itself and depends on nothing else. In this sense, we say that *verum* participates in *veritas*. The same principle is applied to more categories such as chastity, eternity, beauty, and goodness in Question XXIII:

> Everything chaste is chaste by reason of chastity, everything eternal by reason of eternity, everything beautiful by reason of beauty, everything good by reason of goodness; therefore also everything wise by reason of wisdom and everything like by reason of likeness.

The statement that "everything chaste is chaste by reason of chastity" means that a particular chaste thing is not chaste by itself but is chaste by participating in the Form of chastity. On the basis of the three-factor model, we can say that if factor #1 is chastity, the transcendent Form, then factor #3 is the particular thing that receives a limited form of chastity, which is factor #2. It is true that factor #3 is chaste, but the way in which it is chaste differs fundamentally from the way in which factor #1 is chaste. Augustine makes the following clarification to help us understand his concept of participation:

> [W]hat is chaste is said to be so by reason of chastity in two ways—either because it *produces* it, so that it is chaste by reason of the chastity which it produces and for which it is the source and cause of its existence, but otherwise when something is chaste on account of its participation in chastity, because sometimes it can be unchaste.[22]

Here, Augustine makes at least two crucial distinctions between chastity itself and a chaste thing that participates in chastity. The first distinction has to with *self-sufficiency*. That which is chaste on its own produces chastity itself and is the source of chastity, since its chastity does not come from outside but from itself. It is thus absolutely self-sufficient in terms of chastity. In comparison, that which participates in chastity does not produce chastity itself but receives it from another—it is not self-sufficient and depends on a source other than itself. Augustine makes this point clearer later in *De Trinitate*, in which he asserts that the human soul must always cling to God: "For it is not sufficient to itself, nor is anything at all sufficient to him who departs from Him who is alone sufficient."[23] The soul, which participates in God and is insufficient by itself, must depend upon God, who alone is perfectly self-sufficient.

The second distinction has to do with *necessity* or *immutability*. Chastity itself is necessarily chaste because it is chaste by nature and can never become unchaste. But that which participates in chastity is not chaste necessarily but can become unchaste through a change or corruption. This principle also applies to other qualities such as eternal, beautiful, good, or wise:

> [T]hose things which, on account of their participation, are chaste or eternal or beautiful or good or wise admit, as it is said, of being able to be not chaste or eternal or beautiful or good or wise. But chastity, eternity, beauty, goodness and wisdom in no way admit of either corruption or, as I might say, temporality or wickedness or malice.[24]

In Augustine's thought, then, abstract nouns such as chastity, eternity, beauty, goodness, and wisdom seem to correspond to the Platonic Forms, through participation in which particular things become chaste, eternal, beautiful, good, or wise. Individual things are mutable because they are not the Forms themselves but receive limited qualities from the immutable Forms and hence are liable to change. In this respect, Augustine's concept of participation is in continuity with that of Plato. On one significant point, however, Augustine's account of participation deviates from the latter: whereas in Plato, different Forms such as chastity, beauty, goodness, and wisdom seem independent of one another; in Augustine, they are not only unified but identical in God.[25] These Forms are no longer separate but simply different names for the same God, who is by nature simple. Augustine makes this point clear in *On the Literal Interpretation of Genesis: An Unfinished Book*, written in about 393 AD:

> [W]hatever things are chaste are chaste by participation in it. This chastity is surely in God where there is also that wisdom which is not wise by participation; rather, by participation in it, every wise soul is wise.[26]

Hence, even in Augustine's early conception of participation, there is already discontinuity from Plato. While Plato uses participation to describe the relationship between particular things and the universal Forms, Augustine uses it primarily to describe the relationship between God and creatures. Creatures become chaste, beautiful, good, and wise by participating in God, in whom the Forms of chastity, beauty, goodness, and wisdom cohere and become one. In Augustine's thought, then, the idea of participation is inseparable from the doctrine of creation, which is a fundamental difference between his metaphysics of participation and that of Plato.

Later Thought

As a key idea in his thought, participation plays a more crucial role in Augustine's later works such as *The City of God*, where the language of participation is employed frequently. For instance, he states that the human soul receives intellectual light by participation in the divine light. God is the One "who makes the rational and intellectual soul, of which kind is that of human beings, blessed by participation in His unchangeable and incorporeal light."[27] In a comment on the Gospel of John, he writes: "This distinction sufficiently shows that the rational or intellectual soul, such as John had, cannot be its own light, but shines by its *participation* in another and true Light."[28] The "true Light" refers to Christ, by participation in whom human souls become rational. Human intelligence is not self-sufficient—it receives light from Christ and depends on him.

Augustine's extensive use of participation can also be found in *De Trinitate*. In Book Eight, when discussing the relationship between particular goods and "the Good," he explicitly employs the notion of participation:

> There would, therefore, be no changeable goods, unless there were an unchangeable Good. When you hear then of this good and that good which may not even be good in other respects, and if it were possible to put aside those goods which are good by participation in the Good, and to see the Good itself of which they are good by participation . . . if, therefore, I repeat, you could put these goods aside and perceive the Good in itself, you would see God.[29]

In this passage, Augustine clearly identifies "the Good itself" with God, who provides the ultimate basis for other goods, which participate in "the Good." Changeable and particular goods cannot be good on their own, but must receive limited goodness from God, the Good itself. In other words, the Good must first exist in order that changeable goods may exist. This priority is not temporal but ontological, for the existence of changeable goods completely depends on God, the unchanging Good.

In *De Trinitate*, the most important passage on participation is Book 5, chapter 10, in which Augustine discusses why we should not speak of God as three essences but one. First, he distinguishes between two kinds of reality— great things on the one hand and "greatness" on the other—using the theory of participation. What he wishes to emphasize is that while particular great things are *composite*, greatness itself is *simple*. Participation in this sense is a relationship between multiplicity and simplicity. With regard to particular great things, Augustine writes:

> For in things which are great by a participation in greatness, to be is one thing and to be great is another, as a great house, a great mountain, and a great soul;

in these things, then, the greatness is one thing, and that which is great by greatness is another thing.[30]

In those things, there is a clear distinction between their essence and the
property of being great. In a house, being great is not part of the essence or
definition of the house; rather, it is accidental to the house, since a house is
not necessarily a great house. The nature of house and the property of being
great are two different things. In other words, a great house is a composite
thing, not a simple one.

By contrast, greatness itself, by participation in which a great house
becomes great, is not a composite thing but a simple one, because the property of being great is its very nature and essence. Greatness is necessarily
great in itself and by itself:

> Certainly, this greatness is primarily great, and in a much higher degree than the
> things which are great by a participation in it. But God is not great by a great-
> ness, which is not that which He Himself is. . . . He is great by that greatness
> which is *identical* with Himself. Hence, as we do not speak of three essences,
> so we do not speak of three greatnesses, for in God to be is the *same* as to
> be great. . . . He is great by Himself being great, for He Himself is His own
> greatness.[31]

Hence, in contrast to a great house, which is a composite thing, the greatness of God is no longer composite but simple, because God is great not by
participation in a greatness other than Himself. In God, there is no distinction
between *to be* and *to be great*—the two are identical and refer to the same
thing. For this reason, God's greatness is a simple reality, by participation
in which all things become great. But apart from being great, God is also
chaste, good, wise, and so on. Hence, in God, to be is also identical to be
chaste, good, and wise. All the perfections are identical in God, who is absolutely simple. In Augustine's later thought, *divine simplicity* becomes more
prominent in his concept of participation, which will be discussed later in
this chapter.

We notice, therefore, a certain development in Augustine's theory of
participation. In his early thought, there is more continuity between his concept of participation and that of Plato. In his later thought, while retaining
the fundamental features of Platonic participation, he departs from Plato by
placing more emphasis to the absolute unity of things in God. The foundation that undergirds this departure is the Christian doctrine of *creatio ex
nihilo*.

CREATIO EX NIHILO AND
PARTICIPATION IN AUGUSTINE

In Augustine's thought, the concepts of creation and participation are essentially inseparable. Just as he often expresses the truths of creation in terms of participation, he conceives participation in the light of creation. It is this connection between the two that distinguishes Augustine's concept of participation from the straightforwardly Platonic one. The foundational role of *creatio ex nihilo* in Augustine's theology has now been increasingly recognized,[32] but how it reshapes his concept of participation remains largely unexplored. In the rest of the chapter, we will first examine how he understands *creatio ex nihilo* and then discuss how he transforms Plato's theory of participation in the light of the doctrine of creation. [33]

Creatio ex nihilo

A benchmark of Christian orthodoxy, *creatio ex nihilo* holds that all things other than God are created by God freely, absolutely out of nothing.[34] In stressing the ontological divide between God and creatures, this doctrine constitutes not only the opening confession of the Nicene Creed but also the theological grid in which other central doctrines are expounded and defended, such as the divinity of Christ.[35] The origin of the doctrine, however, is a matter of debate. While some scholars argue that the teaching of *creatio ex nihilo* can be directly found in the Bible,[36] others suggest that Scripture in general is concerned little with metaphysics and that the doctrine became explicit as a result of early Christians' attempt to defend the biblical picture of God against Greek philosophy.[37] The scholarly consensus, however, is that the teaching did not originate from Greek cosmology; rather, it was the result of Christian reaction against Hellenism in the light of biblical revelation.[38] As Soskice puts it,

> The development of *creatio ex nihilo* by Jewish and Christian writers was a riposte to the Greek consensus that from nothing nothing comes—*ex nihilo nihil fit*—which threatened not only their understanding of cosmic origins but also the teaching on divine freedom and sovereignty.[39]

Indeed, this doctrine can be summarized in the following points, each of which is a corrective to aspects of Greek philosophy that contradict the biblical teachings or to heretical movements that threaten orthodoxy.

1. Against the Platonic and Aristotelian views of matter being preexistent or eternal, *creatio ex nihilo* stresses that everything, including matter,

is created by God and therefore intrinsically contingent. God does not merely give form to preexistent matter, but brings matter itself out of nothing.

2. Against the dualism of Gnosticism and Manichaeism, *creatio ex nihilo* endorses a radical monotheism, affirming that God is the sole Creator of all that is. Since God is good, whatever he creates is also good, even though what he creates is not as good as himself.

3. Against the metaphysics of emanation,[40] *creatio ex nihilo* emphasizes that God freely creates all things out of nothing. There is neither external incentive nor internal need compelling God to create, since God is complete and perfect in himself.

4. Against pantheism, which tends to blur the distinction between God and creatures, *creatio ex nihilo* stresses a fundamental "ontological" divide between God and everything else. God, the Creator, is wholly transcendent from the created order. Transcendent as he is, God is nonetheless not detached but intimately close to the creation.

Standing within the orthodox tradition, Augustine fully embraces these core tenets of *creatio ex nihilo* and adopts them as the foundational theological framework in which he thinks of all of reality—God and everything in relation to him. Building upon his predecessors' work,[41] Augustine makes important contributions to this doctrine, as the idea of creation has been in the forefront of his mind throughout his life. In fact, Augustine seems to be so preoccupied with the question of creation that he undertakes an exposition on the opening chapters of Genesis at least five times.[42] In many places, not only does he explicitly affirm the teaching of *creatio ex nihilo* but offers further expositions on its meaning. In *On Genesis against the Manichees*, he writes:

> So, too, all the things that God has made are very good, but they are not good in the same way that God is good, because he is their maker, while they are made. Nor did he give birth to them out of himself so that they are what he is; rather he made them out of *nothing* so that they are equal neither to him by whom they have been made, nor to his Son through whom they have been made.[43]

In this passage, by stating that creatures have been made out of nothing, Augustine emphasizes the complete ontological divide between the Creator and creatures, rejecting all sorts of pantheism and emanation. Meanwhile, because everything is created by God, nothing is intrinsically evil and all that truly exists is good. For Augustine, therefore, *creatio ex nihilo* is the ultimate affirmation of the goodness of creation and thereby a decisive refutation of Manichaeism. This understanding is evident in *Of True Religion*:

Who made them? He who supremely is. Who is he? God, the immutable
Trinity, made them through his supreme wisdom and preserves them by
supreme loving-kindness. Why did he make them? In order that they might
exist. Existence as such is good, and supreme existence is the chief good. From
what did he make them? *Out of nothing*. . . . That out of which God created all
things had neither form nor species, and was simply nothing. . . . Therefore, if
the world was made out of some unformed matter, that matter was made *out of
absolutely nothing.*[44]

In contrast to the common Greek view that prime matter is eternal and
uncreated, Augustine is emphatic that even if God created things out of
unformed matter, unformed matter itself is not self-existent but was brought
into existence by God from nothing. God needs no material cause to create;
neither does God create out of necessity as if he needed creatures. "He has no
need for the creatures which He has made, but, rather, created them out of His
own unmotivated goodness."[45] Since all things are created by God through his
goodness, existence as such must be good. A thing is good insofar as it exists.
As such, to assume the existence of an absolute evil being is a logical contradiction, which, for Augustine, lies at the heart of the Manichean fallacy.
Indeed, it is *creatio ex nihilo* that serves as the foundation for his extensive
anti-Manichean polemic.[46]

While wholeheartedly embracing the main tenets of *creatio ex nihilo*,
Augustine in the process of combating Manichaeism develops a unique
metaphysic of being, namely the identification of being with goodness,
which has far-reaching impacts for Christian thought.[47] In Plato, goodness is
beyond being, as he asserts that "goodness itself is not essence but still transcends essence in dignity and surpassing power."[48] Likewise, Neoplatonism
places the Good above being. On this point, Augustine clearly departs from
the Platonic tradition. For him, goodness must be ultimately identical to
being, for God, who is "the Good," is at the same time the Creator of all
that is—"Being itself."[49] In God, therefore, Goodness and Being are the
same. On created levels, goodness and being are also convertible: because
God creates all things from nothing and to create is to bestow existence on
a thing by the good Creator, we are compelled to conclude that existence as
such is good. Existence is a gift of goodness from God, who is the Supreme
Goodness. On the other hand, since goodness is identified with being, evil—
the opposite of good—must be non-being or negation of existence. For this
reason, absolute evil that is completely devoid of goodness cannot exist, for
should it exist, it must contain some degree of goodness. Evil thus cannot
exist apart from good. One of Augustine's most sophisticated expositions
on the nature of good and evil can be found in *Enchiridion on Faith, Hope
and Love*:

All things that exist, therefore, seeing that the Creator of them all is supremely good, are themselves good. But because they are not, like their Creator, supremely and unchangeably good, their good may be diminished and increased. But for good to be diminished is an evil, although, however much it may be diminished, it is necessary, if the being is to continue, that some good should remain to constitute the being. . . . Therefore, so long as a being is in a process of corruption, there is in it some good of which it is being deprived. . . . Every being, therefore, is a good. . . . And if it be wholly consumed by corruption, then the corruption itself must cease to exist, as there is no being left in which it can dwell.[50]

Nothing, then, can be evil except something which is good. . . . Therefore every being, even if it be a defective one, *in so far as it is a being is good*, and in so far as it is defective is evil.[51]

Note that the identification of being with good is developed in the context of an exposition of creation, for immediately before this passage Augustine asserts that "in regard to nature it is not necessary for the Christian to know more than that the goodness of the Creator is the cause of all things."[52] His metaphysic of being does not rise out of philosophical speculation but the doctrine of creation. Insofar as the doctrine of creation is foundational to Augustine's thought, his concept of participation is inevitably shaped by the truths of creation.

Creation and Participation

Needless to say, Augustine is heavily indebted to Platonism[53] for his concept of participation. As discussed above, Augustine essentially borrows the three-factor structure of participation from Plato: the Form or underived source of perfection, the participating subject that receives the limited perfection, and the limited perfection that exists immanently in the subject. As the Platonic insight was further developed by Plotinus, it became a core principle in Neoplatonic philosophy—the idea of a first principle with an unlimited capacity to diffuse its goodness in limited fashion to the whole of reality—which, as Norris Clarke observes, "was passed down to the medieval Christian thinkers, in varying degrees of explicitness, clarity, and adaptation to the Christian view of the universe."[54] In many ways, Augustine's idea of participation rests upon the Neoplatonic structure: the unlimited source of perfection (God), a participating subject possessing the perfection in a limited mode (the creature), and the reception of limited perfection in the subject that depends on the source (participatory relation).

His indebtedness to Platonism notwithstanding, to have a full picture of Augustine's concept of participation, we must not overlook the significant transformation he brings to the notion. In particular, we must examine how he moves beyond (Neo)Platonism by re-visioning the essential components of participatory ontology in the light of the Christian doctrine of creation. Insofar as *creatio ex nihilo* is a consequence of Christianity's critical engagement with Greek philosophy,[55] Augustine's concept of participation challenges the Platonic tradition in a number of respects.[56] While acknowledging the continuity between the Augustinian and Platonic ideas of participation, in this book we will primarily focus on the *discontinuity* between them. As detailed discussions will be provided in the subsequent chapters, in what follows I will summarize the ways in which Augustine modifies the (Neo) Platonic theory of participation, thereby providing a more adequate solution to the problem of the One and the Many.

1. Augustine transforms the Platonic conception of the One—the nature of unity. Within the Platonic tradition, Neoplatonism is especially known for its elevation of the One above Being, as Plotinus repeatedly stresses that the One cannot be named because it transcends Being.[57] On this point, Augustine disagrees sharply, since for him the One is identical to Being. Such disagreement has profound implications for the problem of the One and the Many. The rest of this chapter will discuss the topic in detail.

2. In contrast to the Neoplatonic tendency to devalue multiplicity, Augustine's metaphysics of participation stresses the goodness of multiple creatures and the nonexistence of evil. While Plotinus locates matter as the source of evil,[58] Augustine recognizes goodness in even unformed matter, because matter itself is created by God out of nothing.[59] Nothing is inherently evil. It is true that Augustine tends to prioritize spirit over matter and the One over the Many in a Platonic fashion, but, as we will see, he resolutely defends the essential goodness of matter. Hence, it can be argued that Augustine makes an important progress in affirming the goodness of multiplicity and matter, which will be the topic of chapter 2.

3. Perhaps, the most significant change Augustine brings to the theory of participation is the relationship between the One and the Many. While in both Plato and Plotinus an insoluble tension exists between the transcendence and immanence of the One in relation to the Many, Augustine is able to resolve the conflict and harmonize the two. His source of inspiration is *creatio ex nihilo*, which undergirds a simultaneously transcendent and immanent relation between God and creation. This theme will be discussed in chapter 3.

UNITY IN AUGUSTINE'S METAPHYSICS
OF PARTICIPATION

Since the metaphysics of participation begins with the One, it is natural for us to first examine the concept of unity in Augustine's idea of participation. Insofar as Augustine draws heavily from Plato and Neoplatonism when developing his participatory ontology, he naturally prioritizes unity and regards the One as the first and highest principle of reality. For instance, in a much Neoplatonic fashion, Augustine makes the One the guiding concept in *Of True Religion*, acting not only as the origin of all things but the goal of life, truth, and being.[60] Also following Plotinus, in *Confessions* he defines sin as falling away the One, which results in the soul being distracted by multiplicity.[61] Despite such continuity, Augustine's understanding of unity deviates from that of (Neo)Platonism in at least two significant respects: the first concerning the relationship between unity and being; the second, divine simplicity.

Unity and Being

A defining feature of Neoplatonic metaphysics is to place the One or the Good above Being.[62] For instance, Plato asserts that "the good itself is not essence but still transcends essence in dignity and surpassing power."[63] Following Plato,[64] Plotinus affirms that the One is beyond Being, since the One cannot be named "except that it may be described as transcending Being."[65] The absolutely simple One is beyond Being, which involves multiplicity and is thus not completely simple. Being belongs to the realm of the Intellect, which is below the One, and is thus not the highest principle of reality. For Augustine, however, nothing is higher than Being, for God has declared to be Being Himself in the Scripture (*Exodus* 3:14) and the Creator who bestows existence to all things. In the light of the biblical revelation, Augustine is compelled to assert that Being is the highest principle and repeatedly refers to God as "Being" and "He Who supremely is."[66] For Augustine, God's self-revelation as "I AM THAT I AM" is closely associated with the doctrine of creation, a tradition that goes back at least to the first-century Jewish philosopher Philo, who consistently ties *Exodus* 3:14 with the creation account in Genesis. As Philo understands it, to call God "Being" is to simply claim that God is the Creator that brought all things into existence out of nothing.[67] Likewise, for Augustine, God's name "Being" is anchored in the fact that He is the Creator. In *City of God*, in order to refute the teaching that apostate angels come from a first cause other than God, Augustine writes:

> But we shall more readily and easily avoid the great impiety of this error to the extent that we are able fully to understand what God said through the agency of the angel when he sent Moses to the children of Israel: "I AM THAT I AM."

For God is the Supreme Being—that is, He supremely *is*; and He is therefore
immutable. He gave being to the things that He created from *nothing*, then, but
not a supreme being like His own.[68]

It is clear from the passage that, for Augustine, understanding God as "the
Supreme Being" is inseparable from *creatio ex nihilo*—the former bespeaks
God's nature and the latter, God's proper action. They are simply two sides of
the same reality and mutually explanatory. On the one hand, because God is
Being, it is appropriate for him to create, that is, to bestow existence to things
that would not otherwise exist. On the other hand, the act of creation most
clearly reveals God's nature as Being:

> This being so, then, God, Who supremely is, and Who therefore made every
> being which does not exist supremely (for no being that was made *out of noth-*
> *ing* could be His equal; or, indeed, exist at all had He not made it), is not to be
> reproached with the faults which trouble us. Rather, He is to be praised when
> we contemplate all the natures which He has made.[69]

The fundamental motivation for Augustine to identify Being with God—
the highest principle of all things—is therefore *creatio ex nihilo*, which
compels him to depart from the Platonic tradition that places One above
Being.[70] It has been suggested by scholars that Augustine's identification of
Being with God was influenced by Porphyry and the Christian philosopher
Marius Victorinus. It is true that while Plotinus placed the One beyond
being, Porphyry argued that one cannot think of anything beyond being and
that it thus was reasonable to think of the One as the Supreme Being. And
so it is possible that Porphyry's idea was passed on to Augustine through
Victorinus's translation.[71] But there is no clear evidence that Augustine drew
directly from Porphyry's texts in formulating the principle of identification
between the One with Being. As someone whose thought is rooted in creation, Augustine would have most likely anchored it in the biblical teaching
of creation. From the fact that God as the Creator—the Being Itself—is
supremely one, it would be a natural step for Augustine to arrive at the
position that God is both the One and the Being—hence the convertibility
between unity and being.

Given Augustine's emphasis on Being, it is sometimes tempting to interpret
his metaphysics as decisively "existential," as if Being is more fundamental
than the One or the Good.[72] Such an interpretation is equally groundless. It
is true that for Augustine Being is the highest principle, but like Plotinus, he
also gives absolute supremacy to the One, as he consistently refers to God as
"the One." In *TR*, one of Augustine's early writings, "the One" functions as
the guiding principle.[73]

One God alone I worship, the sole principle of all things. . . . Let our religion bind us to the *one* omnipotent God. . . . In him and with him we venerate the Truth, who is in all respects like him, and who is the Form of all things that have been made by the *One*, and that endeavor after *unity*. . . . We worship *one* God from whom, through whom, and in whom we have our being. . . . We worship *one* God by whom we were made, and his likeness by whom we are formed for *unity*, and his peace whereby we cleave to *unity*.[74]

In case one may argue that Augustine's early thought is too heavily indebted to Platonism, we can point out that he still identifies God as "the One" in his later works. In *Confessions*, by calling Christ "the Son of man who is mediator between you the One and us the many,"[75] he suggests that, in contrast to creatures that are many, God is "the One." In a language that resembles Plotinus, he writes of his experience of turning away from God: "I turned from unity in you to be lost in multiplicity."[76] Likewise, toward the end of *Confessions*, he calls God "the One" and "the Good" in a Platonic fashion: "But you God, one and good, have never ceased to do good. . . . But you, the Good, in need of no other good, are ever at rest since you yourself are your own rest."[77] In his more mature works, the identification of God as "the One" is made even clearer. Toward the end of *DT*, Augustine writes:

But when we shall come to You, these 'many things' which we say 'and fall short' shall cease; and You as One shall remain, You who are all in all; and without ceasing we shall say one thing, praising You in the one, we who have also been made one in You.[78]

Hence, while it is true that Augustine refuses to place the One above Being, it does not follow that he places Being above the One. Although Augustine departs from the standard Platonic notion of Being, he does not completely discard the Platonic tradition that identifies the One or the Good with the first principle of all things. In this respect, the only change he makes is to identify the One with the Creator God of revelation. As the Creator of all things, God is also the absolute source of unity, and it is thus fully consistent with the doctrine of creation for Augustine to identify God as the One. Being and Unity are equally fundamental to God, who is at once Being and the One. In Augustine's thought, therefore, Being becomes identical to Unity in God.

But by identifying the One with Being, Augustine makes important shifts in the metaphysics of participation with respect to the question of the One and the Many.[79]

1. In making the One identical to Being in God, Augustine introduces *efficient causality* into the relationship between the One and the Many. It is

well-known that in Plato the Ideas have only exemplary causality, but no efficient causality, toward sensible things. While Plato asserts that the Many participate in the One, he never satisfactorily clarifies the relation between them, and as a result his theory of participation faces various challenges[80] and is severely criticized by Aristotle.[81] Neither in Plotinus's metaphysics is the One the efficient cause of the Many. In Plotinus's system, where all things are derived from the One, it seems natural to see the One as the efficient cause of the Many. This understanding, however, is a misreading of Plotinus—one that turns "the Plotinian emanation of the multiple from the One into a Christian emanation of beings from Being."[82] Even if, as Lloyd Gerson argues, the One may be seen as the efficient cause of *existence* of all things, it is clear that the One is not the efficient cause of *being* (essence) of things,[83] since to make the One the principle of being would introduce multiplicity into the One and destroy its absolute simplicity. If the One, which is above Being, is not the efficient cause of *being* of things, much less can it be the efficient cause of multiplicity. *Contra* Aristotle, Plotinus thus argues that the One cannot even be said to possess self-knowing, for knowledge already involves a manifold.[84] Hence, neither Plato nor Plotinus perceives the One as the efficient cause of the Many.

By contrast, Augustine explicitly assigns efficient causality to the One, who is identical to Being. Following earlier Christian thinkers, Augustine holds that efficient causality rests upon the reality of existence—only that which really exists has an efficient cause. For this reason, he urges us not to "seek an efficient cause of an evil will. For its cause is not efficient, but deficient, because the evil will is not an effect of something."[85] For the same reason, Augustine argues that creatures have efficient causality insofar as they have being:

> [T]he more they have being, and the more good they do—the more, that is, they effect—the more they have efficient causes. On the other hand, insofar as they lack being, and for this reason do evil—for what, in this case, do they achieve but emptiness?—they have deficient causes.[86]

If the ability to be an efficient cause is proportional to its degree of being, God—the Supreme Being—must have supreme ability as an efficient cause. This is consistent with the fact that God is the cause of all things out of nothing, because among all efficient causes, no cause is greater than that which brings things into being from nothing. In Augustine's thought, therefore, the One, which is identical to the Being, is the efficient cause of the Many, which undergirds a profoundly intimate relationship between the One and the Many.

In contrast to Platonism, in which the One is often seen as separate from the Many, Augustine provides a much closer relationship between the two. Ultimately, it is the doctrine of creation that enables Augustine to identify the One with Being, thus introducing a new understanding of the One's relation with Many, a theme that will be further expounded in chapter 3.

2. In identifying the One with Being, Augustine denies the reality of Absolute Evil or absolute multiplicity, as is affirmed by Plotinus.[87] While Augustine and Plotinus agree on the principle that insofar as a thing is a being it is good, they diverge on the nature of Absolute Evil. The image of all things flowing from the One often gives one an impression that Plotinus must deny the existence of Absolute Evil, as he claims that evil is non-being. However, Plotinus reminds us: "By this Non-Being, of course, we are not to understand something that simply does not exist." In fact, he argues that Absolute Evil must exist:

> For if Evil can enter into other things, it must have in a certain sense a prior existence, even though it may not be an essence. As there is Good, the Absolute, as well as Good, the quality, so, together with the derived evil entering into something not itself, there must be the Absolute Evil.[88]

For many, this passage may seem puzzling. Isn't Plotinus's system monism? How can there be an Absolute Evil when all things come out of the One? In fact, those who ask such questions fail to understand Plotinus's concept of the One in relation to Being. To ask such questions, they think within the Christian framework, where beings emanate from Being. However, as we have stressed, for Plotinus, the One is beyond Being and as such the *reality* of one thing is not determined by its being but by its relation to the One. Accordingly, just as there is a reality, namely the One, that is *above* Being, there must be a reality that is *below* Being at the other end of the spectrum. In other words, just as the One is not Being but nonetheless real, Absolute Evil—the opposite of the One—is likewise not being but have real existence too.[89] In a system where the One is more fundamental than Being, it is natural to posit the reality of Absolute Evil outside the realm of Being.

But what is the Absolute Evil? Plotinus identifies it as Matter, the "Undetermination-Absolute, some Absolute Formlesss," which is entirely "below all the patterns, forms, shapes, measurements and limits."[90] In identifying matter as absolute chaos and evil, Plotinus believes in the existence of absolute multiplicity that is totally deprived of all Forms, order or unity. Multiplicity is the ultimate source of evil.

Augustine is however fundamentally at odds with Plotinus on this point. For not only does he deny the existence of Absolute Evil; he also rejects the notion of absolute multiplicity, since insofar as a thing exists, it has a certain degree of unity. Guided by *creatio ex nihilo*, Augustine develops the unique metaphysics that identifies "being" with "unity" for the whole of reality. On the highest level, God, the Supreme Being, is the Supreme Unity and is absolutely simple, which results in the idea of divine simplicity. On lower levels, a creature's degree of unity is proportional to its degree of existence—something has unity insofar as it exists. This is made clear when Augustine writes:

> Other things may be said to be like unity in so far as they have being, and in so far as they are true. . . . Since things are true in so far as they have being, and have being in so far they resemble the source of all unity, that is, the Form of all things that have being.[91]

It is significant that Augustine first claims that things have unity insofar as they have being, but immediately adds that things have being insofar as they have unity or resemble the perfect unity. In all creatures, unity and being are thus mutually dependent and convertible. For when a creature participates in God's being, it also participates in God's unity. It is the level of participation of a creature in God that determines its degrees of being and unity, which are in fact one. In contrast to God, who *is* Being and Unity, a creature participates in God and *has* being and unity, which fall short of God's full Being and Unity. Participation is a creature's necessary relation to God, through which it receives limited unity from God:

> Every corporeal thing is a true body but a false unity. For it is not supremely one and does not completely imitate unity. And yet it would not be a body either if it did not have some unity. Besides it could have no unity unless it derived it from supreme unity.[92]

Since anything that exists has a degree of unity, which participates in God's perfect existence and unity, absolute multiplicity cannot exist. For if a thing is completely deprived of unity, it must be completely devoid of being and cease to exist. Unlike Plotinus, who holds that there is reality beyond the domain of being, Augustine insists that nothing real exists outside the realm of being. For Augustine, non-being is simply equivalent to non-reality. He states that *essentia* comes from the verb *esse* (to be), as *sapientia* (wisdom) comes from *sapere* (to be wise). Non-being is simply the negation of existence. Non-being does not exist, because there is *no* being contrary to God—Being Itself:

> To that Nature which supremely is, therefore, and by Whom all else that is was made, no nature is contrary . . . for that which is contrary to what is, is not-being.

And so there is no being contrary to God, the Supreme Being, and the Author of all beings of whatever kind.[93]

In this respect, then, Augustine is decisively at odds with Plotinus, although he is indebted to the latter in many ways. While Plotinus posits the existence of Absolute Evil or absolute multiplicity as contrary to the One, Augustine argues that there is nothing that is directly contrary to the One or Being. By identifying unity with being, Augustine makes a significant modification on a crucial aspect of Plotinus's metaphysics. Just as absolute evil does not exist, neither does pure multiplicity. All creatures, insofar as they exist, must contain a certain degree of unity. All things in the created order are a necessary combination of unity and multiplicity. Even on the lowest level, matter is not absolute multiplicity but a mixture of one and many. For this reason, in contrast to Plotinus, who regards matter as the cause of evil, Augustine views matter as a good participating in the Supreme Good and One.

3. By identifying the One with Being, as will be discussed in detail later, Augustine provides a different concept of transcendence of the One in relation to the Many. In Plotinus, since the One is above Being, all properties of being are excluded from the One, which cannot even know itself. For "anything that is thought of as the most utterly simplex of all, cannot have self-intellection; to have that would mean being multiple. The Transcendent, thus, neither knows itself nor is known in itself."[94] Although the One is the source "from which the manifold rises,"[95] it is the negation of the Many. By contrast, Augustine, by identifying the One with Being, does not see the One as the direct negation of the Many. While the One (God) differs the Many (creation), the One nonetheless contains in itself all the qualities of the Many in an infinitely eminent mode. In Augustine's logic, since all beings have perfections, Being Itself, the source of all beings, must have the perfections unlimitedly. The One that is Being must possess the attributes of being supremely. For Augustine, therefore, the One cannot be directly contrary to the Many, which means that the relation between the One and the Many is "non-contrastive."[96] The One transcends the Many—not by negation but by eminence. The One, the ultimate source of the Many, must possess the perfections of the Many eminently and undividedly. The Many is not excluded by the One but exists "in" the One,[97] which brings us to the concept of divine simplicity.

Divine Simplicity

One of the direct consequences of identifying unity with being is Augustine's idea of divine simplicity, which, as we will see, has a decisive influence on

Aquinas. The logic is straightforward: since unity is equivalent to being, God, the Supreme Being, must be supremely unified, or in other words, absolutely simple. The notion of divine simplicity is a crucial theme in Augustine's thought, especially in his later works. One of his most concentrated treatments of divine simplicity can be found in *CG*, Book 11, in which he argues that God alone is simple, while creatures are not:

> There is, then, a Good which alone is simple, and therefore alone immutable, and this is God. By this Good all other goods have been created; but they are not simple, and therefore are not immutable.[98]

But how do we distinguish a simple being from a non-simple being? In other words, what are the fundamental marks of simplicity? Augustine states that a being is "called simple because *it is what it has*."[99] God is such a being. "He is said to be alive, for He has life, and He is Himself the life which He has." Augustine goes on to explain:

> It is for this reason, then, that the nature of the Trinity is called simple, because it has not anything that it can lose, and because it is not something different from what it has, in a way that a vessel is different from its liquid or a body from its colour or the air from its light or heat, or the mind from its wisdom. For none of these things is what it has: the vessel is not liquid; the body is not colour; the air is not light or heat; the mind is not wisdom.[100]

To clarify Augustine's reasoning, it seems helpful to employ Aristotle's distinction between substance and accident. Substance defines a thing and describes its essence. For instance, humanity is the substance of a person, as it defines the nature of a person. Accidents, on the other hand, are non-essential to a thing, as it can possess or lose them. For instance, hair color is an accident to a person, because its change does not affect the essence of a person. In Augustine's thought, there is no distinction between substance and accidents in a simple being, since "what it is" (substance) and "what it has" (accidents) become indistinguishable. Thus, the formula "it is what it has" means that a simple being has no accidents and never undergoes a change: it is immutable. For this reason, Augustine places "immutability" right after "simplicity" in the quote above. This interpretation of simplicity is confirmed by Augustine himself: "But in God nothing is said to be according to the accident, because there is nothing changeable in Him."[101] Immutability, one of the core principles in Augustine's thought, is thus rooted in his concept of divine simplicity.[102]

Just as immutability rests upon divine simplicity, mutability is associated with creaturely non-simplicity. A creature is intrinsically mutable because its being is not simple, for what it has is not equal to what it is—it can lose what it has. By contrast, God can never lose what he has, since what he has is identical to what he is:

> For in the human soul to be is not the same as to be strong, or prudent, or just, or temperate, for there can be a soul without any of these virtues. But for God to be is the same as to be strong, or to be just, or to be wise, and to be whatever else you may say of that simple multiplicity, or that multiple simplicity, whereby His substance is signified.[103]

Because God is simple, while we say God *has* life and wisdom, it is more accurate to say that God *is* life and wisdom, for the so-called properties or attributes of God are not additions to God but are God Himself. In other words, God's substance is identical to his qualities. Divine simplicity means no separation between God's substance and attributes—they are one and the same:

> But we indeed use many different words concerning God, in order to bring out that He is great, good, wise, blessed, true, and whatever else He may be called that is not unworthy of Him. But His greatness is the same as His wisdom, for He is not great by bulk, but by power. Similarly, His goodness is the same as His wisdom and greatness; and His truth is the same as all these qualities. And in Him it is not one thing to be blessed, and another thing to be great, or to be wise, or to be true, or to be good, or in a word be to Himself.[104]

Finally, to illustrate the radical nature of divine simplicity, Augustine shockingly claims that each Person in the Trinity alone is not less than the three Persons together:

> Since, therefore, the Father alone, or the Son alone, or the Holy Spirit alone is just as great as the Father, the Son, and the Holy Spirit together, He is not be called threefold in any sense. Bodies, on the contrary, increase by a union of themselves. . . . God does not thereby become greater than each one separately, for there is nothing whereby that perfection can increase.[105]

This radical idea of divine simplicity marks an important progress in the concept of unity. For Plato, as principles of unity, the Forms or Ideas are nonetheless varied and arguably not completely unified among themselves. In Augustine, God "the One"—the ultimate unifying principle of all of reality— is truly and absolutely unified in himself, which pushes metaphysics toward a new level of unity. All things are now unified by the absolutely simple God. In addition, such a Unity is truly comprehensive and all-embracing, for even matter, which is outside the realm of unity in Plato's thought, now falls under the unifying effect of the Augustinian One, God, who created matter out of nothing. Likewise, by denying the reality of absolute evil or multiplicity, as in Plotinus's system, Augustine places all of reality into unity, emphasizing that there is no nature contrary to the One God. Only this Unity can hold all of reality together. More importantly, this all-unifying One in its simplicity is not mere negation or deprivation of multiplicity. On the contrary, the One is infinitely rich and active, as the One is the Supreme Being that possesses all the qualities of being in infinite eminence and plenitude. Only this One, who is Being Itself, avoids the aloofness of the Plotinian One and relates to the Many in a profoundly intimate fashion. The One does not compromise but sustains the integrity and substantiality of the Many.

From what was discussed above, we can see that Augustine's concept of participation is not straightforwardly Platonic or Neoplatonic. Although indebted to Platonism, especially in his early thought, Augustine certainly moves beyond Platonism by reframing participatory ontology in the light of the doctrine of *creatio ex nihilo*. In their attempts to revive participatory ontology, both RO and Boersma rely heavily on Platonism, but have not paid enough attention to the differences that Augustine has made to the concept of participation. Departing from the Platonic tradition of placing one above being, Augustine identifies unity with being and thus arrives at a significantly different idea of unity from that of Platonism. The Augustinian One is no longer the Plotinian One, but the One that contains and embraces infinite riches of multiplicity. The One is not the antithesis of the Many but its ground. But to allow the Many to truly participate in the One, we also need a different concept of the Many. This will take us to the next chapter, in which we will discuss how Augustine differs from the Platonists in his understanding of multiplicity.

NOTES

1. Vernon Bourke, *Augustine's View of Reality* (Villanova, PA: Villanova University Press, 1964), 117.

2. Agonstino Trapé, *Patrology*, vol. 4, ed. Angelo Di Berardino (Allen, TX: Christian Classics, 1986), 408.

3. David V. Meconi, "St. Augustine's Early Theory of Participation," *Augustinian Studies* 27 (1996): 83. Articles that have touched on Augustine's concept of participation include: Ianuarius Di Somma, "De naturali participatione divini luminis in mente humana secundum S. Augustinum et S. Thoman," *Gregorianum* 7 (1926): 321–38; M. Annice, "Historical Sketch"; Patricia Wilson-Kastner, "Grace as Participation in the Divine Life in the Theology of Augustine of Hippo," *Augustinian Studies* 7 (1976): 135–52; Juan Pegueroles, "Participatión y conocimiento de Dios

en la predicación de San Agustín," *Espíritu* 27 (1979): 5–26; Gerald Bonner, "Augustine's Conception of Deification," *Journal of Theological Studies* 37 (1986): 369–86; Roland Teske, "The Image and Likeness of God in St. Augustine's *De Genesi ad litteram liber imperfectus*," *Augustinianum* 30 (1990): 441–51; Claudio Moreschini, "Neoplatonismo e cristianesimo: 'Partecipare d Dio' secondo Boezio e Agostino," *Sicilia e Italia suburbicaria tra IV e VIII secolo*, ed., Salvatore Pricoco et al. (Soveria Mannelli: Rubbettino Editore, 1991), 283–95. In *Augustine's Early Theology of Image: A Study of in the Development of Pro-Nicene Theology* (Oxford: Oxford University Press, 2016), Gerald P. Boersma also treats of Augustine's participation, but his focus is on the image part of participation. The most explicit, concentrated study of the subject can be found in Meconi, "Augustine's Early Theory of Participation," but even this article is only a brief analysis of one short text from the Augustinian corpus.

4. James F. Anderson has complained that "metaphysical dimension of Augustine's thought has received little special attention among scholars" (*St. Augustine and Being: A Metaphysical Essay* [Hague: Martinus Nifhoff, 1965], preface).

In comparison, more scholarly attention has been given to Augustine's concept of deification. See Mary N. Marrocco, "Participation in the Divine Life in St. Augustine's *De Trinitate* and Selected Contemporary Homiletic Discourses" (PhD diss., University of St. Michael's College, 2000); David Meconi, *The One Christ: St. Augustine's Theology of Deification* (Washington, DC: Catholic University of America Press, 2013).

5. For a more detailed account on this topic, see Annice, "Historical Sketch of Participation."

6. *Republic* X, 596 a6–7.

7. Cornelio Fabro, "The Intensive Hermeneutics of Thomistic Philosophy: The Notion of Participation," trans. B. M. Bonansea, *Review of Metaphysics*, 27 no. 3 (1974): 449.

8. Kathryn Tanner, *Christ the Key* (Cambridge: Cambridge University Press, 2010), 8–9.

9. For a detailed analysis of the centrality of participation in Athanasius's thought, see Alan L. Kolp, "Participation: A Unifying Concept in the Theology of Athanasius," PhD diss., Harvard University, 1976. Cf. Athanasius, *On the Incarnation of the Word* in Nicene and Post-Nicene Fathers, 2nd ser., vol. 4, ed. Archibald Robsertson (Peabody, MA: Hendrickson, 1994), §§7–10.

10. Athanasius, *Four Discourses against the Arians* in Nicene and Post-Nicene Fathers, Discourse 1, chapter 5, section 16, cit. Tanner, 6.

11. Julie Canlis, "Being Made Human: The Significance of Creation for Irenaeus's Doctrine of Participation," *Scottish Journal of Theology* no. 4 (2005): 434–54.

12. Irenaeus, *Against Heresies* in Ante-Nicene Fathers, vol. 1, ed. Alexander Roberts and James Donaldson (Peabody, MA: Hendrickson, 1994), IV. 11.2, cit. in Ibid., 436.

13. Canlis, "Being Made Human," 447.

14. Meconi, "Augustine's Early Theory of Participation," 82. Computer search shows that some forms of "participation" occur 666 times within the Augustinian corpus.

15. Ibid.

16. One of the main reasons for me to focus on metaphysical participation is that while the language of participation in the sense of deification has direct biblical references, the metaphysical sense of participation does not; rather, it is a result of systematic consideration of the metaphysical implications of *creatio ex nihilo* in connection to the Greek philosophical theory of participation.

17. In his important study, David Meconi has investigated the continuity between Plato's concept of participation and that of Augustine (Meconi, "Augustine's Early Theory"), but the discontinuity between them has not been sufficiently examined, which is the focus of this chapter. To be clear, to examine how Augustine's theory differs from Plato's, we do not assume that Augustine read Plato and modified his concept of participation directly. Rather, we understand that his knowledge of Plato was primarily second-handed and between him and Plato stood a long tradition of Middle Platonism, Neoplatonism, and Christian Platonism. In this sense, Augustine's transformation of Plato's participatory ontology was not necessarily original, but to large extent built upon the work laid down by many thinkers before him. It must be noted, however, that we are not interested in tracing the historical development of the theory of participation from Plato to Augustine. Rather, our focus is to simply examine the difference between the two thinkers' concepts of participation based on an analysis of Augustine's texts.

18. On this point, I am indebted to Meconi's article above.

19. *Phaedo*, 100 D.

20. Meconi, "Augustine's Early Theory," 93–5.

21. Augustine, "Miscellany of Eighty-Three Questions," in *Responses to Miscellaneous Questions*, trans. Boniface Ramsey (Hyde Park, NY: New City Press, 2008), question 1.

22. Ibid., question 23.

23. Augustine, *The Trinity*, trans. Stephen McKenna (Washington, DC: Catholic University of America Press, 1963), 10.5.

24. Augustine, "Eighty-Three Questions," question 23.

25. Again, we acknowledge that Augustine was not completely original on this point. Thinkers before him had already contributed to the unification of the Platonic forms. Nevertheless, Augustine did play a significant role in placing the Platonic forms into God's Mind, which, as we will see later, was influential to Aquinas and constituted an important step in resolving the tension between creaturely multiplicity and divine simplicity, even though Augustine's solution was not completely successful.

26. Augustine, *On the Literal Interpretation of Genesis: An Unfinished Book* in *Saint Augustine on Genesis*, trans. Roland J. Teske (Washington, DC: Catholic University of America Press, 1991), chapter 16.

27. Augustine, *The City of God against the Pagans*, ed. and trans. R. W. Dyson (Cambridge: Cambridge University Press, 1998), 8.1 (thereafter CG.)

28. Ibid., 10.2, emphasis added.

29. *DT*, 8.3.

30. *DT*, 5.10.

31. *DT*, 5.10, emphases added.

32. See Carol Harrison, "The Role of *creatio ex nihilo* in Augustine's *Confessions*," in *Le Confessions Di Agostino (402-2002): Bilancio e Prospective* (Roma: Institutum Patristicum Augustinianu, 2003), 415–19; chapter 4 of her *Rethinking Augustine's Early Theology: An Argument for Continuity* (Oxford: Oxford University Press, 2006); N. Joseph Torchia, *Creatio ex Nihilo and the Theology of St. Augustine: The Anti-Manichaean Polemic and beyond* (New York: Peter Lang, 1999); Rowan D. Williams, "'Good for Nothing'? Augustine on Creation," *Augustinian Studies* 25 (1994): 9–24; William A. Christian, "Augustine on the Creation of the World," *Harvard Theological Review* 47, no. 1 (1953): 1–25.

33. Again, we note that Augustine's progress from Plato was mediated by the works of MiddlePlatonists, Neoplatonists, and Christian Platonists.

34. Note that I use "are" instead of "were" before "created by God." This is because, though it is certainly a Christian confession that the world began, Aquinas points out that the idea of the temporal beginning of the world need not to be an intrinsic part of *creatio ex nihilo*—it is not a logical contradiction that God creates an eternal universe. See Thomas Aquinas, *Aquinas on Creation: Writings on the "Sentences" of Peter Lombard 2.1.1*, trans. Steven E. Baldner and William E. Carroll (Toronto: Pontifical Institute of Medieval Studies, 1997), article 5.

35. Harrison, *Early Theology*, 79.

36. Paul Copan and William L. Craig, *Creation out of Nothing: A Biblical, Philosophical and Scientific Exploration* (Grand Rapids, MI: Baker Academic, 2004).

37. Gerhard May, *Creation Ex Nihilo: The Doctrine of 'Creation out of Nothing' in Early Christian Thought*, trans. A. S. Worrall (Edinburgh: T&T Clark, 1994); Ernan McMullin, "Creation *ex nihilo*: Early History," in *Creation and the God of Abraham*, ed. David B. Burrell et al. (Cambridge: Cambridge University Press, 2010), 11–23.

38. See, for instance, Frances Young, "'*Creatio Ex Nihilo*': A Context for the Emergence of the Christian Doctrine of Creation," *Scottish Journal of Theology* 44, no. 2 (1991): 139–51.

39. Janet M. Soskice, "*Creatio ex nihilo*: Jewish and Christian Foundations," in *Creation and God*, ed. Burrell et al., 30–31.

40. There is scholarly dispute on whether the term "emanation" is appropriate for Neoplatonism. For instance, Gerson argued that Plotinus's system is not emanationist but essentially creationist (Lloyd P. Gerson, "Plotinus's Metaphysics: Emanation or Creation?" *The Review of Metaphysics* 46, no. 3 (1993): 570–4.) Thus, instead of naming emanation as specifically Neoplatonic, here I use the general term of "metaphysics of emanat."

41. See Torchia, *Creatio ex nihilo*, ch.1.

42. The first is *On Genesis against the Manichees* (388/9); the second, *On the Literal Interpretation of Genesis: An Unfinished Book* (393); the third, the last three

books of *Confessions* (397–400); the fourth, *The Literal Meaning of Genesis* (404–20); and finally, the eleventh and twelfth books of *City of God*.

43. *On Genesis against the Manichees*, 1.2, emphasis added.

44. Augustine, "Of True Religion," in *Augustine: Early Writings*, trans. John H. Burleigh (Philadelphia: Westminster, 1953), 241–2, emphases added.

45. *CG*, 12.18.

46. Torchia, *Creatio ex nihilo*.

47. This principle was explicitly expounded by Thomas Aquinas eight centuries later (*Summa theologiae* 1.48.1).

48. *Republic*, VI, 509B.

49. *CG*, 12.16.

50. Augustine, *The Enchiridion on Faith, Hope and Love*, trans. J. B. Shaw (Washington, D.C.: Regnery, 1961), chapter 12.

51. Ibid., chapter 13, emphases added.

52. Ibid., chapter 9.

53. By Platonism, I mean the Platonic tradition that ranges from Platonism, Middle Platonism to Neoplatonism. In *Confessions* 8.2.3, Augustine tells of his encounter of "the Platonic books," which revolutionizes his thought. As John Rist suggests, "the Platonic books" may have been a small portion of Plotinus's *Ennead*, and while Augustine's "Platonism" "runs deep . . . his acquaintance with Plato's own writings was largely second-handed." See John M. Rist, *Augustine: Ancient Thought Baptized* (Cambridge: Cambridge University Press, 1994), 3, 8–9.

54. W. Norris Clarke, "The Meaning of Participation in St. Thomas," in *Explorations in Metaphysics: Being-God-Person* (South Bend, IN: University of Notre Dame Press, 1995), 91.

55. See Young, "*Creatio Ex Nihilo*," 139–51.

56. While Augustine in many places speaks highly of Platonists, in his later thought, especially "in the years after 400," as Rist points out, "we can identify in Augustine both a renewed emphasis on the weaknesses of the Platonists and a more sober estimate of their strengths." Rist, *Augustine*, 16.

57. *Enneads*, 5.4.1.

58. *Enneads*, 1.8.8. While there are debates over what Plotinus means by "matter" and "evil," it is undisputable that he unambiguously identifies matter as the primary evil. See John Rist, "Plotinus and Augustine on Evil," in *Plotino ed il Neoplatonismo in Oriente e in Occidente* (Rome: Accademia Nazionale dei Lincei, 1974), 495.

59. *True Religion*, 241.

60. Josef Lössl, "The One (*unum*) – A Guiding Concept in *De uera religion*: An Outline of the Text and the History of Its Interpretation," *Revue des Études Augustiniennes* 40 (1994), 100.

61. *Confessions*, 11.29.39.

62. Anderson, *Augustine and Being*, 4.

63. *Republic*, VI, 509 B.

64. *Parmenides*, 144 E.

65. *Enneads*, 5.4.1.

66. See *True Religion*, 241; *Confessions*, 7.10.16; *Trinity*, 5.2; *CG*, 12.2. In a short paragraph in *CG*, 12.6, Augustine calls God "Him Whom supremely is" four times.

67. Janet M. Soskice, "Augustine on Knowing God and Knowing the Self," in *Faithful Reading: New Essays in Theology in Honour of Fergus Kerr, O.P.*, ed. Thomas O'Loughlin, Karen Kilby and Simon Oliver (London: T&T Clark, 2012), 7–8.

68. *CG*, 12.2, emphases added.

69. Ibid., 12.5, emphases added.

70. Etienne Gilson, *Being and Some Philosophers* (Toronto: The Institute of Medieval Studies, 1952), 31. Gilson observes that Augustine "departed from Plotinus on the fundamental principle of the primacy of Being."

71. Lössl, "The One – A Guiding Concept," 92–3.

72. See, for instance, Anderson, *Augustine and Being*, 5. Anderson proclaims that "in a Christian metaphysics, what-is is one, good, true, etc., because it *is*, not conversely," but it seems too far a stretch to turn Augustine's metaphysics of being into that of Aquinas.

73. Lössl, "The One – A Guiding Concept."

74. *TR*, 55.113, emphases added.

75. *Confessions*, 11.29.39.

76. *Confessions*, 2.1.1.

77. *Confessions*, 13.37.52.

78. *DT*, 15.8.

79. As noted above, Augustine's advance on Platonism in this respect builds upon the contributions laid down by many thinkers before him.

80. In *Parmenides*, 130-35, Socrates has difficulty in responding to Parmenides' objections.

81. *Metaphysics* I, 9.

82. Gilson, *Being and Philosophers*, 23.

83. Gerson, "Plotinus's Metaphysics," 570–4.

84. *Enneads*, 5.3.12.

85. *CG*, 12.7.

86. Ibid., 12.8.

87. For a detailed discussion of the difference between Plotinus's and Augustine's views of evil, see Rist, "Plotinus and Augustine."

88. *Enneads*, 1.8.3.

89. In Plotinus's system, the existence of absolute evil (matter) is compelled by logical necessity: "If the One is the first in a series there must be a last in that series," which "will be the contrary of the first." Rist, "Plotinus and Augustine," 498.

90. *Enneads*, 1.8.3.

91. *TR*, 35.65.

92. Ibid., 34.63.

93. *CG*, 12.2.

94. *Enneads*, 5.3.13.

95. *Enneads*, 5.3.12.

96. Kathryn Tanner, *God and Creation in Christian Theology*: *Tyranny or Empowerment* (Minneapolis: Fortress, 2005), 46.

97. Augustine describes God's wisdom as that "which is simple in its multiplicity and uniform in its variety." *CG*, 12.19. Likewise, he calls God's substance "that simple multiplicity, or that multiple simplicity" in *DT*, 6.4.

98. *CG*, 11.10.

99. Ibid., emphases added.

100. Ibid.

101. *DT*, 5.5.

102. Trapé lists "interiority, participation and immutability" as three fundamental principles of Augustine's philosophy. Trapé, *Patrology*, 407.

103. *DT*, 6.4.

104. *DT*, 6.7.

105. Ibid., 6.8.

Chapter 2

Multiplicity and Matter in Augustine's Participatory Ontology[1]

For nine years, Augustine had been a follower of Manicheanism before he was converted to Christianity and, as a Christian, he was under the heavy influence of Platonism. Because of these associations, there is a widespread impression that Augustine has a particularly low view of matter and diversity. Adolph Harnack, for instance, maintains that "Augustine's system is in truth that of the Gnostics, the ancestors of the Manichees."[1] Likewise, an Aquinas scholar has suggested that Augustine "never seems to have freed himself entirely from the Manichaean conviction of cosmic evil."[2] Colin Gunton adds his complaint about Augustine's disdain for matter and plurality. "[T]he signs of a Platonic transcendentality," he argues, "which denies or subverts the rights of plurality are to be found" in Augustine's thought, which tends toward "a rather gnostic view of matter."[3]

On such readings, Augustine never fully escapes the influence of Platonism and Gnosticism and inherits their contempt for multiplicity and matter. This interpretation, however, overlooks the profound difference between the Augustinian concept of matter and plurality and that of Platonism. In fact, Augustine significantly transforms the Platonic concept of multiplicity and firmly defends the goodness of matter against "the Platonist."[4] Augustine's appropriation of Platonic participation is not slavish but critical, as the doctrine of creation compels him to depart from straightforward Platonism. Within the framework of *creatio ex nihilo*, he cannot simply disparage multiplicity and matter as "the Platonists" do, since all that exists has been created by God and must be intrinsically good. But to understand Augustine's concept of multiplicity and matter, we must first examine the distinction between multiplicity and non-simplicity in his metaphysical thought.

45

THE NATURE OF MULTIPLICITY IN
AUGUSTINE'S THOUGHT

Multiplicity vs. Non-simplicity

As we saw in the preceding chapter, for Augustine, simplicity is the defining feature of divine nature. God's essence is identical to his perfections and for this reason what is divine must be truly simple:

> According to this, therefore, those things which are fundamentally and truly divine are called simple, because in them quality and substance are one and the same, and because they are divine, or wise, or blessed without participation in anything which is not themselves.[5]

By contrast, a created nature is not simple, because it does not possess its qualities by reason of its own nature but by something else. For instance, a piece of metal does not become hot by itself but because of a fire nearby. We may say that the metal participates in the heat of fire, which is hot by nature. Likewise, all creatures, whose nature is non-simple, must participate in God, who alone is simple. Hence, just as simplicity is intrinsic to divine nature, non-simplicity is accordingly the mark of a created nature. We have thus two sides of participation: one is divine nature, which is simple and participates in nothing else; the other is created nature, which is non-simple and must participate in God.

For Augustine, then, the fundamental distinction between God and creatures is that while the former is simple, the latter are not. We must note, however, that the distinction between simplicity and non-simplicity is not the same as the distinction between unity and multiplicity, because for Augustine non-simplicity is not the same as multiplicity. It is true that he sometimes uses the two concepts—non-simplicity and multiplicity—interchangeably. For instance, when discussing the nature of bodily things, he claims that "the nature of the body is essentially manifold, and not at all simple" (*multiplex esse conuincitur natura corporis, simplex autem nullo modo*).[6] Likewise, he maintains that a spiritual creature such as the soul, while simpler than the body, is nonetheless "not simple, but multiple" (*non simplecem sed multiplicem*).[7] In these places, multiplicity seems to be identical to non-simplicity. In Augustine's mature thought, however, there is a subtle difference between these two concepts. For if multiplicity were indeed identical to non-simplicity, then God, being simple, would absolutely have nothing to do with multiplicity. However, on more than one occasion, Augustine maintains that God himself contains manifold. For instance, he writes that "in Holy Scripture, it is true, the Spirit of Wisdom is called '*manifold*' because it contains *many things* within itself."[8] If God himself is said to be "manifold," then multiplicity cannot be strictly identical to non-simplicity, for God is simple.

But how can God be one and many simultaneously? To understand this, we have to review what we discussed about Augustine's concept of the One. As mentioned in the preceding chapter, the Augustinian One is the not the same as the Plotinian One, from which multiplicity is utterly excluded. The Augustinian One, although simple, nonetheless contains multiplicity within itself. This understanding is made clear in the text below:

> [T]he Spirit of Wisdom is called "manifold" because it contains many things within itself. What it contains, however, it also is, and, being one, it is all these things. For wisdom is not many things, but one thing, in which there are immense and infinite treasures of intelligible things, and in which reside all the invisible and immutable Forms of the visible and mutable things made by it.[9]

The Spirit, who is divine in nature, is *manifold*, because it contains multiple Forms in infinite plenitude. It is thus clear that for Augustine, divine simplicity by no means excludes multiplicity—it includes and embraces multiplicity. God is multiplicity in simplicity. For this reason, Augustine speaks of God as "that simple multiplicity or that multiple simplicity" (*simplici multipliciate uel multiplici simplicitate*).[10] For him, the fundamental difference between God and creatures is not between the One and the Many (between unity and multiplicity) but between simplicity and non-simplicity. The opposite of unity is not multiplicity but disunity or divisibility. In other words, the essence of non-simplicity is *divisibility*, which becomes evident if we examine his exposition of the non-simplicity of creatures.

First, with regards to corporeal things, Augustine writes that they are not simple because they are made of separable or divisible parts:

> Whatever comes into contact with a bodily sense is proved to be not one but many, for it is corporeal and therefore has innumerable parts. I am not going to speak of parts so minute as to be almost unrealizable; but, however small the object may be, it has at least a right-hand part and a left-hand part, an upper and a lower part, a further and a nearer part, one part at the end and another at the middle. We must admit that these parts exist in any body however small, and accordingly we must agree that no corporeal object is a true and absolute unity.[11]

Augustine explains that bodies fail to be true unity because they can always be divided into parts which are separable from one another by space. However small, insofar as one thing is a body, it necessarily contains divisible parts and is inherently divisible. It is spatial extension that makes a body divisible, because "everything that is a body is certainly made up of parts so that one part in it is greater, another less, and the whole is greater than any part, no matter which it is or how great it is."[12] Apart from spatial extension, division between different qualities of a body, such as size and shape, also makes it divisible:

[For] in every single body, size is one thing, color another and shape another. The color and the shape can remain the same, even though the size becomes smaller; likewise the shape and the size can remain unchanged, even if the color is changed . . . and whatever other qualities are said to be in the body can all be changed at the same time, or some can be changed at the same time without any change in the rest. From this it follows that the nature of the body is essentially manifold, and not at all simple.[13]

For corporeal things, then, it is their inner divisibility that constitutes non-simplicity. They are non-simple because they are composed of separable parts and qualities. Insofar as they are bodies, things cannot possess full unity and as such Augustine argues that "every corporeal thing is a true body but a false unity."[14]

Next, in contrast to corporeal things, spiritual creatures, such as angels and the soul, have no spatial extension and are not restrained by physical boundaries. Nor do they have sensible qualities such as color and shape. In this sense, Augustine admits that a spiritual being "is more simple than the body . . . because it is not spread out in bulk over a determined amount of space." Nonetheless, he asserts that "the soul is also manifold and not simple," because it can lose its qualities:

But since even in the soul to be skillful is one thing, to be indolent another, and to be keen another; and since memory is one thing, desire another, fear another, joy another, sadness another, and since numberless things can be found in the soul in numberless ways, some without others, some more, and some less, it is obvious that its nature is not simple, but manifold. For nothing simple is changeable, but every creature is changeable.[15]

Hence, although a spiritual creature does not have different parts, it is still non-simple, because its essence is separable from its qualities and it undergoes a change when it acquires or loses them. Using Aristotelian concepts, we can say that there is a distinction between substance and accidents in spiritual creatures. The essence of a soul is separable from qualities such as wisdom and justice, since a soul is always a soul, regardless of the fact whether it has wisdom or justice or not. In this sense, qualities of wisdom and justice are accidental to a soul. Hence, it is the *divisibility* between substance and accidents that makes spiritual creatures non-simple.

Finally, divine nature is absolutely simple, because there is neither division between substance and accidents, nor division between being and perfections—they are one and the same in God. God is thus supremely indivisible in himself. In contrast, all creatures are by nature divisible. Just as simplicity is the defining feature of divine nature, divisibility is the defining feature of a created nature. For everything, its degree of divisibility is inversely proportional to its degree of being. Being in its highest way, "that which is (*id quod est*),"[16] is perfectly simple and absolutely non-divisible; all other beings are non-simple and divisible. In this connection, the degree of divisibility also corresponds to the degree of mutability: the more divisible something is, the more mutable it is.[17] It is within this framework that Augustine distinguishes between three kinds of being—God, spiritual creatures, and corporeal creatures—in a descending order. God, who is completely simple and indivisible, is immutable and eternal. Corporeal things, being most divisible, are most mutable and perishable. In between, spiritual creatures, although immortal, are nonetheless mutable and non-simple.

For Augustine, therefore, it is not multiplicity but divisibility that constitutes the essence of non-simplicity. Although he sometimes uses non-simplicity and multiplicity interchangeably, it is divisibility or non-simplicity that defines the created nature. This insight, still somewhat implicit in Augustine, as we will see, was made explicit by his medieval successor, Aquinas, eight centuries later. With rigorous tools of Aristotelian logic, Aquinas managed to bring this Augustinian insight into full light.

Multiplicity and *creatio ex nihilo*

The doctrine of *creatio ex nihilo* holds that all that is real has its origin in God, which means that nothing truly exists in the creation can be contrary to God. For this reason, created multiplicity cannot be the direct opposite of divine simplicity. The negation of simplicity is not multiplicity but non-simplicity, the essence of which is divisibility. As a result, in contrast to the Neoplatonic position, Augustine develops a significantly different concept of multiplicity in relation to God's simplicity in the light of the doctrine of creation. Whereas Neoplatonism holds that multiplicity is entirely excluded by the One, Augustine affirms that multiplicity does not contradict the simplicity of the One, but is already contained in the One. For Augustine, the One, who is the Creator of all, is simultaneously unity and multiplicity, and as such God is called "simple multiplicity or multiple simplicity."[18] God is not a monad, but contains an infinite plenitude of perfections which exist in an absolutely indivisible mode. It is this complete indivisibility, as we have seen, that undergirds the concept of divine simplicity.

In contrast, multiplicity in creation is not perfectly unified but separable or divisible. As such, no creatures have full unity or simplicity. However, insofar as they exist, different parts or qualities are held together in unity, otherwise they would not exist at all. What distinguishes creatures from God is therefore not multiplicity but divisibility. In a certain sense, both God and creatures contain multiplicity, but while God's multiplicity is supremely unified, creatures' multiplicity is unified to a limited extent and their unity is not perfect but divisible and mutable.

In Augustine's metaphysics of participation, then, creatures participate in God with respect to both unity and multiplicity. They participate in God's unity insofar as they have a unified being, without which they would not exist. They participate in God's multiplicity insofar as they receive multiple qualities from God such as wisdom, goodness, and justice, which exist supremely in God. Since these perfections in creatures are finite, they are separable and divisible among themselves. Despite such divisibility, there is still unity among the perfections, for insofar as they participate in God, the perfections are unified to a certain degree. Even in a creature, wisdom cannot be utterly separable from goodness or justice—they are unified to some degree. All creatures thus participate in God's unity and multiplicity and are a combination of the One and the Many. Just as created unity reflects God's unity, created multiplicity reflects God's multiplicity.

Hence, the Christian doctrine of creation compels Augustine to transform the metaphysics of participation and to embark on a journey, although in an initial stage, of developing a profoundly different view of multiplicity from that of Neoplatonism. On this journey, as we will see, Aquinas travels further, but in many ways he is indebted to the decisive step that his predecessor has made in reshaping the Neoplatonic tradition.

Multiplicity in Plotinus and Augustine

To some extent, Plotinus's entire philosophical endeavor is to answer the question of how the Many derives from the One. Synthesizing Plato's theory of participation with Aristotle's notion of causality, Plotinus makes the One not only the principle of unity but also the source of the Many.[19] His system on the surface seems consistent with the Christian view of reality. A closer examination of his philosophy, however, reveals a significantly different conception of the Many in relation to the One from that of the Christian tradition. In Plotinus, the Many is utterly excluded from the One and multiplicity is more of a *deflection* from than a product of the One, which is absolutely simple. The One alone is perfect and the degree of perfection of everything else is inversely proportional to its distance from the One. The further anything is from the One, the more manifold and imperfect it is.[20] In contrast to the perfect One, any degree of multiplicity is understood as an imperfection. For this reason, as discussed in the preceding chapter, Plotinus sees matter, which is the furthest removed from the One, as absolute multiplicity and thereby Absolute Evil.[21] In fact, matter is not located in the domain of being but in that of non-being.[22] To return to the One—"the passing of solitary to solitary"[23]—the soul must rid itself of matter and multiplicity. To see the One, we must "cut away everything."[24] Multiplicity is annihilated for the sake of unity and it can be argued that Plotinus's metaphysics contains a tragic dimension, as articulated by David Hart:

> For if the truth of things is their pristine likeness in substance (in positive ground) to the ultimate ground, then all difference is not only accidental, but false (though perhaps probatively false): to arrive at the truth, one must suffer the annihilation of particularity. . . . Truth's dynamism is destruction, a laying waste of all of finite being's ornate intricacies, erasing the world from the space between the vanishing point of the One and the vanishing point of the *nous* in their barren correspondence.[25]

In Plotinus, therefore, multiplicity *per se* has no positive ground or substantial reality insofar as it is the negation of unity; neither does multiplicity contain any amount of goodness insofar as it is a deviation and deflection from the One.[26] Multiplicity as such is the source of evil and something to be denied and rejected.

It must be noted that the fact that Plotinus has a low view of multiplicity does not mean that he has a Gnostic vision of the sensible world. On the contrary, he has an impressively high regard for the physical universe and disagrees sharply with the Gnostics over the goodness and beauty of the cosmos. In his polemic against the Gnostics, he berates their blindness toward the glory of the universe:

> [W]ho will be so lethargic and unresponsive in his sensitivities that, upon seeing all the beauty in the sensible world, and its symmetry and its great state of order, and the pattern made visible among the stars, even though they are so far away, he does not thereupon take notice and be seized by reverential awe of how marvelous these things are, and how marvelous their source is?[27]

It is true that the sensible world is not as good as the intelligible world, but we should not put the former—an image of the intelligible world—on par with the latter. Nevertheless, the universe is a good image of the intelligible world:

> What other image of the intelligible world could there be that is finer than this? For what other fire could be a better image of the intelligible Fire apart from

the sensible fire? And what other earth apart from the sensible earth could come next after the Earth in the intelligible world? And what sphere could be more precise, more dignified, and more well-ordered in its revolution after the one in the intelligible world that contains intelligible cosmos? And what other sun after the intelligible Sun could be ranked ahead this visible sun?[28]

It is therefore evident that Plotinus, like his predecessor Plato, affirms the order and beauty of the cosmos, which places him outside of the Gnostic camp. Unlike the Gnostics, who see a stark separation between the sensible world and the intelligible world, Plotinus views the sensible world as participating in the intelligible world and truly illuminated by the soul of the universe.[29] The universe is good because of the illumination and presence of the intelligible soul.

The universe is good, however, *not* because of its physicality and multiplicity. For physicality itself is not good and makes no contribution to the goodness of the world. It is thus natural for Plotinus to affirm, like Plato, the beauty of the physical world on the one hand, and to disdain, also like Plato, embodiment and physicality on the other hand. Even in his polemic against the Gnostics, Plotinus acknowledges that it is legitimate for them to "despise the nature of the body because they heard Plato disparaging body for the many ways in which it obstructs the soul," and urges them to look beyond the corporeal nature of the cosmos and consider its intelligible dimension.[30] In fact, Plotinus devotes a treatise in *Enneads* to reconciling a seeming contradiction in Plato's thought—seeing the body as a prison or cave on the one hand and hailing the physical cosmos as a blessed god on the other.[31] There, he argues that whereas the soul of the universe administers the cosmos as a whole with intellect only, the soul of an individual attends to a particular body with discursive reasoning and hence suffers distractions from the body. It is thus clear that while Plotinus affirms the goodness of the cosmos, he is in continuity with Plato in viewing physicality and multiplicity as a burden and source of distraction.

In Plotinus's thought, therefore, we indeed find a source of contempt for matter and plurality, which, as we have seen, is the foundation for the Reformed thinkers' suspicion of Platonism and RO's appropriation of Platonism in developing participatory ontology. The suspicion is warranted, because uncritical appropriation of Platonism may indeed lead to a concept of participation that undermines physicality and multiplicity. As such, I have argued that contemporary theologians of participation should rely more on Augustine, because while Augustine adopts the concept and key structures of participation from Platonism, he significantly reshapes the important aspects of the theory, especially the nature multiplicity and physicality.

It is true that some of Augustine's language, especially in his earlier and middle works such as *Confessions* and *Of True Religion*, resembles that of Plotinus. In particular, scholars observe that *Confessions*, which depicts the odyssey of the soul's return to the One from distractions of multiplicity, seems to echo Plotinus's project in *Enneads*.[32] Indeed, in Book II, Augustine writes of his experience of turning away from God in a seemingly Plotinian fashion: "You gathered me together from the state of disintegration in which I had been fruitlessly divided. I turned from unity in you to be lost in multiplicity."[33] In Book IX, he writes:

> In your repose which forgets all toil because there is none beside you, nor are we to look for the multiplicity of other things which are not what you are. For "you, Lord, have established me in hope by means of unity."

Likewise, he speaks of Christ as "mediator between you the One and us the many, who live in a multiplicity of distractions by many things."[34] In those places, it appears that Augustine, just like Plotinus, deems multiplicity negatively and dismissively.

If we look more closely, however, we will understand that Augustine does not see multiplicity in the same way as Plotinus does. In fact, Augustine does not see multiplicity *per se* as the source of trouble, since matter and diversity as God's creation are not evil but essentially good. Rather, it is the will (*voluntas*) of the soul that is the cause of trouble[35] when it decides to seek and enjoy created goods rather than the Creator, whom alone should be enjoyed.[36] It is for this reason that each quote above contains a verb: "turn," "look for," or "live," which indicates an action—a result of the will. The real trouble is not multiplicity as such, but the soul's decision to "turn" away from God, to "look for the multiplicity of other things," or to "live" in a way in which one does not seek God but created goods. Thus, for Augustine, it is not multiplicity but idolatry—making creatures rather than God our ultimate concern—that is at the heart of sin. Multiplicity in creation is good in itself, but if we choose to enjoy it for its own sake instead of God, we commit sin and produce evil. For this reason, Augustine emphasizes that God alone is to be enjoyed, whereas creatures are to be used. It is out of the same concern that he admonishes the soul not to look for creaturely multiplicity but turn to God.

Hence, while sometimes using language that echoes that of Plotinus, Augustine—especially in his more mature writings—develops a profoundly different understanding of multiplicity from the latter. First, while Plotinus never assigns multiplicity to the One, Augustine clearly attributes multiplicity to both God and creatures.[37] In this sense, multiplicity in Augustine's thought can be seen as a *transcendental*,[38] which, as we shall see, is later made more explicit by Aquinas.[39] On this understanding, multiplicity is not merely creaturely finitude, but first exists supremely within God. Divine multiplicity is the source of creaturely multiplicity. Needless to say, no ontological continuity exists between divine and created multiplicity and yet the doctrine of creation requires a correspondence and causal relation between them, just as there is a correspondence and causal relationship between divine and human wisdom. Using Aquinas's term, we may say that there is an "analogy" between creaturely and divine multiplicity.[40] This understanding is lacking, however, in Plotinus, who conceives no analogy between multiplicity and the One. The doctrine of *creatio ex nihilo* compels Augustine to depart from Plotinus and establish a positive connection between creaturely multiplicity and divine simplicity.

Second, unlike Plotinus, who sees multiplicity as purely negative in comparison to the One, Augustine gives positive reality to multiplicity. In Plotinus, manifold things that proceed from the One have goodness insofar as they participate in Unity. Their goodness, however, has nothing to do with their multiplicity, which is the measurement of their distance from unity and goodness. In other words, multiplicity as such is not a *reality* but the measurement of distance from reality—the One. Multiplicity *per se* has no ground in reality but is a deviation from reality. In a certain sense, the place of multiplicity in Plotinus is equivalent to that of evil in Augustine.[41] Just as Augustine states that evil is nothing but "the absence of good,"[42] Plotinus regards multiplicity as nothing but the absence of unity and goodness. It is for this reason that multiplicity and matter are considered as the source of evil. Multiplicity must be purged before the soul returns to the One. By contrast, for Augustine, because multiplicity exists supremely in God, multiplicity is not the corruption of being but a substance in itself. Divine multiplicity is supremely substantial, since God is supremely Being. Creaturely multiplicity is also substantial, since it is created by and participates in God. On this understanding, creaturely multiplicity and diversity are by no means evil but part of the good creation. Multiplicity in itself is good, real, and substantial and does not need to be abolished when creatures return to God.

In the framework of creation, Augustine is thus compelled to reject Plotinus's dismissive view of multiplicity and affirm its goodness and substantiality. This difference between Augustine and Plotinus (and Neoplatonists in general) is most evident in their sharp divergence on the nature of the body in relation to evil. Given that there is a widespread impression that Augustine has a low view of matter, it is important that we investigate how his view of the body differs from that of "the Platonists."[43]

AUGUSTINE ON THE GOODNESS
OF MATTER (THE BODY)

Due to his alleged associations with Platonism, Augustine has gained a reputation for holding a tragically low view of matter and the body.[44] This impression partially comes from the fact that he states that he is only concerned with "God and the soul,"[45] stressing that the soul is superior to the body.[46] A surface reading of these texts may leave one with a sense that he never fully departs from Manichaeism and Gnosticism or that his view of materiality is in continuity with Platonism. Augustine seems to embrace a sub-Christian worldview that denies the dignity of materiality and the goodness of creation.

A closer reading of Augustine's text, however, especially the middle section of *City of God*, reveals a profound difference between his view of the body and that of "the Platonists." Despite his generally high regard for Plato and Platonism, Augustine engages in a painstaking debate with the Platonists[47] over the body's relation to evil. Contrary to the position above, Augustine firmly defends the goodness of the body, which separates him not only from Gnostics and Manicheans but also from the Platonists, who see the body as the source of disturbance for the soul. While he believes that the Platonists have obtained many truths, Augustine is convinced that their view of the body is fundamentally mistaken. In *Confessions*, he recounts that while in the "books of the Platonists" he finds biblical teachings such as the preexistence of the Word, through whom all things were created, he does not read the truth of the Incarnation and chides the Platonists for being too proud to accept the Word made flesh.[48] The goodness of the physical body constitutes a key theme in Augustine's theology, especially in its later stage, in which he becomes more critical of the Platonic tradition.

The Body or Its Corruptibility

In Plotinus, matter—absolute multiplicity—is the "Absolute Evil" and the source of all evils.[49] On this understanding, matter is blamed as the cause of wickedness.[50] To be sure, in Neoplatonism matter is not identical to corporeal things such as the world and the human body.[51] Nonetheless, since corporeal things are closest to unformed matter in the scale of reality, Plotinus claims: "The bodily Kind, in that it partakes of Matter, is an evil thing"[52] and Platonists in general believe that "the ills of the soul derive from the body."[53]

Those who accuse Augustine of having a semi-Gnostic view of the body will be surprised to realize that it is on the goodness of the body that he takes up a most painstaking polemic against the Platonists, whom are otherwise praised by him to have held doctrines that are close to Christian truths.[54] In his dispute with the Platonists, Augustine first presents their position:

> But the philosophers . . . mock us because we say that the separation of soul and body is to be considered among its punishments. They do so because they deem that the soul's blessedness is perfected only when it is entirely rid of the body, and returns to God simple and alone and, as it were, naked.[55]

The Christian teaching on death—the separation of body and soul—as a punishment is derided by the Platonists, because they think that the soul's separation from the body is not a punishment but a blessing and that the soul's blessedness is attained only when it is detached from the body. In presenting his adversaries' position, Augustine seems to have Plotinus in mind, since the sentence "returns to God simple and alone and, as it were, naked" noticeably echoes *Enneads*. Against this understanding, Augustine argues insightfully that,

> it is not the body, but the body's corruptibility, which is a burden to the soul. Hence that verse of Scripture which we quoted in an earlier book: "For the corruptible body presseth down the soul." The word "corruptible" is here added to show that the soul is pressed down not by the body *simply as such*, but by the body as it has become by reason of sin and its consequent punishment.[56]

Here, Augustine skillfully distinguishes between the body as such and the body's corruption, arguing that it is the latter—not the former—that constitutes the burden for the soul. The source of the trouble is not the body *per se* but the corruptibility of the body, which in fact is a result of the first sin. In doing so, Augustine offers an insightful critique of the Platonists' view of the body as the source of evil and defends the Christian teaching on bodily resurrection. It is not the body but its corruptibility that will be overcome in blessedness:

> To obtain blessedness, therefore, we need not be rid of every kind of body, but only the corruptible, irksome, painful, dying body: not of such bodies as the goodness of God made for the first human beings, but only of such as the punishment of sin has imposed upon us.[57]

In the blessed state, we have "bodies which, though earthly, are nonetheless now incorruptible: bodies which they can move as they wish, and place where they wish, with the greatest ease."[58] In Scripture, resurrected bodies that finally become incorruptible and immortal are called "spiritual bodies." Spiritual bodies become immortal since the corruptibility of the body has been removed, but they are still physical bodies, nonetheless. Augustine explains the nature of spiritual bodies in the following passage:

> For just as the spirit is not improperly called carnal when it serves the flesh, so shall the flesh rightly be called spiritual when it serves spirit. This is not because flesh will be converted into spirit. . . . Rather, it is because it will be subject to the spirit with a supreme and marvelous readiness to obey, and will fulfill its will in the most assured knowledge of indestructible immortality, with all distress, all corruptibility and all reluctance gone.[59]

To safeguard from misinterpretations of spiritual bodies, Augustine is emphatic that it is not that the body will turn into a spirit, but that the body— while remaining its fleshly nature—will become completely obedient to the spirit, because its corruptible and rebellious nature has been removed. In contrast to the Platonist position, Augustine repeatedly emphasizes that the bodily nature, which is God's good creation, remains in spiritual bodies, as is evident in resurrected Christ:

> [For] even after the Resurrection, when He was now in spiritual, yet nonetheless real, flesh, He took food and drink with His disciples. . . . Hence, they will be spiritual not because they will cease to be bodies, but because they will be sustained by a quickening Spirit.[60]

Hence, in distinguishing between the body *per se* and its corruptibility, Augustine decisively departs from the Platonists and firmly defends the goodness of the body. Compelled by the doctrine of creation, he cannot simply disregard the body as the Platonists do, but must affirm its intrinsic value—a nature that has been created to be good. In his defense of the body, Augustine in effect develops a significantly different theory of the cause of evil from that of the Platonists.

Nature or Will

Augustine argues that it is not the body but the corruptibility of the body that is responsible for the vices of the soul. The question remains, however—what causes the body's corruptibility? The Platonists suggest that corruptibility is the very nature of flesh. By contrast, Augustine argues that corruptibility is not part of the nature of flesh, but the result of sin, which is caused by the *will* of the soul. This explanation offers a profoundly different view on the origin of evil. Whereas the Platonists locate the source of evil in matter and in the body, Augustine places the cause of evil in the will of the soul. As

Paul Henry points out, the Platonic tradition, following Socrates, holds an intellectualist view of ethics, in which virtue is seen as knowledge and vice as ignorance, and the role of will is completely absent. "Neither Socrates nor Plato took sufficient note of the will-factor. In their teaching there is no place . . . for sin and plenary responsibility," because "the Intellect, with which the soul in the higher phase of its life is identified, is without sin and strictly incapable of sinning."[61] In such a framework, evil is not caused by the will but by the intrinsic weakness of the body. Augustine, however, is at odds with this position:

> Now someone may say that the flesh is the cause of moral evils of every kind, because it is thanks to the influences of the flesh that the soul lives as it does. But he who says this has not considered the whole nature of man with sufficient care.... Nonetheless, those who suppose that the ills of the soul derive from the body are in error.[62]

In response to the Platonists' position, as expounded by Virgil, which views the body as the source of disturbances for the mind, such as desire, fear, joy, and grief, Augustine asserts firmly:

> Our faith, however, is something *very different*. For the corruption of the body, which presseth down the soul, was not the cause of the first sin, but its punishment; nor was it corruptible flesh that made the soul sinful, but the sinful soul that made the flesh corruptible.[63]

To refute the Platonists, Augustine reverses the order of cause and effect: while the Platonists blame the body as the cause of vices in the soul, Augustine considers the soul as the cause of the corruption of the body. In other words, for Augustine, the body's corruptibility, which has negative effects on the soul, is not the cause but an effect of sin. But what is the cause of the first sin? Again, it is not the flesh but the soul. Sin is not a bodily matter but a *spiritual* one. This understanding is made clear in the following argument:

> Thus, though this corruption of the flesh results in some incitements to sin and in sinful desires themselves, we still must not attribute to the flesh all the vices of a wicked life. Otherwise, we should absolve the devil from all such vices, since he has no flesh.[64]

Augustine's strategy is *reductio ad absurdum*: if we were to concede to our adversaries that all vices are caused by the flesh, a logical conclusion would be that Satan is completely without sin, because he does not have a body. But this is absurd according to what we know from revelation and hence the assumption that the flesh is the cause of evil is false. With this argument, Augustine reaffirms the Christian position that the source of evil is not the body but the soul:

> For the apostle says that hatred, variance, jealousy, wrath and envy are works of the flesh, and the source and origin of all these evils is *pride*, which reigns in the devil even though he is without flesh. . . . It is not, then, by having flesh, which the devil does not have, that man has become like the devil. Rather it is by living according to his own self; that is, according to man. For the devil chose to live according to self when he did not abide in the truth.[65]

Augustine makes it clear that the ultimate origin of sin is pride, which is certainly not a bodily matter but a spiritual one. Pride is a condition of the soul, whereby it chooses to live not according to God, but according to man. Augustine uses the word "choose" to suggest that the decision is not made by necessity but by the will. He repeatedly emphasizes the centrality of the will in ethics:

> What is important here is the quality of a man's will. For if the will is perverse, the emotions will be perverse; but if it is righteous, the emotions will not only be blameless, but praiseworthy. The will is engaged in all of them; indeed, they are all no more than acts of the will.[66]

With this shift, Augustine reinterprets the so-called four most notable disturbances of the mind: desire, joy, fear, and grief. He points out that the feelings are not essentially bad; they can be good as well—whether they are good or bad depends on the associated will:

> A righteous will, then, is a good love; a perverted will is an evil love. Therefore, love striving to possess what it loves is desire; love possessing and enjoying what it loves is joy; love fleeing what is adverse to it is fear; and love undergoing such adversity when it occurs is grief. Accordingly, these feelings are bad if the love is bad, and good if it is good.[67]

By introducing the crucial role of will into ethics, Augustine provides a significantly different view of the origin of evil.[68] In the intellectualist tradition, in which all things are under necessity, no freedom of will is allowed and as a result vices must derive from the nature of things—it is the inherent defects or imperfections in the nature of things that become the source of evil. Nature in itself is to be blamed. Because matter—the body—is located at the bottom in the scale of reality, it is simply a natural conclusion that the body is the origin of vices. In such a system, the goodness of nature—especially of the body—is inevitably compromised. It is true that, as Augustine admits, the Platonists do not go as far as the Manicheans in deeming the body as the natural substance of evil.[69] However, by assigning the body as the cause of vices in the soul, they indeed downplay the goodness of the body—and hence the goodness of creation. It is on this point that Augustine takes issues with the Platonists. By introducing the factor of the will into the system, Augustine shifts the burden from the body to the will, arguing that it is the will—not the body—that is responsible for vices, and that nature as such, be it the soul or the body, is essentially good. As such, although he is indebted to Platonism in many ways, Augustine firmly disassociates himself from the Platonic tradition on the essential goodness of the body. Neither the soul nor the body in itself is intrinsically evil, because both were created from nothing by the good Creator:

> [T]he first evil act of the will, since it preceded all other evil acts in man, consisted rather in its falling away from the work of God. . . . Moreover, though an evil will is not according to *nature*, but contrary to nature because it is a defect, it nonetheless belongs to the nature of which it is a defect, for it cannot exist except in a nature. But it can only exist in a nature which the Creator created *out of nothing*. . . . For, although God formed man out of the dust of the earth, the earth itself and all earthly matter were derived *from nothing at all*; and when man was made, God gave to his body a soul which was made *out of nothing*.[70]

All natures, whether they are corporeal or incorporeal, are good in themselves, because they were created by God and participate in God's goodness. For this reason, Augustine asserts that all natures, including the body, will not perish but will last permanently:

> For, there, the gifts of *nature*—that is, the gifts bestowed upon our *nature* by the Creator of all natures—will be not only good but also everlasting. And this is true not only of the spirit, which is healed by wisdom, but of *the body* also, which will be renewed by resurrection.[71]

In another passage, Augustine stresses that nature, as created by God, is essentially good and will not be destroyed in the consummation:

> For when this world passes away, this will not come about by the utter destruction of things, but by their transformation. This is why the apostle says, "For the figure of this world passeth away. I would have you be without anxiety." It is, then, the figure, not the *nature*, that passeth away.[72]

In fact, Augustine's emphasis on the intrinsic goodness of nature is so radical that he asserts that even the nature in which the devil exists is good and will not be completely removed by God in the eternal punishment:

> There exists, then, a nature in which there is no evil, and in which evil cannot exist at all. But there cannot exist a nature in which there is no good. In so far as it is a nature, not even the nature of the devil himself is evil. . . . The good imparted by God, which the devil has in his nature, does not remove him from God's justice, by which his punishment is ordained; nor does God punish the good which He has created, but the evil which the devil has committed. Moreover, God does not take away everything that He gave to that nature. He removes something, yet He leaves something also, so that there may be something left to feel pain at what has been taken away.[73]

Substance or Accidents

To better understand Augustine's debate with the Platonists over the goodness of nature, it is perhaps helpful to re-examine the issue in terms of the distinction between substance and accidents. For Augustine, the body is a substance and an essential part of human nature, while the corruptibility of the body is an accident, which is not caused by the nature of the body, but by something external. Corruptibility does not arise from within the body but from without and as such is accidental to the body. For this reason, in the resurrection, the corruption of the body will be removed, but the substance of the body will be preserved:

> I believe that whatever deformity was present in it . . . will be restored in such a way that, while the integrity of the body's substance is preserved, the deformity will perish.

> There, all defects will be corrected . . . Whatever is more than fitting will be removed, but without prejudice to the integrity of the body's substance.[74]

The same understanding applies to the relationship between nature and evil. For Augustine, created natures are substances, while evil is an accident that is not caused by a nature but something external to the nature. Because nature is substantial, evil must be non-substantial. For this reason, he is emphatic about the non-substantiality of evil.[75] With the distinction between substance and accidents, Augustine develops a unique understanding of nature's relation to evil. Because nature is substantial to something and evil is accidental to it, nature cannot be the cause of evil. Evil does not arise within nature; it arises outside of nature.

In the Platonic system, in which everything is under necessity, evil must derive from the nature of things. Evil does not arise outside of nature but from within. Nature itself is faulty: it contains elements of evil and is a mixture of goodness and evil. Since the Absolute Evil is real, just as the Absolute Good is real,[76] reality is a continuum between the two extremes—the Absolute Good and the Absolute Evil:

> There must then be The Good—good unmixed—and the Mingled Good and Bad, and the Rather Bad than Good, this last ending with the Utterly Bad we have been seeking, just as that in which Evil constitutes the lesser part tends, by that lessening, towards the Good.[77]

On this understanding, evil is simply part of the nature of all things other than the One or the Good Itself. The body, which is closest to the Absolute Evil, is mostly evil. In a sense, we may say that for Plotinus evil is essential to the body, but for Augustine it is accidental. This understanding is clearly expressed by Augustine himself in *Enchiridion:*

> For what is that which we call evil but the absence of good? In the bodies of animals, disease and wounds mean nothing but the absence of health; for when a cure is effected, that does not mean that the evils which were present—namely, the diseases and wounds—go away from the body and dwell elsewhere: they altogether cease to exist; for the wound or disease is not a substance, but a defect in the fleshly *substance*—the flesh itself being a *substance*, and therefore something good, of which those evils—that is, privations of the good which we call health—are *accidents*.[78]

Hence, while Augustine is inspired by Platonism when developing his theory of participation, he arrives at a significantly different understanding of matter and the body in relation to the One. For Augustine, matter and multiplicity must be good because they are products of a Triune God, who intentionally brought them into being through his Goodness and Wisdom. The goodness of matter and plurality is anchored in the Trinitarian creation.

GOODNESS OF MATTER AND
TRINITARIAN CREATION

As discussed above, at the heart of Augustine's dispute with the Platonists over the nature of the body lies his insistence on the goodness of creation. Because all that exists is created by God and must be good, Augustine cannot agree with the Platonists that nature itself is culpable, since doing so would imply that God himself is the author of evil. In defending the goodness of nature, Augustine is thus essentially defending God's goodness in creation. But what makes Augustine's idea of creation distinct from Plotinus's model? It can be argued that to a certain extent Plotinus's metaphysics may be called creationist, since the Plotinian One is the first principle for the existence of all things, which comes close to the Christian sense of creationism.[79] However, the One is not the first cause of the *being* of all things and it is on this point that the Plotinian One fundamentally differs from the Christian God, who is the first cause for both the being and existence of all things. Unlike the Simplex One, which allows no multiplicity, the Christian God is a Triune Creator, who brings all things into being through the cooperative act of the Father, the Son, and the Spirit. To be specific, in Augustine's theology, creation is motivated by God's Will (the Holy Spirit) and carried out through His Wisdom (the Son), which lays the foundation for the goodness of materiality and multiplicity.[80]

God's Good Will in Creation

In Augustine's thought, the goodness of creation (particularly of matter and multiplicity) is in the first place rooted in the goodness of the Divine Will. God's act of creation is neither motivated by any internal necessity nor by any external need. Rather, in line with the orthodox conception of *creatio ex nihilo*, Augustine affirms the absolute freedom of God in creation:

> In this way, perhaps, He demonstrated in a marvelous fashion, to those who are able to see such things, that He has no need of the creatures which He has made, but, rather, created them out of His own unmotivated goodness; for He abode without created things for an eternity which had no beginning, yet His blessedness was no less complete.[81]

Not only is Augustine emphatic about God's freedom, as is indicated by the word "unmotivated"; he also makes it clear that God creates things out of his good will. In other words, although God does not need to create, he decides to do so purely from his good will, which underscores the fact that God's creation is deeply intentional. Since God's will or intention is supremely good in itself, it bestows goodness on the essence of all creatures. Hence, all created natures are essentially good, not only because of the goodness of God's essence, but also because of the goodness of his will, which intends goodness for all creatures. As the intentional "author of all natures,"[82] God's good will or intention secures the order and goodness of creation. Nature is good and

orderly because it is so arranged by the will of God. Even miracles are in fact
consistent with nature, as is ordained by God's will:

> Indeed, men say that all portents are contrary to nature. They are not so, however;
> for how is that contrary to nature which happens by the *will* of God, since the
> *will* of so great a Creator is certainly the nature of every created thing? A portent,
> therefore, is an occurrence contrary not to nature, but to nature as we know it.[83]

Similarly, Augustine marvels at the orderliness of the world: "What is there so
closely regulated by the Author of the nature of the heavens and earth as the
ordered course of the stars? What is there so securely established by laws so certain and unvarying?"[84] The whole creation is stamped with the good will of God.

In Augustine's thought, God's good will is particularly connected to the
Holy Spirit: "[I]f the will of God is also to be specially attributed to any
Person in the Trinity, then this name, just as love, belongs most appropriately
to the Holy Spirit."[85] This understanding is made evident in his commentary
of Genesis 1:

> Hence, when there is mention of the Spirit of God, whereby the Divine
> Goodness and Love are to be understood, perhaps He is said to be stirring
> above creation, so that God may be thought of as loving the work to be pro-
> duced not out of any need or necessity, but solely out of the largeness of His
> bounty.[86]

In Augustine's understanding, the special but not exclusive work of the Spirit
is to communicate God's goodness and love toward creation. But God's will
to communicate his goodness is rooted in his absolute freedom in creation, for
God does not create under any obligation but purely from his good will. As
Augustine puts it, "God has a benevolence that is sovereign, holy, and just;
and it is not out of any need but out of His goodness that His love is directed
towards His works."[87] The Holy Spirit is thus crucial for creation, since it
is through the Spirit that God's benevolence and goodness are bestowed on
creation. The goodness of creation completely depends on the work of the
Spirit, because "there is no good thing except that which is subject to the
divine goodness of the Spirit."[88]

Hence, in emphasizing the role of God's will in creation, Augustine is in
effect affirming the indispensable work of the Holy Spirit in creation, which
secures creatures' participation in God's goodness and offers the ultimate
ground for the goodness of matter and multiplicity. Accordingly, it could be
argued that it is the lack of the Spirit in the Simplex One that makes Plotinus's
model incapable of providing a solid foundation for the essential goodness
of all things.

Divine Knowledge in Creation

As we have seen, the Plotinian One is beyond knowledge, for knowledge requires difference and multiplicity. Not only is the One without knowledge of its emanations; it has no knowledge of itself either, for even self-knowledge implies diversity. Utterly transcendent, the One is completely aloof toward all things below. The picture is totally different, however, for Augustine, who insists that God's knowledge is the very foundation for creation:

> But He does not, therefore, know all His creatures, both spiritual and corporeal, because they are, but they, therefore, are because He knows them. For He was not ignorant of what He was going to create. He created, therefore, because He knew; He did not know because He created. He did not know them differently when they were created, than which they were to be created, for nothing has been added to His wisdom from them; it has remained the same as it was, while they came into existence as they should and when they should. So it is also written in the Book of Ecclesiastes: "All things were known to him before they were created, so also after they were perfected."[89]

Augustine is emphatic that God's knowledge differs essentially from that of humans in that while the latter derives from existent things, the former precedes them—not necessarily temporally but ontologically. Before creatures come to existence, God already has the knowledge not only of the creation as a whole but of each particular thing, for God does not create blindly but according to his predetermined plan. It is thanks to the preexisting divine knowledge that things exist in the way they are. God's knowledge is the basis for the existence and nature of all things. Each creature is good because it is created through God's knowledge of it. The whole creation is good because it is produced and ordained by God's wisdom and knowledge.

Since the wisdom and knowledge of God are particularly linked to the Word, through which all things were made (John 1:1), Augustine's emphasis on the importance of God's knowledge in creation underlies his Christocentric vision of creation. "[T]he Word of God should be specially called also the wisdom of God, even though the Father and the Holy Spirit are wisdom," for Paul calls Christ "the power of God and the wisdom of God."[90] In his exegesis of Genesis 1, Augustine identifies Christ not only as the "Beginning," in which the origin of creatures is located and through which all things exist, but also as the "Divine Wisdom" and "Divine Exemplar," which all things imitate and from which they receive their forms. Christ is the Model after which all creatures are made. Not only is he the paradigm of creation; he is also the goal. Christ draws creatures to himself and brings them to perfection:

[T]he Word recalls His imperfect creature to Himself, so that it may not be
formless but may be formed according to the various works of creation which
He produced in due order. In this conversion and formation the creature in its
own way imitates the Divine Word.[91]

If the Holy Spirit is God's Will for the goodness of creation, Christ is
the Form or the paradigm of goodness for creation. Creation is good not
only because God has intended so, but also because God made it after the
supreme model of goodness. Using Aquinas's term, we can say that Christ
is the exemplary cause of goodness in creation. As the perfect image of the
Father and the Wisdom of God, Christ gives all of creation its proper form
and nature, ensuring that "the Father's creation takes shape according to the
Father's will."[92] It is thus through Christ that all of creation receives its truth,
beauty, and goodness; it is also through Christ that the nature of creation is
restored and perfected.

In conclusion, with his Trinitarian conception of creation, Augustine provides a profoundly different picture from Plotinus's model. Divine knowledge and will are essential in Augustine's theology of creation. Creation is an
intentional act of God's communication of goodness to creation through the
Holy Spirit. While the Plotinian One has no knowledge of things, God produces each creature and the creation as a whole through his knowledge and
wisdom, in which all creatures participate. Ultimately, it is thus the Trinitarian
vision of creation that lies at the heart of the difference between Augustine's
theology of creation and that of Plotinus. It is also the Trinitarian creationism
that provides the ground for the goodness of matter and multiplicity.

Because creation is intentional and purposeful, the hierarchy in creation
is not the result of an ontological fall, but the purposeful result of divine
wisdom. As such, the superiority of the soul to the body in Augustine's
thought need not be interpreted as evidence for his low view of matter, as his
critics have suggested. Rather, to place the body below the soul, Augustine
simply keeps each creation in its proper place in the hierarchy of creation,
as established by divine wisdom, and values them as much as they deserve.
Augustine places the soul above the body because he believes that God has
created the world in such a way that the soul is superior to the body. To place
the body above the soul is to deviate from reality, as ordained and intended
by God, and is to show contempt for God's wisdom. On the other hand, it is
equally an insult to God's wisdom and will to deny the value and goodness
of the body. It is for this reason that Augustine undertakes the painstaking
task of refuting the Platonists who consider the body as an imperfection and
thereby the cause of evil. To see the body as intrinsically defective implies
that God's will and wisdom in creation is faulty, which is blasphemy. In his
polemic with the Platonists over the goodness of the body, Augustine is thus

doing nothing less than defending the goodness and truthfulness of God's will and wisdom in creation.

Hence, those who accuse Augustine of having a low view of matter and multiplicity fail to understand the subtle but decisive difference between his view of multiplicity and that of the Platonists. As discussed above, it is true that both Plato and Plotinus have a largely disparaging view of the body and as such the Reformed theologians' concern over RO's appropriation of Platonic participation is legitimate. However, the same concern cannot be directly applied to Augustine. For although he is indebted to Platonism for the principle and structures of participation, he significantly modifies some key aspects of the theory—particularly the nature of multiplicity—in the light of the Christian doctrine of creation, which enables him to affirm the goodness of matter and plurality. So instead of appropriating the straightforwardly Platonic concept of participation, contemporary theologians should retrieve more of Augustine's already Christianized metaphysics of participation. Anchored in *creatio ex nihilo*, Augustine's participatory ontology constitutes a significant step forward from its Platonic roots. In fact, the advance on Platonism is even more evident in Augustine's treatment of transcendence and immanence, which brings us to the next chapter.

NOTES

1. Adolph V. Harnack, "Analysis and Historical Appraisal of the *Enchiridion*," in *Enchiridion*, 167, n.1.

2. A. M. Fairweather, introduction to *Nature and Grace: Selections from the* Summa Theologica *of Thomas Aquinas*, trans. and ed., A. M. Fairweather (London: SCM, 1954), 21.

3. Gunton, *One, Three and Many*, 137–8. Of course, Gunton is not alone in critiquing Augustine's view of matter and plurality—in a way, he is a representative of many contemporary authors who have the same or similar opinions about Augustine.

4. In *Confessions* as well as in *CG*, Augustine mentioned "the Platonists," by which he possibly meant Neoplatonists such as Plotinus and Porphyry. While his acquaintance with Plato was largely second-hand, Augustine at least read certain portions of Plotinus's *Enneads* and a good deal of Porphyry (Rist, *Augustine*, 9, n.11).

5. *CG*, 11.10.

6. *DT*, 6.6; Latin text: *Corpus Christianorum*, Series Latina 50, VI, 8 (Turnhout, 1968).

7. Ibid.

8. *CG*, 11.10, emphases added; see also *DT*, 6.4.

9. *CG*, 11.10.

10. *DT*, 6.4; Latin text: *Corpus Christianorum*, Series Latina 50, VI, 6.

11. *Of Free Will*, 8.22.

12. *DT*, 6, 6.

13. Ibid.

14. *Of True Religion*, 34.63.

15. *DT*, 6.6.

16. *Confessions*, 7.17.23.

17. As MacDonald observes, "The attribute that Augustine links most closely to true being is immutability. He very often discusses them together, and he takes them to be mutually entailing." Scott MacDonald, "The Divine Nature," in *The Cambridge Companion to Augustine*, ed. Eleanore Stump and Norman Kretzmann (Cambridge: Cambridge University Press, 2001), 84.

18. *DT*, 6.4.

19. As modern scholarship shows, Middle-Platonism and Neo-Platonism may be explained as developments in which "Platonic, Aristotelian and Stoic theories coalesced into a coherent and convincing worldview." TH. G. Sinnige, "Gnostic Influences in the Early Works of Plotinus and Augustine," in David T. Runia, ed., *Plotinus amid Gnostics and Christians* (Amsterdam: Free University Press, 1984), 73.

20. *Enneads*, 5.3.15; see also Schindler, "What's the Difference," 13.

21. *Enneads*, 1.8.3.

22. A. H. Armstrong, *The Architecture of the Intelligible Universe in the Philosophy of Plotinus* (Cambridge: Cambridge University Press, 1940), 111–12.

23. *Enneads*, 6.9.11.

24. *Enneads*, V.3.17.

25. David B. Hart, "The Offering of Names: Metaphysics, Nihilism, and Analogy" in *Reason and Reasons of Faith*, ed. Paul J. Griffiths and Reinhard Hütter (New York and London: T & T Clark, 2005), 288–9.

26. Schindler, "What's the Difference," 14.

27. Plotinus, *The Enneads*, ed. Lloyd P. Gerson, trans. George Boys-Stones, etc. (Cambridge: Cambridge University Press, 2019), 2.9.16. Thereafter, this version will appear as *Enneads* (Gerson version).

28. Ibid., 2.9.4.

29. Ibid., 2.9.3.

30. Ibid., 2.9.17.

31. Ibid., 4.8.

32. See, for instance, Henry Chadwick, introduction to *Confessions*, xxi. For this reason, Chadwick throughout the book seeks to identify references where Augustine is indebted to Plotinus.

33. *Confessions*, 2.1.2.

34. *Confessions*, 11.29.39.

35. Rist observes that "it is well known that Augustine locates the origin of moral evil in the *voluntas*, whether of men or angels" (Rist, "Plotinus and Augustine on Evil," 505). A good discussion of this theme is given by Wei Hua, "On the Rise of Augustine's Concept of *Volutuas*," *Sino-Christian Studies* 15 (2013): 111–30. As Hua points out, the centrality of "the will" in Augustine's moral theory has been widely recognized by modern scholarship. See Terrence H. Irwin, "Who Discovered the Will," *Philosophical Perspective* 6

(1992): 454–73; Simon Harrison, *Augustine's Way into the Will: The Theological and Philosophical Significance of* De libero aribitrio (Oxford: Oxford University Press, 2006). More discussion on this point will be provided later in this chapter.

36. Augustine, *de Doctrina Christiana*, 1.22.

37. For instance, Augustine speaks of God's essence as "simple multiplicity and multiple simplicity" in *Trinity*, 6.4.

38. A transcendental is an idea that can be applied universally to all of reality. "The Many" is called a transcendental, for in Augustine's thought "the Many" is applied to both God and creatures. Contrast Gunton's verdict on Augustine: "Unity, but not plurality, is transcendental" (*One, Three and Many*, 138).

39. For a detailed discussion of transcendentals in Aquinas, see Jan A. Aertsen, *Aquinas on Transcendentals*.

40. For Aquinas's discussion of analogy, see *ST* 1.3.

41. For a comparative study on evil in Plotinus and Augustine, see Rist, "Plotinus and Augustine."

42. *Enchiridion*, XI.

43. As noted above, by "the Platonists" Augustine meant certain Neoplatonists such as Plotinus and Porphyry.

44. See the beginning of the chapter.

45. *Soliloquies*, I.

46. See, for instance, *Trinity*, 11.5.

47. Hereafter, I will no longer use quotation marks around the Platonists but use the phrase to mean the Neoplatonists Augustine has in mind.

48. *Confessions*, 7.9.13–14.

49. *Enneads*, 1.8.3.

50. Note that while there is a general consensus that for Plotinus matter is the source of evil, there are debates on what matter is and in what sense matter is the origin of evil. See, for instance, the debate between O'Brien and Rist: David O'Brien, *The Origin of Matter and the Origin of Evil in Plotinus's Criticism of the Gnostics* (Paris: Épiméthé Paris Presses Universitaires de, 1990); Rist, "Plotinus and Augustine on Evil." I will not engage fully in the controversy over the interpretations of Plotinus; rather, I will examine the issue from Augustine's perspective, that is, from how he understands "the Platonists."

51. McKenna suggests that Jules Simon's statement "Matter is rather a demand of thought than a reality of existence" is closer to truth than the common misunderstanding that thinks of matter as being "material." See "Exacts from the Explanatory Matter in the First Edition," in *Enneads*, xxxi.

52. *Enneads*, 1.8.3.

53. *CG*, 14.3. This is Augustine's interpretation of the Neoplatonist position.

54. *Of True Religion*, 7; *CG*, 8.5, where Augustine asserts: "No one has come closer to us than the Platonists."

55. *CG*, 13.6.

56. Ibid, emphasis added.

57. Ibid., 13.17.

58. Ibid., 13.18.

59. Ibid., 13.20.

60. Ibid., 13.22.

61. Paul Henry, S.J., "Introduction: The Place of Plotinus in the History of Thought," in *Enneads*, xxxviii.

62. *CG*, 14.3. In *Confessions* 5.10.20; 7.17.22, Augustine likewise asserts that evil originates in the voluntary part of the soul.

63. *CG*, 14.3.

64. Ibid.

65. Ibid.

66. Ibid., 14.6.

67. Ibid., 14.7.

68. For a discussion of Augustine's innovation in the role of the will in ethics, see Irwin, "Who Discovered the Will."

69. *CG*, 14.5.

70. Ibid., 14.11, emphases added.

71. Ibid., 19.10, emphases added.

72. Ibid., 20.14, emphasis added.

73. Ibid., 19.13.

74. *CG*, 22.19.

75. *Enchiridion*, chap. 11–14; Rowan Williams, "Insubstantial Evil," in *Augustine and His Critics: Essays in Honour of Gerald Bonner*, ed. Robert Dodaro and George Lawless (London: Routledge, 2000), 105–23.

76. In *Enneads*, 1.8.14, Plotinus averts: "To deny Evil a place among realities is necessarily to do away with the Good as well, and even to deny the existence of anything desirable."

77. Ibid.

78. *Enchiridion*, chapter 11, emphases added.

79. Gerson, "Plotinus's Metaphysics," 574.

80. Indeed, in Augustine's thought, God's good will and knowledge are central to creation. He makes this point clear: "According to His own *will*, however, which, together with His *foreknowledge*, is eternal, God has certainly already made all things in heaven and on earth which He has *willed*: not only things past and present, but also things future" (*CG*, 22. 4, emphases added).

81. *CG*, 12.18.

82. Ibid., 21.7.

83. Ibid., 21.8.

84. Ibid.

85. *DT*, 15.20.

86. *Literal Meaning of Genesis*, 1.7.13.

87. Ibid., 1.5.11.

88. Scott A. Dunham, *The Trinity and Creation in Augustine: An Ecological Analysis* (Albany, NY: State University of New York Press, 2008), 68.

89. *DT*, 15.13.

90. Ibid., 15.17.

91. *Literal Meaning of Genesis*, 1.4.

92. Dunham, *Trinity and Creation*, 79.

Chapter 3

Transcendence and Immanence in Augustine's Participatory Ontology

In the last two chapters, we have discussed Augustine's concepts of unity and plurality in his theology of participation. In contrast to Platonic philosophy, Augustine's theology does not elevate the One at the cost of the Many, since in the creationist framework, unity is no longer the opposite of diversity. God's unity contains multiplicity,[1] which, as we will see, is possible only because of God's absolute transcendence. So, foundational to Augustine's advance over Platonism is the unique Christian concept of transcendence. In this chapter, we will discuss how Augustine revolutionizes the concepts of transcendence and immanence in the light of the doctrine of creation. First, we will look at an irreducible tension between transcendence and immanence in Greek philosophy.

TRANSCENDENCE AND IMMANENCE IN GREEK PHILOSOPHY

Greek philosophy began with the recognition of transcendence, without which there would be no philosophy. When pre-Socratic philosophers such as Thales and Anaximander asked, "What is the fundamental stuff out of which things are made?" they assumed the existence of a single first cause beneath the manifold of things. This first cause gives unity to the world. But how can the world be unified and yet diversified? Hence, one of the first and most fundamental philosophical problems is the problem of the One and the Many or the relationship between unity and diversity. But to posit a first cause of things, we assume that the cause is somehow different from the world. In other words, the first cause should transcend the world. Searching for the transcendent cause is at the foundation of Greek philosophy.

71

While Greek philosophy is a departure from Greek mythology, it is profoundly influenced by the latter. The first cause is often identified as god or some sort of deity[2] and the relation between divinity and the world is a central problem in Greek philosophy. In her important study, Kathryn Tanner offers a taxonomy of Greek concepts of divinity's relation with the world. The first type, namely "univocal predication," perceives divinity as "a kind of being distinct from others within the matrix of the same cosmos."[3] Divinity is then "that which is most powerful, self-sufficient and unchanging among beings."[4] An example of this kind of deity is the fiery substance in Stoicism. Being in close contact with the world, the deity is truly immanent. But its immanence is gained at the cost of its transcendence, since the difference between the deity and the world is a difference between two things within the same spectrum. The deity may be the greatest or highest thing, but is nevertheless part of the cosmos. In other words, the difference between the deity and the world is quantitative and the deity does not truly transcend the cosmos.

The tension between divinity's transcendence and immanence is even sharper in the second type of relation. This type of relation places deity or Ideas in direct opposition to the visible world, as is represented by Plato's theory of the two worlds. "The Being of knowable Ideas is simply contrasted with the physical world of Becoming apprehended in sense perception and opinion."[5] Whereas sensible things in the world change and perish, the Ideas exist perfectly and permanently. In this type of relation, divinity's difference and transcendence from the world is more prominent, but its immanence is severely limited such that it is often conceived as utterly detached from the world. For instance, Plato's realm of Ideas is seen as separate from the sensible world. Likewise, Aristotle's unmoved Mover is utterly indifferent to the world. As the final cause of the world, the Aristotelian God thinks only of his own thoughts and is completely isolated from the world. In such contrastive conceptions, transcendence is achieved at the expense of immanence. To secure his difference from the world, God is distanced from the world.

In the first two kinds of relation, then, God's transcendence and immanence "vary inversely in degree. The more transcendent God is the less God is directly involved with the world."[6] There is a third kind of relation that proposes "a radical transcendence of God that is *non-contrastive*," which goes beyond the first two kinds. While univocal predication assumes God's continuity with the world,[7] direct opposition is also appropriate only "for distinguishing beings within the world." But "if God transcends the world, God must transcend that sort of characterization, too."[8] Plotinus seems to have this transcendence in view when he speaks of the One that is simple and unnamable. The One is beyond everything and is thus unspeakable and unknowable. In addition, as the source of everything, in which all things participate, the

One is considered present to all things.[9] The One is thus at once transcendent and immanent in relation to the world.

In reality, however, Plotinus's conception of the One seems to oscillate between univocal and contrastive predications.[10] On the one hand, he describes the emanation of things from the One in terms of water coming from a fountain or radiation from a light source, which arguably assumes certain ontic continuity between the One and its emanations.[11] Then on this understanding, there seems to be a univocal relation between the One and the beings. On the other hand, Plotinus speaks of the One in terms of absolute negation of multiplicity and places the simplicity of the One and the multiplicity of beings in direct opposition. This contrastive reasoning is especially evident in his concept of the Absolute Evil. In his argument for the existence of the Absolute Evil, Plotinus reasons that since the One, which is pure simplicity, exists, the opposite of the One, which is pure multiplicity, must also exist. Pure multiplicity is nothing but the Absolute Evil. Hence, although Plotinus envisions a non-contrastive transcendence, his thinking falls back into contrastive terms and the tension between transcendence and immanence remains. The One is utterly transcendent, but its immanence in things is questionable. For while the One is the ultimate source of all things, its only direct product is the Mind, and all lower things come into existence through intermediary agents. Although the One is said to be present to all, it can be argued that it is infinitely distanced from multiplicity.[12] Hence, the opposition between transcendence and immanence still remains in Plotinus. In this context, we turn to Augustine's concept of transcendence and immanence. As we will see, with the framework of *creatio ex nihilo*, Augustine develops a truly non-contrastive view of God's relation with creation, which finally helps him resolve the tension between transcendence and immanence.

TRANSCENDENCE IN AUGUSTINE'S THOUGHT

Augustine's Concept of Transcendence

The transcendence of God is key to Augustine's thought and permeates his writings. He treats of this topic in many places, but one of his most concentrated discussions of God's transcendent nature is found in the *Confessions*. According to Augustine himself, in a cultural milieu saturated by materialism, he had difficulty in grasping the concept of transcendence and came to know the transcendent God only after a long and tortuous path. Roughly speaking, his idea of transcendence went through the same three stages, as discussed above, namely univocal, contrastive, and non-contrastive predictions. At first, he was unable to think of God except in terms of material objects: "When I wanted to think of my God, I knew of no way of doing so except as a physical mass."[13] At this stage, his conception of God was univocal in relation to the material world. For although he understood God to be infinite, he conceived of him as something physical occupying infinite space, holding a sort of pantheistic worldview:

> Although you were not in the shape of the human body, I nevertheless felt forced to imagine something physical occupying space diffused either in the world or even through infinite space outside the world. . . . I conceived even you, life of my life, as a large being, permeating infinite space on every side, penetrating the entire mass of the world, and outside this extending in all directions for immense distances without end; so earth had you, heaven had you, everything had you.[14]

However, in *conf.* 7.10.16-21.27, Augustine tells us that, triggered by "the Platonic books," his thought underwent a revolution. In particular, the Neoplatonic teaching on the spirituality of reality freed him from materialism, enabling him to conceive of God beyond material categories.[15] Moving beyond materialistic, univocal conceptions of God, Augustine arrived at the second stage, namely contrastive predications, which is evident in his description of "the immutable light":

> I . . . saw *above* that same eye of my soul the immutable light *higher* than my mind—not the light of everyday, obvious to anyone, nor a larger version of the same kind which would, as it were, have given out a much brighter light and filled everything with its magnitude. It was not that light, but a different thing, *utterly different* from all our kinds of light. It *transcended* my mind, not in the way that oil floats on water, nor as heaven is above earth.[16]

In this passage, Augustine tackles the nearly impossible task of describing the indescribable transcendence of God. First, he contrasts the immutable light with corporeal lights. The immutable light is incorporeal and cannot be understood as "larger" or "brighter" than corporeal lights. For to say that it is larger or brighter than physical lights is to place it on the same ontological level as the latter. Because the immutable light is "utterly different from all our kinds of light," all univocal predications fail. Excluding univocal, materialistic conceptions of God, Augustine has now arrived at contrastive models of transcendence.

However, Augustine takes an even further step, stressing that the immutable light transcends his mind. In emphasizing the immateriality of God, people could conceive of God as a spirit that does not differ fundamentally from the human mind. To exclude such misconceptions, Augustine stresses that God is not on the same ontological level as the mind but radically "above" or "higher" than the mind. At this point, he comes close to a non-contrastive conception of transcendence but still struggles to describe this radical transcendence with a contrastive language. On the one hand, he cannot help but employ contrastive terms such as "above" or "higher," without which he would not be able to talk about God at all. On the other hand, he carefully differentiates the true meaning of transcendence from what such phrases normally signify. Hence, after stating that the immutable light is "above" or "higher" than his mind, he goes on to explain that it transcends the mind "not in the way that oil floats on water, nor as heaven is above earth." The language here is primarily negative. Realizing that it is impossible to describe God's transcendence positively, he resorts to the apophatic tradition. For to say that God does not transcend the mind "in a way that oil floats on water" is not to offer any positive information about God's transcendence, but to dissuade us from thinking that God is above the mind in the same way that oil is above water. For there is no ontological continuity between God and the mind—a fundamental "gap" exists between them.[17]

The ontological gap between God and the mind, however, does not mean that God is removed or detached from the mind. As such, after stating that God transcends his mind "*not* in a way that oil floats on water," Augustine immediately adds that nor does God transcend "as heaven is above earth."[18] If "heaven" here refers to the sky, the distance between heaven and earth would be spatial. Then to say that God is not above his mind as heaven is above earth, Augustine seems to emphasize that the distance between God and his mind is not spatial,[19] nor in the same ontological spectrum. But for Augustine "heaven" often means the spiritual realm in contrast to the physical world,[20] and as such the statement above would mean that the distance between God and the mind is not the same as the distance between the spiritual and the physical. Rather, it is the ontological divide between the Creator and creation, which is infinitely greater than any difference between creatures. However great the difference between a spiritual creature and a physical one—say, between an angel and a worm—may be, it is infinitely dwarfed by the ontological difference between God and the angel. God's transcendence over creatures cannot be measured through differences between creatures. In short, God's transcendence transcends all creaturely differences. At this stage, Augustine finally arrives at a non-contrastive conception of God's transcendence.

Transcendence and *creatio ex nihilo*

As discussed above, Plotinus had the vision of non-contrastive transcendence and yet did not achieve it. Augustine moved beyond Plotinus. It is true that Augustine's concept of transcendence was indebted to the Platonists, for it was the Platonic notion of spiritual reality that liberated him from materialistic concepts of God and enabled him to obtain a glimpse of the transcendent light. So, it is reasonable to say that Neoplatonism played a crucial role in catalyzing a breakthrough in Augustine's idea of transcendence. The most pivotal foundation for his concept of transcendence, however, is not Neoplatonism but the Christian doctrine of *creatio ex nihilo*. Although much of Augustine's language in *Confessions* has Neoplatonic traces, the fundamental theme in his concept of transcendence, as Harrison suggests,

> is *not*, in fact, strictly a Platonic one: it is the conviction that God is Being, to whom all other beings owe their existence, and that there is an ontological divide between creation and Creator; creation is brought into being *out of nothing* and is mutable and temporal, whereas God is the transcendent, eternal and immutable Creator on whom all else depends.[21]

Indeed, after stating that the immutable light transcends his mind "not in a way that oil floats on water, nor as heaven is above earth," Augustine continues to expound on God's transcendence in a way that is profoundly non-platonic:

> It was superior because it *made* me, and I was inferior because I was *made* by it. . . . When I first came to know you, you raised me up to make me see that what I saw is *Being*, and that I who saw am not yet Being.[22]

If God's transcendence cannot be understood contrastively in terms of differences within the creation, Augustine now makes it clear that God's transcendence can only be understood in terms of the ontological divide between the Creator and creation. The ultimate difference in reality is therefore not the difference between two things in the physical realm or between the spirit and the matter, but the difference between the Maker and what is made. The difference between God and the world cannot be contrastive, because the Creator is not the negation of creation but the infinite source of all things— the Being Itself. This understanding is made clear in Augustine's description of God in the Ostia vision:

> Our minds were lifted up by an ardent affection towards eternal being itself. Step by step we climbed beyond all corporeal objects and the heaven itself, where sun, moon, and stars shed light on the earth. We ascended even further by internal reflection and dialogue and wonder at your works, and we entered into our own minds. We moved up beyond them so as to attain to the region of inexhaustible abundance where you feed Israel eternally with truth for food. There life is the Wisdom by which all creatures come into being.[23]

Here, not only does Augustine confirm that God transcends corporeal things and the mind; he also explicitly asserts that God's transcendence is rooted in the fact that he is the Creator, which means that the foundation of his concept of transcendence is not Neoplatonism but the doctrine of creation. When insisting that "the immutable light" was superior because "it *made* me," he makes it clear that the light was not the Neoplatonic One, but the Creator.[24] More specifically, this Creator is the Wisdom (Christ), through whom all things came into being. Anchoring God's transcendence in Christ is a far cry from the Plotinian tradition.

Even if Plotinus's metaphysics may be called "creationist" in a certain sense,[25] the emanations are not intentional products but overflows out of the One.[26] As it is difficult to maintain a complete chasm between the First Principle and its outflow, there is arguably ontic continuity between the One and its emanations. In such a system, the only way to highlight the transcendence of the One is to stress the difference between the One and the world and place them in contrastive oppositions. The tendency to set up contraries is evident in Plotinus's treatise on evil, where he repeatedly uses the word "contrary." Plotinus seeks to show that the opposite of the Good is the Absolute Evil and that it exists. To do so, he first defines evil as "something contrary to that which is good" and then explains how there can be something contrary to the Good:

But if the Good is Substance, or transcends Substance, how could there be a *contrary* of it? That there is no *contrary* substance in the case of a particular substance has been shown securely by induction, but this has not been shown generally for substance. What, then, will be universally *contrary* to substance and, generally, to the primary ones?

In fact, it is non-substance that is *contrary* to substance, and it is the nature and principle of evil that is *contrary* to the nature of the Good. For both are principles, the one of evils and the other of goods and everything within each nature is a *contrary* of the other.[27]

Contrastive thinking is exhibited explicitly in the passage above. Although there is no contrary of a particular substance, Plotinus argues, the contrary of universal substance or the Good, namely the Absolute Evil, is real. It seems odd that he would posit the existence of non-substance. But we must remember that for Plotinus the One is above Being and as such being or substance is not the ultimate measure of reality. Hence, the Absolute Good and the Absolute Evil are both outside the domain of Being and yet both exist. Just as the One, which is *above* being, is real, the Absolute Evil, which is *below* being, is likewise real. To refute those who deny the existence of the Absolute

Evil, Plotinus maintains: "As there is Good, the Absolute, as well as Good, the quality, so, together with the derived evil entering into something not itself, there must be the Absolute Evil."[28] Both the Good and the Absolute Evil must exist, because they are the limits and the principles of all goods and evils. Just as all good things participate in the Good, all evil things participate in the Absolute Evil.

It is thus clear that foundational to Plotinus's metaphysical system is the opposition between the Good and the Evil, which is the basis for all other contraries.

> Things, therefore, that have been separated and have nothing in common and stand at the greatest distance from each other in their natures are contraries. . . . [T]hey are separated from each other as much as possible and is construed from their being placed opposite to each other and this produces the contraries.[29]

It can therefore be argued that at the heart of Plotinus's metaphysics is some type of dualism—a dualism between the Good and the Evil—although it differs fundamentally from the dualism of Gnosticism. But this dualism is certainly the ground for contrastive oppositions between the One and everything else. To stress the transcendence of the One, Plotinus has to resort to contrastive exclusion or opposition, stressing that the One is entirely exclusive of multiplicity. As a result, while Plotinus presumably perceives a non-contrastive concept of transcendence, he is not free from the dialectic between transcendence and immanence, as imbedded in Greek philosophy.[30] The tension is inevitable for a system that elevates the One above Being and places it in contrastive relation with the emanations.

By contrast, only in a system in which the One is identical to Being can we find a transcendent One/Being that is non-contrastive to beings. The Christian doctrine of *creatio ex nihilo*, as we have seen, provides such a system. Because all things have been created from nothing by the God, the Being Itself, there is no contrary to being and there is no opposition between God and creatures. This insight is clearly understood by Augustine when he discusses God's relation with creatures. For Augustine, since God, the first principle of everything, is the Being Itself, being is the ultimate measure of all reality and as such there is no such thing as "the Absolute Evil." Nor are there two principles of the Good and the Evil, in which all things participate. All things participate God, who freely brought them into being from nothing. No ontic continuity exists between God and creation, because "all things were made not of the very substance of God but out of nothing."[31] The fact that creatures were created out of nothing means that no nature can be directly contrary to God. Hence, in contrast to Plotinus, Augustine explicitly denies the existence of contraries to God:

For God is the Supreme Being—that is, He supremely *is*; and He is therefore immutable. He gave being to the things that He created from nothing, then, but not a supreme being like His own. . . . To that Nature which supremely is, therefore, and by Whom all else that is was made, no nature is contrary save that which is not; for that which is contrary to what is, is not-being. And so *there is no being contrary to God,* the Supreme Being, and the Author of all beings of whatever kind.[32]

For Augustine, "non-being," which is contrary to being, does not really exist. From the fact "that which is contrary to what is, is not-being," he directly arrives at the conclusion that "there is *no* being contrary to God." For he takes it for granted that "non-being" is identical to "non-reality," an assumption that Plotinus would vehemently reject. This discrepancy between the two thinkers' understanding of non-being betrays a fundamental difference between two metaphysical systems, which again undergirds their diverging views of transcendence. In Plotinus's system, where the One is beyond Being, transcendence is categorized in terms of opposition; in Augustine's system, where the One, identical to Being, created all things out of nothing, transcendence can finally be conceived non-contrastively. Because there is nothing contrary to God, nothing in the creation can be directly opposed to God. It is this conviction that compels Augustine to refute the stark dualism of Manichaeism. It is also the conviction that helps him depart from Plotinus's dualistic tendencies. With the doctrine of *creatio ex nihilo*, Augustine is thus able to move beyond Plotinus and arrive at a truly non-contrastive concept of transcendence, which also helps resolve the tension between transcendence and immanence in Plotinus's philosophy.

IMMANENCE IN AUGUSTINE'S THOUGHT

Plotinus on Immanence

As discussed above, a problematic in traditional Greek philosophy is that the transcendence and immanence of God are "mutually exclusive. . . . The more transcendent God is the less God is directly involved with the world."[33] Even Plotinus, as we have seen, is not free from this problem. It is true that he speaks of the One's immanence: since all things participate in the One, the One must be present to all.[34] In effect, however, because the One is utterly devoid of multiplicity, all things, insofar as they are being, contain multiplicity and are estranged from the One. As such, although the One is presumably present to the Many, the Many cannot be present to the One, unless it purges multiplicity. In other words, the Many must cease to be "many" in order to be present to the One. Plotinus expresses this understanding in the passage below:

> Thus the Supreme as containing no otherness is ever present with us; we with it when we put otherness away. It is not that the Supreme reaches out to us seeking our communion: we reach towards the Supreme; it is we that become present.[35]

It can be thus argued that the One is not truly immanent to the Many; rather, the One is present only to *itself*. The One is present to things only because they are participants of the One, that is, they contain unity—part of the One—in a pantheistic sense. Since the One cannot be separated, it must be present to an "extension" of itself, as it were, which exists at the core of all beings. It is in this sense that the One is always present to all. The Supreme is said to be "ever present with us" only because we have the Supreme within us or, in other words, we contain diluted dimensions of the Supreme. But the Supreme One is not present to multiplicity *as such*, because the One is utterly devoid of multiplicity. Absolute multiplicity is thus seen as furthest removed from the One. In the end, in a system where unity and multiplicity are opposites, the One cannot be truly immanent to the Many *per se*; the One is present only to the unity of things, but absolutely detached from their multiplicity. Multiplicity as such, the opposite of unity, is a negation of reality. Hence, in all things, which are composites of unity and multiplicity, unity constitutes reality, whereas multiplicity is simply a deficiency or imperfection. As Schindler puts it,

> [F]or Plotinus, unity alone is perfect, and all other things are perfect precisely to the extent that they relate to this unity, which means that their imperfection, conversely, is measured by their difference or distance from it.[36]

On this understanding, the One is near to something insofar as it has unity but distant from it insofar as it has multiplicity. The more multiple a being is, the further it is removed from the One. Although the One is said to be present to all beings, they are in fact blocked from the One by their multiplicity. Multiplicity is an obstacle between the One and all things. For this reason, Plotinus asserts that we must "put otherness away"[37] when we return to the One. It can be argued that the One is not truly immanent but infinitely distant from the emanations.

Augustine on Immanence

Augustine is emphatic about God's radical transcendence and the ontological chasm between God and the world. Does his emphasis of God's infinite transcendence make God less immanent to the world? Or does the ontological chasm between God and creation entail a detachment of God from the world? To answer the questions, we must first look at a passage in *Confessions*, in which Augustine wrestles with the question of how the transcendent God can be intimate to him. When invoking God to come to him, he asks how God—the infinite Creator—can come to him, who is but a tiny piece of creation:

> But what place is there in me where my God can enter into me? "God made heaven and earth" (Gen. 1:1). Where may he come to me? Lord, my God, is there any room in me which can contain you? Can heaven and earth, which you have made and in which you have made me, contain you? Without you, whatever exists would not exist. Then can what exists contain you? I also have being. So why do I request you to come to me when, unless you were *within* me, I would have no being at all. . . . Accordingly, my God, I would have no being, I would not have any existence, unless you were *in* me. Or rather, I would have no being if I were not *in* you "of whom are all things, through whom are all things, *in* whom are all things" (Rom. 11: 36). . . . How can I call on you to come if I am already *in* you?[38]

Augustine realizes that when he calls upon God, he is essentially asking God to come "into" him. But the immediate dilemma is: how can a creature contain God, when even heaven and earth cannot contain him? How can what is infinite enter into what is finite? Recognizing the infinity of God, Augustine is stressing the radical transcendence of God over creation. On the other hand, in a paradoxical fashion, he confesses that the Creator must be already "within" him, for unless God is already intimately present to him, he would not exist at all. This reality is true for all creatures: the very fact they exist means that God is already most immanently present to them. As the Creator of all things, God must sustain their existence in a most intimate fashion—that is, God must exist at the foundation of their being—for them to continue to exist. For a creature to exist and continue to exist, God must be profoundly immanent. Hence for Augustine, God's radical transcendence must go hand in hand with his radical immanence. He realizes that, as the Creator who creates all things out of nothing and sustains their existence, God must be at once transcendent and immanent. For this reason, he speaks of God as "most high, utterly good, utterly powerful, most omnipotent, most merciful and most just, *deeply hidden* yet *most intimately present*."[39] This idea of immanence differs significantly from that of Plotinus.

As we have seen, the Plotinian One is not truly immanent to the Many, since the One is present only to unity, not to multiplicity. In Augustine, however, the transcendent One—the Creator God—is truly immanent to the Many. As Being Itself, God is intimately present to all things—both in unity and multiplicity. Since the Creator God is not the Plotinian Simplex but the ultimate source of both unity and multiplicity, multiplicity is by no means removed from God. God is immanent to both unity and multiplicity.

In addition, even if the Plotinian One were present to the Many, the Many cannot be said to be present to the One, which is completely devoid of multiplicity. In Plotinus, the One's immanence is thus at best one-way: the immanence of the One to the Many is coupled with the distance of the Many from the One.[40] But in Augustine, immanence is two-directional. Not only is God "within" the creature; the latter also exists "in" God: "I would have no being if I were not *in* you . . . *in* whom are all things. . . . How can I tell you to come to me if I am already *in* you?" The Many is immanent to the One, just as the One is immanent to the Many. Such a conception of immanence is decisively un-Plotinian. For in Plotinus, the opposition between the One and the Many means that immanence cannot be mutual, but in Augustine the One and the Many are no longer oppositional, and it is thus possible to have mutual immanence—a creature can be said to be in God and God in the creature.[41] The mutual immanence reveals a much more intimate relationship between God and creation.

Hierarchy and Immanence

The fact that God is immanent in all things does not mean that there is no hierarchy in creation. Like Plotinus, Augustine sees the world hierarchically, which is reflected in his well-known theory of three levels of reality and in his repeated emphasis on the superiority of the soul over the body. On the surface, this Augustinian hierarchy of reality does not seem different from the Plotinian "great chain of beings."[42] If we take a closer look, however, we find a profound difference between the two types of hierarchy. In Augustine, the hierarchy is real only with respect to creatures but not to God. But in Plotinus, the hierarchy is real with respect to God (the One) also. As we have seen, in Plotinus's system, the degree of reality of things is inversely proportional to their distance to the One, which corresponds to their level of diversity or multiplicity. The more multiple a thing is, the less reality it contains and the further removed from the One. The hierarchy of being is *real* with respect to the One. The One is really closer to the Mind than to matter. In Augustine's thought, however, God is equally close to immaterial things and material things, as he exists most intimately in all things. As Denys Turner puts it,

> all things are also in a certain sense *equidistant* from the God whose action sustains them *equally* in existence as opposed to the nothingness "from which" they are created. For there is no such kind of thing as the kind of thing that exists; there is no kind of being, therefore, which, prior to or beyond its character as

pure gift, has any claim on existence because of the kind of being that it is. Hence, even if, given its existence, an angel possesses an existence "more necessary" than that of a worm, from this "absolute" point of view of creation—that it exists at all—an angel has no better claim on existence than a worm has. The "aristocratic" theological language of the angelic hierarchy cannot be justified except in its dialectical tension with, and ultimate subordination to, the "democratic" ontology of creation *ex nihilo*. As "the Cause of all" God stands in the same relation to the whole hierarchy as its Creator: he does not stand as a top being on that hierarchy.[43]

Turner insightfully points out that because God is sustaining the existence of all things in their innermost being, he is equally immanent to them all. In this sense, God is as intimately present to an angel as he is to a worm, because the ontological difference between an angel and a worm does not make the former ontologically closer to God. Hence, there is no ontological hierarchy of things in a real sense before God, since all things are equally and intimately dependent on God for their existence. On the other hand, however, a hierarchy does exist within the creation, for the mode of being of an angel is indeed higher than that of a worm, because the former contains intelligence, while the latter does not. The hierarchy is real with respect to creatures. It is therefore problematic for Turner to proclaim that the "aristocratic" language of hierarchy conflicts with the "democratic ontology of creation *ex nihilo*." The equal distance of all creatures to God by no means nullifies the hierarchical structure *within* the created order and as such there is no inherent conflict between the "democratic ontology of creation *ex nihilo*" and the hierarchical structure in the creation. To illustrate this point, we can think of the relationship between infinity and a series of finite numbers. On the one hand, infinity is equally distant to all finite numbers, because the number 3 is not further away from infinity than 4. On the other hand, with respect to numerical value, 4 is indeed greater than 3—the mathematical sequence is real. The hierarchy of finite numbers within themselves is thus consistent with their equal distance to infinity. Likewise, the "democratic ontology of creation *ex nihilo*" is also consistent with the hierarchy of being in the creation.[44]

The key point, however, is that in Augustine's thought God is equally immanent to all things and *vice versa*. While there is a hierarchy within the creation, God is truly intimate to all things in the hierarchy. Even matter, at the bottom of the hierarchy, is immediately present before God.

Transcendence and Immanence

Now we are in the position to discuss how God's transcendence and immanence, which were dialectical in Greek philosophy, become coherent in

Augustine's thought. As we have discussed, for Augustine, *creatio ex nihilo* is foundational not only to God's transcendence but also to his immanence. God transcends all things, as there is a complete ontological divide between him and the creation. God is immanent to all things, since he must be most intimately present to them in order to sustain their existence. God's transcendence and immanence cohere in *creatio ex nihilo*. It is therefore the doctrine of creation that enables Augustine to overcome the dialectic between transcendence and immanence. As the Creator of all that *is*, God is transcendent and immanent in relation to all things. Augustine clearly expresses this understanding in the passage below:

> Although the Divine Being is beyond words and cannot be spoken of in any way with human language without recourse to expressions of time and place, whereas God is before all time and all place, nevertheless He who made us is nearer to us than many things which have been made. *For in him we live and move and have being.*[45]

The first part of the quote speaks of God's transcendence: God is entirely transcendent and as such is "beyond words," although we must use human language to talk about him. But we cannot adequately speak of God because he is completely different from us. The second part talks about God's immanence. He is closer to us than creatures, because he created us. God's simultaneously transcendent and immanent relation to creatures is anchored in the fact that He is the Creator of all things. In God, transcendence and immanence are simply two sides of the same reality. In fact, it can be argued that God is truly immanent to us *because* he is wholly transcendent or completely different from us. Material things cannot be truly present to us, as Augustine argues, "because they are separated from our sight and touch by reason of obstacles lying between us and them."[46] A corporeal thing can only be in contact with things that are next to it, but cannot be present to things that are removed from it. A spiritual being, however, can be present to multiple corporeal things at once, because it is not restricted by physical boundaries. The difference between a spiritual being and a corporeal one makes it possible for the former to be immanent in the latter. How much more, then, can God, "the wholly other" who transcends all creaturely dimensions, be truly immanent to all creatures simultaneously. God's absolute transcendence ensures his immanence to creation. If God's transcendence were limited, as in univocal and contrastive conceptions, he would not be present to all things. Limited transcendence entails limited immanence; only full transcendence ensures full immanence.

Hence, in Augustine's thought, the transcendence and immanence of God become coherent, because they are anchored in the same truth of creation. All creatures participate in the transcendent God, who is simultaneously immanent to all. This version of participatory ontology is certainly a step forward from Neoplatonism. Not everyone, however, is convinced. A. H. Armstrong, one of the foremost Neoplatonic scholars, argues that Augustine's view of reality constitutes a regression from Platonism. In what follows, I will reflect on and respond to Armstrong's position.

THE IMMANENCE OF GOD AND THE RELEVANCE OF THE COSMOS

In his 1966 Augustine Lecture, *St Augustine and Christian Platonism*, Armstrong makes the following comment on Augustine in relation to Platonism:

> It does seem to me that St. Augustine and, to a great extent, the other Christian thinkers of his age, missed the chance of carrying out a much deeper and more dynamic transformation of Platonism than they in fact effected . . . and that in one respect, their thought about the material universe shows a certain *regression* in comparison with that of pagan Platonism, or at least fails to make the necessary Christian advance.[47]

This regression, Armstrong explains, lies in the fact that while the material world was regarded holy and sacred in the cosmic religion of Platonism, Augustine and other Christian thinkers of his time, while rejecting pantheism, dampened "the sense of the holiness, the religious relevance of the cosmos as a whole, and with it, inevitably, the sense of holiness of ordinary human life and bodily activities."[48] This inattention to God's immediate presence in all things in the world resulted in a "Christian narrowness" that moved our attention "away from God's work in the world" and focused almost exclusively on "his work for souls in the Church." In comparison to the Church and spiritual life, the natural world and mundane things became irrelevant to the Christian faith. In the process of the de-sacralization, the "natural" was sacrificed at the altar of the "supernatural."[49]

On the one hand, I would dispute Armstrong's assertion that Augustine's view of the material world constitutes a regression from that of pagan Platonism. First, for Neoplatonists, the universe is sacred only because the world, in its unity, is a diffused extension of the One, but matter *per se*, which is the obstacle for our return to the One, is to be rejected. The veneration of the cosmos is always coupled with the rejection of materiality. In contrast, to defend the goodness of creation, especially matter, Augustine criticizes the Platonists, who blamed matter as the source of evil. For Augustine, the world is good, not because it is an extension of the divine, but because it is created to be good by the good Creator. Matter's relation to God is not oppositional, as in Neoplatonism, but harmonious, since matter also reflects the goodness of God.[50] This view of matter is certainly an advance over Neoplatonism. In addition, we must remember that it is from Neoplatonism that Augustine learns the inward approach to God.[51] So his tendency to move away from the world and focus on his inner life originates in Platonism, as is evident in passages of Plotinus.[52] If this is the case, it is difficult to say that Augustine's lack of interest in the world is a regression from pagan Platonism. At best, we can say that he has not moved *far enough* from Platonism, but his view of reality is certainly not a regression. In this respect, then, Armstrong's critique of Augustine seems unjustified.

On the other hand, there is perhaps some validity in Armstrong's complaint about Augustine. Although Augustine understands the goodness of matter and God's immanence in all things, it can be argued that his vision of the world is still too Platonic and does not fully recognize the religious significance of matter, especially in his early thought. In *Soliloquies*, for instance, he asserts that he desires to know "nothing more" than "God and the soul."[53] Of course, it can be argued that such statements underscore his thorough theocentric view of reality. What is potentially problematic, however, is his lack of interest in the material world in contrast to his enthusiasm for spirituality, as if the latter provided a superior access to God. This view of reality arguably reflects the residue of a Neoplatonism that has not been fully transformed by the Christian worldview of *creatio ex nihilo*.[54] For if we truly adopt "the democratic ontology of creation *ex nihilo*,"[55] as Turner suggests, it becomes clear that God is equally immanent to material and spiritual things, which means that incorporeal things do not necessarily provide a privileged access to God than corporeal things. In the pursuit of God, we do not need to prioritize spiritual things over material things, and we can experience God's immediate presence through material things as well as through spiritual things. This view of reality is not prominent, if not absent, in Augustine's early thought.

To some extent, the implications of *creatio ex nihilo*, especially the religious relevance of the cosmos and God's immediate presence in the world, become more prominent in Augustine's later thought. The last four books of *Confessions*, for instance, concern not only the redemption of the soul but also of the whole world. The journey of the soul's return to God, as portrayed in the first nine books, is essentially a microcosm of the same journey of the whole cosmos.[56] In this sense, the theme of redemption in *Confessions* goes beyond that of the soul and reaches a cosmic level, which comes close to the concept of cosmic redemption in Maximus the Confessor. Moreover, the sense of God's immediate presence in all things becomes more evident in Augustine's later works, especially in *City of God*, where he writes:

> Neither heaven nor earth, neither angel nor man, not even the inward parts of the smallest and most inconsiderable animal, nor the feather of a bird, nor a tiny flower of a plant nor the leaf on the tree, has God left unprovided with a harmony and, as it were, a peace among its parts.[57]

In another place, he makes it even clearer: "It is His hidden power, *pervading* all things and undefilably *present in them all*,"[58] which shows an acute awareness of God's pervasive presence in all things. It seems that God's profound immanence becomes more significant in Augustine's mature theology.

Despite the progression, on the whole, a sacramental vision of the cosmos is not evident in Augustine's thought. It can be argued that Augustine falls short of the "sacramental ontology" that Boersma seeks to retrieve. Sacramental ontology refers to the worldview that sees the world as a sacrament of God, who is truly present in the world, just as Christ is truly present in the Eucharist. Boersma explains that a sacrament differs from a symbol in that while a symbol points toward an external reality, a sacrament points toward something inhering in it. In traditional theology, Christ is considered as truly present in the Eucharistic bread and the Eucharist is thus not merely a symbol but a sacrament of Christ. Likewise, in the "Great Tradition" of the Church, the world was viewed as a sacrament of God. In sacramental ontology, God is considered as truly present in the world and all creatures really connected to God.[59]

Overall, it can be argued that such a sacramental view of the material cosmos is not prominent in Augustine's thought. A sense of sacredness or holiness of the material world is relatively weak, if not absent, in Augustine, even in his mature thought, as is evident in his dubious attitude toward the study of the natural world. For instance, in the *Literal Meaning of Genesis*, one of his mature works, Augustine writes:

> Hence it is that it is more toilsome to discover material creatures than the Creator who made them, since the joy a devout mind finds in the slightest knowledge of God is incomparably greater than anything it could experience in a thorough understanding of all material things. For this reason those who search into this world are rightly *rebuked* in the Book of Wisdom.[60]

It is true that we do not need all the scientific knowledge to become good Christians; it is also true that knowledge of God is much more valuable than knowledge of nature. Nevertheless, it is unnecessary to place the study of

God and the study of nature in opposition, in fear that the latter may drag our focus away from the former.[61] If we truly accept the intimate, immediate presence of God in the world, engagement with nature does not necessarily pull us away from God. If God is equally immanent in material and spiritual things, the study of nature does not move us further away from God; neither do spiritual activities necessarily keep us closer to God. Natural science can be as spiritual as meditation. It can be argued that Augustine's preference of introspection over the study of nature is perhaps not completely consistent with his conviction about the goodness of matter and God's immanence in all the world.

In addition, if God's presence truly permeates and undergirds the material world, the study of nature can provide us with a glimpse of God's wisdom and power in the creation.[62] As such, scientific knowledge is not a distraction but an enhancement to religion. Knowledge of the cosmos is not trivial but deeply relevant to the faith.[63] Such an insight is powerfully expressed by Thomas Aquinas:

> The opinion of those who say with regard to the truth of faith that it is a matter of complete indifference what one thinks about creatures, provided one has a true interpretation of God . . . is notoriously false. For an error about creatures is reflected in a false opinion about God.[64]

While Aquinas's statement is by no means a refutation of Augustine, it nonetheless shows a considerable difference between their visions of the relevance of the cosmos for the knowledge of God.[65] While Augustine is skeptical of material things as a reliable source for our knowledge of God, Aquinas, as we will see, takes sensible things as a starting point for the knowledge of God. To some extent, I suggest, this difference reflects a difference in how thoroughly the implications of *creatio ex nihilo* transform the Neoplatonic metaphysics of participation.[66] The transformation of the Platonic participatory ontology has begun in Augustine: while retaining the basic structure of participation, he has made significant changes, as we have seen in the past three chapters, to the key concepts of unity, multiplicity, and relationship in the light of the doctrine of creation. But the Christianization of participation is somewhat incomplete in Augustine. While *creatio ex nihilo* is central to Augustine's theology, its fullest implications have not been fleshed out in his vision of reality, as is evident in his insufficient recognition of the religious relevance of the cosmos. For a more thorough transformation of participatory ontology, we need to go to his medieval successor, Thomas Aquinas, who enables the implications of *creatio ex nihilo* to shape his worldview more thoroughly. It is to Aquinas's participatory ontology that we will now turn.

NOTES

1. For Augustine, multiplicity is not the opposite of simplicity and as such God even in his simplicity admits multiplicity. For a detailed discussion, see the section "The Nature of Multiplicity in Augustine's Thought" in chapter 2.

2. Needless to say, there is a wide and complicated spectrum in the Greek concepts of *theos* or divinity, some of which can hardly be named "God." We will use "deity," "divinity," or "God" respectively to reflect different conceptions of *theos* in Greek philosophy. For an excellent discussion of the notion of God in different contexts, please see Etienne Gilson's *God and Philosophy* (New Haven, CT: Yale University Press, 2002).

3. Tanner, *God and Creation*, 42.

4. Ibid., 39.

5. Ibid., 40.

6. Ibid., 39.

7. It could be argued that the term "God" should not be used for the Plotinian One. But Plotinus does sometimes refer to "the One" as "God."

8. Ibid., 42.

9. Plotinus, *Enneads*, 6.9.7.

10. Tanner, *God and Creation*, 42.

11. "We call [Nous] the image of the One. . . . It is its image because that which is begotten by the One must possess many of its characteristics and resemble it as light resembles the sun." Plotinus, *Enneads*, 5.1.7.

12. See the section "Plotinus on Immanence" below.

13. *Confessions*, 5.10.19.

14. *Confessions*, 7.1.1–2.

15. While it is not exactly clear which Platonic books triggered his breakthrough, traces of influence from Plotinus, as Chadwick has noted, can be found in various places of *Confessions*.

16. *Confessions*, 7.10.16, emphases added.

17. Again, the word "gap" here needs to be understood analogously. It is not spatial or essential; rather, as we shall see, it underscores the fundamental ontological difference between God and creation.

18. *Confessions*, 7.10.16.

19. In discussing how the Spirit is said to stir above the water, Augustine emphasizes that the Spirit is "said to stir by the transcendent excellence of His power and not by any spatial relation." *Literal Meaning of Genesis* 1.7.13.

20. See Ibid., 1.1.3.

21. Harrison, *Augustine's Early Theology*, 30, emphases added.

22. *Confessions*, 7.10.16, emphases added.

23. *Confessions*, 9.10.24.

24. In another place, he explicitly links God's transcendence with the truths of creation: "My humble tongue makes confession to your transcendent majesty that you were maker of heaven and earth." *Confessions*, 7.1.1.

25. Gerson, "Plotinus's Metaphysics."

26. *Enneads*, 5.1.6.

27. *Enneads*, 1.8.6 (Gerson version), emphases added.

28. *Enneads*, 1.8.3.

29. *Enneads*, 1.8.6 (Gerson version).

30. Tanner, *God and Creation*, 42.

31. *Confessions*, 12.17.25. Likewise, in discussing the nature of created wisdom, Augustine asserts that "it is not derived from you, our God, but in such a way as to be wholly other than you and not Being itself" (*Confessions*, 12.15.21).

32. *CG*, 12.2, emphases added.

33. Tanner, *God and Creation*, 39.

34. "God—we read—is outside of none, present unperceived to all." *Enneads*, 6.9.7.

35. *Enneads*, 6.9.8.

36. Schindler, *"What's the Difference?"* 13.

37. *Enneads*, 6.9.8.

38. *Confessions*, 1.2.2, emphases added.

39. *Confessions*, 1.4.4, emphases added.

40. It is true that Plotinus does speak of the other direction—the Many strives to be present to the One—but, as we have argued, in their return to the One, beings must essentially eliminate their multiplicity. In order to be present to the One, multiplicity must be sacrificed.

41. Needless to say, for Augustine, God's immanence in creation cannot be understood in the same way as creation's immanence in God. God is within a creature because he sustains its existence; a creature is said to be in God because it cannot exist outside of God's presence. Another difference is that God is always present to creatures, but creatures can in a certain sense turn away from God and fall toward nothingness, as is indicated in: "Your omnipotence is never far from us, even when we are far from you." *Confessions*, 2.2.3.

42. To borrow the phrase from Arthur Lovejoy: *The Great Chain of Being: A Study of the History of an Idea* (Cambridge, MA: Harvard University Press, 1936).

43. Denys Turner, *Faith, Reason and the Existence of God* (Cambridge: Cambridge University Press, 2004), 161.

44. This understanding is also reflected in Augustine's exposition of eternity's relation to time. The fact that all things are simultaneously present to eternity does not abolish the real successiveness of time. See *Confessions*, 9.11.13.

45. *Literal Meaning of Genesis*, 5.16.34.

46. Ibid.

47. A. H. Armstrong, *St. Augustine and Christian Platonism*(Villanova: Villanova University Press, 1967), 14, emphasis added.

48. Ibid., 16.

49. Ibid., 18.

50. *Confessions*, 12.8.8.

51. "By the Platonic books I was admonished to return into myself." *Confessions*, 7.10.16.

52. See, for instance, *Enneads*, 5.1.1.

53. *Soliloquies*, 26.

54. While it is true, as Carol Harrison has argued in *Augustine's Early Thought*, that the idea of *creatio ex nihilo* has been central to Augustine since the very beginning of his career, it is likely that the radical implications of the doctrine were not fully recognized by Augustine until later. It takes time for the profundity of this concept, especially a sense of God's immediate presence in the material world, to penetrate into his system of thought.

55. Turner, *Faith, Reason and Existence of God*, 161.

56. Henry Chadwick, introduction to *Confessions*, xxiv.

57. *CG*, 5.11.

58. Ibid., 12.26.

59. Boersma, *Heavenly Participation*, 21–6.

60. *Literal Meaning of Genesis*, 5.16.34, emphasis added. A similar view is found in *Enchiridion*, ch. 9 (written in 421): "When, then, the question is asked what we are to believe in regard to religion, it is not necessary to probe into the nature of things, as was done by those whom the Greeks called *physici*." It is legitimate to distinguish science from Christian doctrine, but since nature is God's creation, the study of nature cannot be entirely irrelevant to religion.

61. Needless to say, in his warning against scientific investigations, Augustine has idolatry in mind. Nonetheless, here he writes mainly for Christians, for whom idolatry should not be a prominent problem or danger. Rather, it is possible for a Christian to seek to understand God better though the study of nature—God's creation.

62. It should be admitted that Augustine indeed, by alluding to Roman 1:20, affirms that we can see traces of God in the created order, but he nonetheless emphasizes that the incorporeal creatures are a superior way of revealing God and warns against those who take an interest in the investigation the physical world. See *DT*, 15.39.

63. This understanding is clear in Boethius, for whom "knowledge of the rational, numerical structure of the universe would lead to knowledge of the divine nature, and to apprehension of God himself." P. G. Walsh, "Introduction," in Boethius, *The Consolation of Philosophy*, trans., P. G. Walsh (Oxford: Oxford University Press, 1999), xxii.

64. *SCG*, 2.3.

65. It is true that in fact Aquinas quotes Augustine in the passage, but Aquinas often quotes previous authors in order to advance his own ideas, which means that his interpretation of an ancient author's passage may differ significantly from what the original author intends to say.

66. Needless to say, this difference is also due to a much greater impact of Aristotle on Aquinas than on Augustine.

Part II

AQUINAS'S PARTICIPATORY ONTOLOGY

Chapter 4

Aquinas's Theology of Participation and the Concept of Unity

In the first part of the book, we have discussed how Augustine transformed the Platonic theory of participation in the light of *creatio ex nihilo*, which results in a participatory ontology that is more suitable for describing God's relationship with the world. In such a theology of participation, creaturely multiplicity is no longer antithetical to divine simplicity and God's transcendence no longer inversely proportional to his immanence. It can thus be argued that Augustine made a key contribution to the Christianization of participatory ontology. This process, however, is incomplete with Augustine. For a more thorough transformation of participation, we must go to Augustine's medieval successor—Aquinas.

Like Augustine, Aquinas makes the doctrine of creation entirely foundational to his system of thought.[1] But he surpasses his predecessor by developing a true metaphysic of creation, which enables him not only to conceptualize and articulate the meaning of creation more precisely but to construct a more distinctively Christian participatory ontology, which can be more conducive to the contemporary retrieval of participatory theology. In this chapter, we will first examine how Aquinas develops his metaphysic of creation and transforms the concept of unity in the light of the doctrine of creation. In the next two chapters, we will investigate the concepts of multiplicity and relationality in Aquinas's participatory ontology.

THE METAPHYSICS OF CREATION AND PARTICIPATION IN AQUINAS

What enables Aquinas to go a step further in transforming participatory ontology is a deeper connection he builds between the notions of creation and participation, both of which are central to his thought. The idea of creation, as Josef Pieper puts it, is a "hidden key" that can unlock the entire system of Aquinas's thought:

> In the philosophy of St. Thomas Aquinas, there is a fundamental idea by which almost all the basic concepts of his vision of the world are determined: the idea of creation, or more precisely, the notion that nothing exists which is not *creatura*, except the Creator Himself; and in addition, that this createdness determines entirely and all-pervasively the inner structure of the creature.[2]

Likewise, the idea of participation is also fundamental to Aquinas.[3] The term "participation" in some form or other appears more than 3,000 times in his writing, especially at key points in his most systematic works: *Summa contra Gentiles* and *Summa theologiae*.[4] Part of the reason why participation is so central to Aquinas is because he believes that it philosophically articulates the essence of creation. For instance, when discussing the efficient cause of creation, Aquinas uses the theory of participation to demonstrate that all things other than God must have been created by God.[5] For Aquinas, then, participation and creation are inherently inseparable and his participatory ontology is essentially his metaphysical interpretation of *creatio ex nihilo*. Hence, to understand Aquinas's concept of participation, we must first examine his metaphysic of creation.

Debt to Previous Thinkers

Returning for a moment to Augustine, we noted that he made significant contributions to the doctrinal development of *creatio ex nihilo*. For not only did he make it explicit that all things—including "formless matter"—are created by God absolutely out of nothing, but he developed the Christian ontology which identifies being with good.[6] In a more technical language, we can say that Augustine understood the nonexistence of material cause in creation, the insubstantiality of evil, and the identification of goodness and being—which offer building blocks for a Christian metaphysic of creation. On the whole, however, Augustine's exposition of *creatio ex nihilo* was far from systematic: although he obtained crucial insights about creation, these insights were not organized to form a clearly structured and coherent system. His limited knowledge of the best of Greek philosophy[7] also prevented him from presenting his insights of creation with philosophical sophistication. It is reasonable to say that while Augustine made important contributions to the development of creation *ex nihilo*, he did not arrive at a metaphysic of creation in a strict sense.[8] This task was to be completed by Aquinas. Building upon Christian, Jewish, and Muslim thinkers and employing Aristotle's philosophy, Aquinas gave *creatio ex nihilo* "its full expression and most sophisticated exposition."[9] In Aquinas, we finally find a true metaphysic of creation.[10]

It goes without saying that Aquinas is indebted to Augustine in many respects, as he embraces almost all of the latter's insights on creation: for instance, the denial of material cause for creation, the dependence of creatures upon God, and the convertibility of being, unity, and goodness. Apart from Augustine, however, Aquinas also draws inspirations from non-Christian philosophers such as Avicenna, Averroës, and Moses Maimonides.[11] Among these three philosophers, Avicenna has the greatest influence on Aquinas.

One of Avicenna's main contributions is his definition of creation as "making something after absolute non-existence."[12] An implication of this definition is that creation is not a physical event but a metaphysical reality, because the operation that brings something from nonexistence into existence is more fundamental than any change in time. This insight proves crucial to Aquinas. He repeatedly emphasizes that creation is not a change and that all the arguments against creation are invalid because they rest on the assumption that creation is a change. For the same reason, Aquinas argues that creation does not necessarily require the temporal beginning of the world.[13] Avicenna's greatest influence on Aquinas, however, is the distinction between essence and existence, which is not only crucial in Aquinas's early thought, as in *On Being and Essence*,[14] but also foundational to the idea of divine simplicity in more mature works such as *Summa theologiae*. For Aquinas, the pivotal difference between God and a creature is that while essence and existence are separable in a creature, they are identical in God. God's nature is therefore "simple." With this distinction, he demonstrates rigorously that all creatures, which by definition are not simple, must be created by and participate in God, who is simple.

Aquinas does not appropriate Avicenna uncritically, however. When adopting the distinction between essence and existence, he shifts the relationship between the two concepts. For Avicenna, as for most Neoplatonic thinkers before him, essence is more fundamental than existence, which is an accident that happens to the essence. In contrast, by defining existence as the act of essence,[15] Aquinas makes existence more fundamental. In the history of metaphysics, if Avicenna can be referred as an "essentialist," Aquinas is then an "existentialist,"[16] for in Aquinas existence is more primary than essence. This shift is profound. As Burrell puts it, Aquinas's metaphysics is "more than a development of Avicenna; it is a fresh start requiring a conception of existing that could no longer be confused with an accident."[17] Giving primacy to existence instead of essence marks a decisive break from a long Platonic tradition, rendering metaphysics more serviceable to Christian theology. Insofar as the Christian doctrine of creation is distinguished from the Platonic teaching of Idea, this shift is a transition from a predominantly Platonic worldview to a more distinctively Christian and creationist one.

This transition would not have occurred, however, if Aquinas had not creatively employed the Aristotelian philosophy. For it is Aristotle that bequeaths Aquinas' sophisticated philosophical tools for articulating the truths of creation with new rigor and precision, even though Aristotle him-self explicitly rejects the notion of creation *ex nihilo.*[18] As is consistent with the way in which he treats all past thinkers, Aquinas admires Aristotle but does not follow him blindly. He embraces Aristotle when he is consistent with Scripture but corrects him when he is not. But more importantly, he is apt to utilize Aristotle's categories to advance his own metaphysical system, which is not merely an extension—but a thorough remaking—of Aristotle's philosophy. The best example in this regard is his pioneering application of the latter's potency-act theory in the relation of essence-existence. Aristotle, who invented the distinction between potency and act, never thought about applying the distinction to existence and essence and as such remained an "essentialist" in his metaphysics. By applying the potency-act distinction to the category of existence/essence and making existence the fundamental concept in metaphysics, Aquinas opens up a world that differs profoundly from that of Aristotle:

> The world [for Aristotle] is a world of substances or things, but the world is eternal and uncreated, and it is against the background of this eternal and uncre-ated world that Aristotle analyses the concept of substance. Aquinas took over the Aristotelian analysis of substance, but at the same time the world for him consisted of *finite* substances, each of which is *totally dependent* on God.[19]

Another example of Aquinas's creative employment of Aristotle can be found in *ST* 1.44, in which he uses the theory of four causes to discuss the causal relation of creation to God.[20] While Aristotle employs his theory for individual things, Aquinas applies it to the whole creation, proving that God is the efficient, exemplary, and final cause for creation. He uses "exemplary cause" instead of "formal cause" to avoid pantheistic implications, which shows that his appropriation of Aristotle is meticulous and critical. His decisive departure from Aristotle, however, is his exposition of the material cause of creation. Aristotle states repeatedly that "there always has to be some underlying thing which is what comes to be."[21] For him, it is impos-sible for something to come from nothing, a conclusion that he claims is accepted by all philosophers.[22] For it is taken for granted by Aristotle and Greek philosophers that pre-existing primary matter serves as the material cause of the world. Aquinas, however, has to disagree with the Philosopher on this point. He insists that there is no material cause for creation, because even matter itself must ultimately have been created by God. Prime matter is not pre-existent or self-existent but was brought into being from nothing. Hence, while embracing Aristotle's idea of material cause, he arrives at an entirely different conclusion—that the Christian doctrine of creation *ex nihilo* is not only rational but also the summit of philosophy. Past philosophers failed to recognize the truth of creation, he suggests, because their thought did not reach the level of metaphysics and hence were unable to arrive at the metaphysical concept of creation.[23] For this reason, Aquinas's first task is to provide a metaphysical definition of creation and here he goes considerably beyond Augustine.

Metaphysic of Creation

Before defining creation, Aquinas has to first expose some of the misconceptions around what "creation" is. The most common misunderstanding is that creation is a sort of change and many of the objections to creation are based on this assumption. To refute these objections, Aquinas points out that creation is not a change. For a change to occur, there must be some pre-existent substrate that undergoes the change. For instance, my skin becomes darker in the sun, but for the change to happen, my skin must first exist and persist throughout the change. Creation, however, presupposes no underlying substrate. Creation is out of nothing and therefore not a change. But if creation is not a change, what is it? Aquinas offers one of his earliest definitions of creation in his commentary on Lombard's *Sentences*. There, he reasons that every imperfect being must "in its entirety, arise from the first and perfect being," which is nothing but God. "This we call to *create*: to produce a thing into being according to its entire substance."[24] According to this definition, creation is to bring the entirety of one thing into existence.

An even clearer definition of creation is given in *Summa theologiae*, where Aquinas explicitly states that "to create is to make something out of nothing":

> [I]t is not enough to consider how some particular being issues from some particular cause, for we should also attend to the issuing of the *whole of being* from the universal cause, which is God; it is this springing forth that we designate by the term "creation."[25]

For Aquinas, creation thus means the production of the entire existence of a creature by God from nothing. Creation is by definition out of nothing. In this sense, "creation" is simply an abbreviation of "*creatio ex nihilo*." Following Augustine, Aquinas affirms that there is no pre-existent matter before God's creation, for matter itself was created by God out of nothing. For "if we consider the coming forth of the whole of being from its first origin, we cannot presuppose to it any being."²⁶ Hence, "creation presupposes nothing in the thing which is said to be created." By contrast, in a change,

> a subject which is a complete being is presupposed. Hence, the causality of the generator or of the alterer does not extend to everything which is found in the thing.... The causality of the Creator, however, extends to everything that is in the thing.²⁷

Creation is more fundamental than a change: a change affects a thing partially, while creation affects its entire being. With this clarification, it becomes clear that the objections to creation are based on the fallacious assumption that creation is a change. The distinction between creation and change has profound implications. The first is that creation does not take place in time. Time is associated with change and, if creation is not a change, then it cannot be measured by time. For this reason, Aquinas is open to the possibility of an eternal world. For him, an everlasting world is not logically contradictory to the fact it has been created, since creation is not necessarily linked with time.²⁸ Another implication is that creation is not a physical event but a metaphysical reality. Creation concerns the existence of things and is metaphysical in nature. As such, creation is not to be confused with any scientific theories such as the Big Bang; nor can it be in a direct conflict with scientific theories such as the theory of evolution.²⁹

Aquinas's most original contribution to the metaphysics of creation, however, perhaps lies in his innovative interpretation of the meaning of *ex nihilo*. The first meaning of *ex nihilo*, he points out, is that there is no material cause for creation. Secondly, he suggests that *ex nihilo* also means that, in all creatures non-being is ontologically prior to being such that without God's creation they would not exist. In other words, non-being is the natural ontological state of creatures:

> [N]on-being is prior to being in the thing which is said to be created. This is not a priority of time or of duration . . . but a priority of *nature*, so that, if the created thing is left to itself, it would not exist, because it only has its being from the causality of the higher cause.³⁰

Creatures therefore cannot exist on their own, since nothing in their nature contains the source for their existence—existence comes from without. They must continually depend upon God. Creation is thus not a onetime event but an ongoing relation to God. At the heart of the doctrine of creation is thus the radical ontological dependence of creatures on God. They depend on God not only for their coming into being but also for their continuing to exist. For this reason, Aquinas suggests that creation and conservation are essentially one operation:

God does not produce things into being by one operation and conserve them in being by another. . . . Whence the operation of God does not differ according as it makes the beginning of being and as it makes the continuation of being.[31]

Going back to Augustine momentarily, we note that he also affirms that creatures continuously depend upon God for their existence and that God's creation and providence are essentially one. Now Aquinas makes it clear that the unity between creation and providence is already contained in the meaning of creation *ex nihilo*. For him, almost all the truths of creation—God's causal relation to creatures, creatures' dependence on God, and God's transcendence and immanence—are contained in the definition of creation. With the definition, he demonstrates most truths about creation with reason:

The immense achievement of Aquinas is to have explained so much of the Christian teaching on creation in philosophical terms. Nearly everything essential to the Christian idea of creation—the existence of the Creator, the uniqueness of the Creator, the fact that the Creator creates without intermediaries, the fact that the creation is properly out of nothing, the fact that the Creator creates freely—is not only philosophically comprehensible . . . but also philosophically demonstrable.[32]

By integrating Aristotle's philosophy with biblical teachings, Aquinas is able to bring the Christian understanding of creation to a new level of sophistication than what Augustine and other past Christian thinkers had achieved. Aquinas is the first one in the history to develop a metaphysic of creation, which allows us to penetrate into the deeper meanings of *creatio ex nihilo*, especially the profound sense of creatures' dependence on God. Created from nothing, a creature is by nature a "being-in-relation" to God, which is the heart of the idea of participation.

Metaphysics of Participation

In Aquinas's thought, creation is deeply intertwined with the theory of participation. To some extent, creation and participation are two sides of the same coin. In creation, we move from God to creatures; in participation, we move from creatures to God. If creation describes the way in which the One produces the Many, participation explains the way in which the Many relate to the One. As such, Aquinas's theology of participation is the reverse side of his metaphysic of creation. Having discussed his metaphysic of creation, we now examine his metaphysics of participation. We first need to clarify what the term "participation" means for Aquinas.

The concept of participation (*methexis*) goes back at least to Plato, who employed this term to describe how different individual things can be called by the same name.[33] For instance, there are different flowers such as rose, orchid, and lily, but they all are called "flowers." In other words, they share the same name "flower" and in a more technical language we say that they participate in "flower." Participation thus accounts for the relation between the One and the Many. In addition to the Platonic heritage, Aquinas adds the Aristotelian theory of causality to participation, making it more dynamic. To participate, he says, "is nothing other than to *receive partially* from another."[34] More specifically, participation describes the relationship between what is particular and what is universal or between what is partial and what is whole. Such understanding is made evident in his exposition of Boethius's *De hebdomadibus*, where he lists three types of participation:

> For "to participate" is, as it were, "to *grasp a part.*" And, therefore, when something receives in a particular way that which belongs to another in a universal way, it is said "to participate" in that, as human being is said to participate in animal because it does not possess the intelligible structure of animal according to its total commonality; and in the same way, Socrates participates in human. And similarly, too, a subject participates in accident, and matter in form, because a substantial form, or an accidental one, which is common by virtue of its own intelligible structure, is determined to this or that subject. And similarly, too, an effect is said "to participate" in its own cause, and especially when it is not equal to the power of its cause, as for example, if we should say that "air participates in the light of the sun" because it does not receive that light with the brilliance it has in the sun.[35]

As we can see from the passage, at the heart of the concept of participation is *relation*. There are different kinds of relation and subsequently different kinds of participation. When the relation is between what is particular and what is universal, participation is primarily conceptual. Socrates participates in humanity not because he is partially human, but because he is a particular human being. When the relation is between what is partial and what is full, participation is ontological or causal and is suitable for describing the relationship between a cause and its effect. This kind of participation, which is most important in Aquinas, is associated with causality. For instance, when we say that air participates in the sun's light, we mean that air receives partial light from the sun. Integrating Plato's idea of participation with Aristotle's causality, this type of participation offers a unique tool for describing the relationship between God and creatures. Aristotle would not have approved of combing causality with the concept of participation, as he explicitly rejects the latter.[36] However, by putting the two seemingly conflicting concepts together, Aquinas creates a synthesis beyond Plato and Aristotle, which allows him to express the truth of creation more aptly.

Neither Plato nor Aristotle has arrived at a full doctrine of creation. Plato's Demiurge merely gives forms to pre-existent matter and Aristotle's God is only the final cause. Both fall short of the concept of *creatio ex nihilo*. Left on its own, neither Plato's theory of participation nor Aristotle's theory of causality can lead to the Christian teaching on creation. The ingenuity of Aquinas is that he integrates the concept of participation with causality and applies it to the category of existence, thereby demonstrating that all creatures owe their existence to God:

> For when we encounter a subject which participates in a reality then this reality must be caused there by a thing which possesses it of its nature, as when, for example, iron is made red-hot by fire. . . . God is sheer existence subsisting of his very nature. And such being . . . cannot but be unique, rather as whiteness would be were it subsistent, for its repetition depends on there being many receiving subjects. We are left with the conclusion that all things other than God are not their own existence but participate in existence.
>
> It follows strictly that all things which are diversified by their diverse participation in existence, so that some are fuller beings than others, are caused by one first being which simply is in the fullest sense of the word.
>
> On these grounds Plato held that before the many you must place the one; and Aristotle that supremely real and true is the cause of everything that is real and true, his illustration being fire, which is *hottest and the cause of heat in everything else.*[37]

In this crucial passage, all the key themes of our discussion—participation,[38] the One and the Many, causality and creation—are deeply interwoven. The goal of this argument is to prove that God is the single cause of existence for all things. But the backbone of the whole argument is the concept of participation, the essence of which is the causal relationship between the One (which possesses a reality fully and by nature) and the Many (which possess the reality partially). Aquinas first establishes the general rule of participation that a partial reality found in a thing must come from something that possesses the reality by nature. Applying the rule to existence, he then reasons that all things that exist partially must receive existence from something that exists by nature, which is God. Hence, God alone is the source of existence for all things.

It is remarkable that Aquinas explicitly acknowledges his indebtedness to Plato and Aristotle. From Plato, he appropriates the Many-to-One relation of participation; from Aristotle, the theory of causality. He integrates these two Greek philosophical theories in order to demonstrate the truth of creation. It

should be noted that the Greek philosophy he receives has already been mediated by Muslim authors, which makes it easier to Christianize participatory
ontology and to use it to articulate the doctrine of creation.

In this sense, his metaphysic of creation is also his metaphysic of participation, because the metaphysical implications of creation are most clearly
captured by the concept of participation. A creature by definition is a being
by participation. In Aquinas, therefore, creation and participation are two
sides of the same reality—the relation between creatures and God. Since they
describe how God, who is entirely simple, relates to the plurality of creation,
creation and participation are also concerned with the question of the One and
the Many. Hence, by transforming the Platonic theory of participation in the
light of the doctrine of creation, he offers a promising solution to the problem
of the One and the Many. In this chapter, we will first discuss the concept of
unity in his participatory ontology.

THE CONCEPT OF UNITY IN AQUINAS'S PARTICIPATORY ONTOLOGY

Before going into a detailed discussion of the concept of unity in Aquinas's
metaphysics of participation, let us look at his approach to the perennial
philosophical debate on the One and the Many.[39] Monists such as Parmenides
and Melissus suggest that reality is one and that diversity is but an illusion.
Aristotle in his *Physics* and *Metaphysics* attempts to refute the Parmenidean
thesis, arguing that there are more than one first principles.[40] In line with
Aristotle, Aquinas critiques the monists.[41] He points out that the monist
position is based on the faulty assumption that the term "being" has only
one meaning, whereas in fact it can be said in multiple senses: substance,
quality, or quantity.[42] In other words, "being" is not univocal but analogical.
The analogy of being thus constitutes an important part of his solution to the
One and the Many. While indebted to Aristotle's insight that "being" has
more than one meaning, his analogy of being is a significant development
from the former. While Aristotle's discussion is restricted to the conceptual
level, Aquinas extends the principle to the ontological level, suggesting that
there are different levels of being with respect to perfection. For instance,
on the one hand, in terms of essence, an angel is more perfect than a worm.
The ontological difference between two species gives rise to a multiplicity
of reality. On the other hand, insofar as both the angel and the worm exist,
there is a commonality between their existence. In other words, they are unified by the fact of existence. But their existence is imperfect in comparison
to the being that exists perfectly. In this sense, they both participate in the
existence of God. In Aquinas's thought, the theory of analogy of being is

thus incorporated into the concept of participation in order to account for "the fact that many different things do indeed exist, and yet that each of them in some way shares in the perfection of being."[43] In this respect, he departs from Aristotle and remains Platonic. For him, participation is indispensable for maintaining a balanced Christian worldview that affirms both creaturely diversity and their unity in God.

But Aquinas's Platonism is already Christianized, as he makes important modifications to all the key aspects of participation—unity, plurality, and relation. In our discussion of Augustine, we already examined how he transforms the concept of unity. By identifying one with being, not only does he introduce a notion of unity that does not exclude plurality, but he also develops a concept of divine simplicity that pushes unity to a new level. Aquinas firmly embraces these Augustinian insights and maintains the principle of convertibility of unity and being. Yet he moves beyond his predecessor by establishing this principle on a more solid metaphysical ground.

Unity and Being

In affirming the convertibility of the One and Being, Aquinas differentiates himself from the Neoplatonic tradition that places the One above Being. For in the Christian context, Aquinas, like Augustine, cannot but identify the One with Being, as they are convinced by revelation that God is the self-existing Being (*ipsum esse*) as well as the One.[44] Being and the One must be identical. This Christian principle, as Gilson has explained it, is fundamentally at odds with the Neoplatonic tradition:

> This is straight Neoplatonism: the first principle is the One, and being comes next as the first of its creatures. Now this is, though self-consistent, yet absolutely inconsistent with the mental universe of Christian thinkers, in which being cannot be the first of all creatures . . . it has to be the Creator Himself, namely God.[45]

In identifying Unity with Being, Aquinas is undoubtedly continuing the legacy of Augustine,[46] whose conviction that God is Being is rooted in the revelation of God's name as "I AM THAT I AM" in Exodus 3:14. On the basis of the same passage, Aquinas asserts that the most appropriate name for God is "He who is" and quotes Augustine in support.[47] Like Augustine, he anchors God's name as Being in the truth of creation.[48] There is a difference, however, between the ways in which the two thinkers arrive at the principle of identification between Unity and Being. While Augustine derives the principle from Scripture, Aquinas gives it a philosophical underpinning. Observing that Aristotle reaches a similar conclusion on philosophical basis,

Aquinas integrates the philosophical argument with biblical insights and provides a sophisticated metaphysical treatment on the relation between "one"
and "being."[49]

First, he borrows an insight from Aristotle that "one" does not add anything substantial but a conceptual difference to "being." In *Metaphysics* IV.2,
Aristotle explains that "one" is the *per se* attribute of being in that "being
and one are the same and one in the sense that they follow upon each other
. . . but not in the sense that they are determined by one concept."[50] In other
words, "one" and "being" are identical in essence but are distinguished conceptually.[51] In *Metaphysics* X.1, Aristotle states that the essence of "one" is
"indivisible" or "undivided" and as such "one" adds a conceptual difference
to "being."[52] Aquinas adopts this position and claims that the substance of
a thing is *one* and *being* through itself.[53] But he moves beyond Aristotle
by offering a more secure metaphysical foundation for the identification of
"being" and "one."[54] An excellent discussion on this topic can be found in
Summa theologiae.

After treating the eternity of God, Aquinas devotes a whole question to
the oneness of God. In the first article, he asks whether one adds anything to
being. After presenting the objections to the convertibility of one and being,
Aquinas writes:

> Oneness (*unum*) adds nothing real to being (*ens*), but simply denies the division
> of it, for to be one means no more than un-division of being (*ens indivisum*).
> [And from this it is clear that one is *convertible* with being (*unum convertitur
> cum ente*) (my translation).][55]

Like Aristotle, Aquinas makes it clear that with respect to reality "one" is
identical to "being," and the only difference that "one" makes to "being" is
conceptual—it expresses the undivided state of being. In a different place,
he explicitly defines "the one" as "being that is not divided."[56] Unity is thus
the negation of division in being. This insight, as we discussed, had already
been understood by Augustine but his conception was somewhat implicit
and at times inconsistent. At the hands of Aquinas, the insight becomes more
explicit: one and being are identical with respect to substance and differ only
conceptually. A thing must be a unity in order to exist.

Aquinas points out that the reason why people refuse to identify "one" with
"being" is because they confuse between two senses of "one" or "unity": (1)
the unity that is convertible with being; (2) the unity that is the first number.
He claims that Avicenna makes this mistake when he, "seeing that the unity
initiating number adds something to substance," thinks that the unity in the
first sense adds something to the substance. But this is false, since "everything is *one* of its very substance," and "the unity convertible with being does

not add anything to being, whilst the unity initiating number adds something belonging to the genus of quantity."[57] Unity is thus convertible with being in the first sense. To support the conclusion, Aquinas provides the following argument:

> For every being (*omne ens*) is either simple or composite. Now simple things are neither actually nor potentially divided, whilst composite things do not exist as long as their constituent parts are divided, but only after these parts have come together to compose the thing. Clearly then everything's existence is grounded in indivision. And this is why things guard their unity as they do their existence.[58]

Aquinas's strategy is to divide things into two categories: simple things and composite ones. With regard to simple things, by the very fact that they are simple, that is, indivisible, their being is necessarily one. For composite things, while they are not simple and thus potentially divisible, their constituent parts must be unified in order to exist, otherwise they would not exist as a whole but disintegrate into separable parts. Along as they exist as a whole, their existence must be a unity. To exist is to be one. For both simple things and composite ones, then, being is in effect convertible with one, because existence is grounded in unity.

Here, Aquinas makes an important distinction between simple things and composite things, which eventually enables to him to distinguish between "undividedness" and "indivisibility" (or between "unity" and "simplicity"). For both simple and composite things being is convertible with unity, but there is a difference between the two kinds of unity: the unity of composite things is the *undividedness* of being, whereas the unity of simple things is the *indivisibility* of being. All things that are indivisible in being are naturally undivided, but the reverse is not true. For things that are undivided in being may be potentially divisible. They *can* become divided if nothing in their nature necessitates the undividedness of being. Hence, in comparison to undividedness, indivisibility is associated with a higher level of unity. As Aquinas sees it, the being of simple things is indivisible because it is undivided both actually and potentially. Simple things are not only undivided but also can never be divided because their being is *by nature* indivisible. In contrast, composite things are potentially divisible, although they are undivided at this point. In other words, their undividedness is conditional but not necessary since they are divisible in principle. Indivisibility is thus more demanding—it is absolute and necessary undividedness. If unity corresponds to undividedness, then simplicity corresponds to indivisibility. Simplicity is the highest level of unity and supreme oneness and as such only God is called simple.[59] This understanding of simplicity has profound implications for Aquinas's discussion of the nature of God. What fundamentally distinguishes God from creatures is not unity (oneness), for both God and creatures have unity, but simplicity, which then leads us to divine simplicity, a key but controversial concept in Aquinas.

Divine Simplicity

As we have seen, the concept of divine simplicity constitutes a crucial aspect of Augustine's thought about God's nature. Like his predecessor, Aquinas embraces divine simplicity as one of the core concepts about God. Building upon the insights from Augustine and many other thinkers before him,[60] Aquinas is able to bring divine simplicity to a new metaphysical height, making it foundational to his treatment of divine attributes. The centrality of divine simplicity is evident in the way he arranges the topics in *Summa theo-logiae*. Having established the existence of God in *ST* 1.2, Aquinas proceeds to investigate God's nature, but the very first question in the section is "the simplicity of God," which lays "the foundation for questions that follow."[61] For in his mind, simplicity is the most distinctive feature of God that sets him apart from creatures. While attributes such as goodness, wisdom, and unity can be possessed by creatures in certain modes,[62] simplicity is attributed to God alone. Simplicity is the defining mark of God's nature, of which other divine attributes are derivatives. It should be noted, however, that simplicity is not a positive predication of God, as Aquinas makes it clear that "we cannot know what God is, but only what he is not."[63] To affirm God's simplicity is to rule out any "compositeness" from him.[64] Hence, when expositing divine simplicity, Aquinas is essentially separating God from all creaturely modes of existence. Divine simplicity underscores the radical ontological difference of God from creatures as well as his absolute transcendence.

Indeed, each of the articles in the question is a denial of composition in God. For instance, article 1 denies the composition of parts in God; article 2, composition of form and matter; article 6, composition of substance and acci-dents. Of all the articles, articles 3 and 4 are most central to divine simplic-ity and deserve special attention. In article 3, Aquinas seeks to demonstrate that God is identical to his nature or essence. First, he argues that, in things composed of form and matter, the thing cannot be identified with its essence. The essence of a person, for instance, is humanity. But an individual person cannot be the same as human nature, for apart from human nature, the person also possesses traits that are particular to her or him. Composite things there-fore cannot be identical to their essence. But things that are not composed of matter and form are identical to their form, because they do not derive any particular traits from matter. For an example, an angel, which by nature is a form without matter, is identical to its essence. For this reason, each angel is its own species. Likewise, God is not composed of form and matter and thus must be "identical with his own godhead, with his own life and with whatever else is similarly said of him."[65]

This article alone, however, does not completely distinguish God from other beings, such as angels. To further define the absolute simplicity of God, in article 4 Aquinas maintains that God's essence is identical to his existence; in other words, it is "God's very nature to exist."[66] He offers three arguments that God *is* not only his essence but also his existence. Of these three arguments, the third is particularly significant, as it employs the theory of participation:

> Thirdly, anything on fire either is itself fire or has caught fire. Similarly, anything that exists either is itself existence or partakes of it. Now, God, as we have seen, exists. If then he is not himself existence, and thus not by nature existent, he will only be a partaker of existence. And so he will not be the primary existence. God therefore is not only his own essence, but also his own existence.[67]

The first sentence sets up the general principle of participation, using the illustration of fire. Applying this principle to the category of existence, Aquinas is then able to arrive at the conclusion that in reality that are only two modes of existence: self-existence and existence by participation (existence derived from an external source). The question is then: which kind of existence is God's existence? If God is not existent by nature, the conclusion would be that he exists by participation, which is evidently false. It is thus necessary that God is self-existent—God *is* his own existence. Because God is his own essence, God's essence must be identical to his existence.

Here, Aquinas establishes the ultimate kind of simplicity—the identification between essence and existence. Only God has absolute simplicity, since his being is so supremely unified that even the fundamental distinction between essence and existence, which holds for all creatures, does not obtain for him. This absolute simplicity alone is called "divine simplicity." Other "simple" beings, such as angels, do not have this kind of simplicity because they do not exist by nature but receive existence from God. No creatures have absolute simplicity as they are necessarily compositions of essence and existence. Such multiplicity is irreducible and is part of the nature of the creation—a defining feature of creatureliness. To secure the fundamental divide between God and creatures, it is thus essential for Aquinas to establish divine simplicity as the starting point for his treatment of divine attributes.

As the epitome of classical theism, Aquinas's idea of divine simplicity has been under heavy fire in modern times.[68] On the one hand, contemporary analytic philosophers have argued that the notion of divine simplicity is internally incoherent or inconsistent.[69] On the other hand, Trinitarian theologians complain that it is problematic to take an abstract concept such as divine simplicity, instead of the economic activities of the Triune God, as the starting point for discussing God.[70] There are also complaints that the idea of divine simplicity gives a solitary, static picture of God, which is a product of Greek metaphysics and has nothing to do with the biblical view of God that is alive and active.[71] In what follows, I will respond to these criticisms by pointing out a weakness common to their arguments—the tendency to see divine simplicity in isolation. In particular, these objections fail to see the essential connection of divine simplicity with other foundational aspects of Aquinas's theology, especially the doctrine of creation. This weakness is particularly evident in Gunton's criticism.

As a representative of modern Trinitarian thinkers who are discontent with classical theism, Gunton suggests that divine simplicity, in elevating God's oneness over his threeness, exemplifies classical theism's obsession with unity and disregard for plurality.[72] As discussed earlier, however, Aquinas distinguishes between the two kinds of "one"—the numerical one and what is equivalent to being—and stresses that "the unity with which number begins is not attributed to God but only material things."[73] So, his concept of divine simply is not about "one" in the numerical sense over against "three," but about the unique mode of God's being that is completely distinguished from creaturely modes. In other words, his emphasis on God's absolute unity is in fact his insistence on God's perfection and absolute transcendence over creation. If one is indeed convertible with being, to say that God is simple is essentially to say that God is supremely Being. This understanding is made clear by Aquinas himself:

> Since to be one is to exist undividedly, anything supremely one must be both supremely existent and supremely undivided. Both characteristics belong to God. He exists supremely, because he has not acquired an existence which his nature has then determined, but is subsistent existence itself, in no way determined. He is also supremely undivided, because as we have seen he is altogether simple, not divided in any way, and this neither actually nor potentially. Clearly then God is supremely one.[74]

In this important passage, Aquinas first restates the definition of "one" and the convertibility of one and being. Then, he reasons that since the degree to which something is one corresponds to the degree to which it exists, what is supremely existent must be supremely one. Since God exists supremely, it follows necessarily that he is supremely one. Here again, he clarifies that God's unity is not in the numerical sense but in the sense of being. God's supreme simplicity is rooted in the fact that he is supreme *existence*. To emphasize God's simplicity is to affirm that God is supremely Being, whose name is revealed as "He who is," which underscores the fact that God is the Creator of all. Hence, for Aquinas, God's simplicity is inseparable from the scriptural revelation of God's name and the foundational doctrine of *creatio ex nihilo.* Those who claim that divine simplicity is baptized Greek metaphysics, alien to the Bible, fail to see its biblical anchor. We must not interpret Aquinas's concept of divine simplicity in an isolated way, but do so in relation to his metaphysics of creation and participation. In Aquinas's mind, divine simplicity highlights the fact that God, as the Creator of all things, is the transcendent source of existence and perfections. Divine simplicity is the supreme perfection.

For this reason, much of the criticism, especially the complaint that divine simplicity gives a solitary, static picture of God is misguided. For Aquinas, to say that God is simple is equivalent to saying that he is supreme existence. Existence is "the ultimate actuality of everything," since "the most perfect thing of all is to exist."[75] Accordingly, divine simplicity is an affirmation of the fact that God is "the most *actual*, and therefore the most perfect, of all things."[76] If composite beings have perfections such as life and activity, God, in his simple and supreme existence, must have the perfections in a supreme mode. As Aquinas puts it, because God "is the primary operative cause of all things, the perfections of everything must pre-exist in him in a higher manner."[77] So, God in his simplicity is in fact the opposite of a static being, as suggested above. This observation is well articulated by Stump:

> The difficulty of thinking one's way up the ladder of being can leave one with the impression that the immutable, impassible, eternal, simple God of Thomistic philosophical theology is frozen, static, inert, unresponsive, and incapable of action. But Aquinas's notion of God is exactly the opposite. If it were not so subject to misinterpretation, one might well say that for Aquinas God is maximally *dynamic*, and not static at all. On Aquinas's views, there is more ability to act—one might say, more action—on the part of a God with the classical divine attributes than there could be on the part of a composite entity acting in time. That is why Aquinas can say that in the *esse* that is God there are all the perfections of all the genera of created things—including responsiveness and action, which are perfections of any *id quod est* with mind and will.[78]

Likewise, those who complain that Aquinas starts with the oneness, instead of the threeness, of God, have also misunderstood the real import of divine simplicity. On their understanding, the concept of divine simplicity is a product of Greek philosophy and a distortion of the biblical view of God.[79] As we have argued, however, Aquinas's divine simplicity is essentially an expression of the radical transcendence of God as the Creator, as anchored in the doctrine of *creatio ex nihilo.* In this sense, divine simplicity is not a metaphysical construct that is alien to the Bible, but arises out of the "biblical metaphysics of creation."[80] To start with divine simplicity in his discussion of God's nature, Aquinas is therefore doing nothing less than beginning with the fact that God is the Creator,[81] as is consistent with the Nicene Creed. It is a confession about the Creator God, and for that matter, it is also the beginning of the Bible. For someone steeped in Scripture and tradition, it is most natural for Aquinas to begin discussing God with the truth of creation, which underpins his idea of divine simplicity. To start from God's oneness instead of his threeness, Aquinas is not privileging metaphysics over revelation nor prioritizing the One against the Many, as Gunton suggests. On the contrary, he is simply in his own terms being faithful to the Bible and tradition, since for him divine simplicity underscores the fact that God is the supreme, transcendent Creator of all that is.

Because it is anchored in the doctrine of creation, Aquinas's idea of divine simplicity is not a mere adoption of Plotinus's concept of the Simplex. Although they both mean absolute unity and use the same word,[82] the ways in which simplicity relates to plurality differ profoundly. Whereas the Plotinian Simplex is utterly devoid of plurality, divine simplicity is all-embracing, possessing "the manifold perfections of all other things."[83] God's simplicity by no means excludes creatures' perfections. On the contrary, Aquinas asserts that "all existent things are contained in a primordial unity in God."[84] Unity is not the negation of plurality but dividedness and as such divine simplicity is not the negation of plurality but divisibility. God in his simplicity possesses multiple perfections in an absolutely indivisible fashion. This insight is expressed by Aquinas himself:

> If the sun, as Dionysius says, possesses in itself, primordially and without diversity, the divers qualities and substances of the things we can sense, while yet maintaining the unity of its own being and the homogeneity of its light, how much more must everything pre-exist in unity of nature in the cause of all? Perfections therefore which are diverse and opposed in themselves, pre-exist as one in God, without detriment to his simplicity.[85]

On this understanding, the One (God) in absolute simplicity is the infinitely abundant source of plurality and diversity, because the plural perfections pre-exist in God in a supremely indivisible mode. Plurality is no longer a deviation of the One but comes from the One, who is not beyond Being but the Supreme Being itself—the Creator of all. In fact, because the One is the immediate source for all things, the Many truly participate in the One. In Plotinus's system, multiplicity must be eliminated from beings when they return to the One; but in Aquinas, when creatures return to God, their diversity and particularity is not abolished but preserved. They do not disappear in the One but truly become themselves. The dialectic between the One and the Many finally ceases. In comparison to the Neoplatonic Simplex, Aquinas's divine simplicity is therefore a significant step forward. In Aquinas's theology of participation, the Many participates in the One not because it is a fall-away from the One but because it is created by the One, the infinite source of plenitude. The One, while completely transcendent, is nonetheless intimate to all things. Only in this system can creatures participate in God without losing their diversity and particularity. This brings us to the next chapter—multiplicity in Aquinas's participatory ontology.

NOTES

1. See Josef Pieper, *The Silence of St. Thomas*, trans. John Murray, S.J. and Daniel O'Connor (South Bend, IN: St. Augustine's Press, 1999), 47–8. Likewise, Rudi te Velde observes that the doctrine of creation is "basic to Thomas's thought" in that it "provides the general metaphysical framework of most of his theological, anthropological and ethical inquires." *Aquinas on God: The 'Divine Science' of the* Summa Theologiae (Aldershot, UK: Ashgate, 2006), 123.

2. Pieper, *Silence of Thomas*, 47.

3. Since the publication of the ground-breaking work of Fabro and Geiger, the centrality of participation in Aquinas's metaphysics has been widely recognized. See Cornelio Fabro, *La nozione metafisca di partecipazione secondo S. Thommaso d'Aquino* (Milan, 1939); 2nd ed. (Turin, 1950), and L.-B. Geiger's *La participation dans la philosophie de s. Thomas d'Aquin* (Paris, 1942). See also W. Norris Clarke, "The Limitation of Act by Potency in St. Thomas: Aristotelianism or Neoplatonism?" *New Scholasticism* 26 (1952): 167–94; idem, "The Meaning of Participation in St. Thomas," *Proceedings of the American Catholic Philosophical Association* 26 (1952), 147–57; John F. Wippel, *The Metaphysical Thought of Thomas Aquinas: from Finite Being to Uncreated Being* (Washington, D.C.: Catholic University of America Press, 2000): 94–131.

4. Hubler, "*Creatio ex nihilo*," 173–4.

5. *ST* 1.44.1.

6. Among other things, *creatio ex nihilo* also means for Augustine a profound sense of God's immanence to creatures. Conversely, it underscores the radical dependence of all creatures on God.

7. Lewis Ayres, *Augustine and the Trinity* (Oxford: Oxford University Press, 2000). As Ayres points out, it is now widely recognized in modern scholarship that Augustine had limited exposure to the best of Greek philosophy.

8. It is perhaps possible to construct a "philosophy of creation" out of Augustine's writings, as is done by Christopher J. O'Toole, *The Philosophy of Creation in the Writings of St. Augustine* (Washington, D.C.: Catholic University of America Press, 1944). We must note, however, that Augustine himself never constructed a systematic philosophy of creation; rather, his thoughts about creation are scattered throughout his writings.

9. Baldner and Carroll, "Preface" to *Aquinas on Creation.*

10. Detailed analyses of Aquinas's philosophy of creation can be found in te Velde, *Participation and Substantiality*; Hubler, "*Creatio ex nihilo*"; Matthew R. McWhorter, "Aquinas's Theology of Creation in *Summa theologiae:* A Study and Defence of Selected Questions" (PhD diss., Ave Maria University, 2011).

11. Baldner and Carroll, introduction to *Aquinas on Creation*, 17–9; Burrell, "Aquinas and Islamic and Jewish Muslim thinkers," 70–81.

12. Quoted in Rahim Acar, "Creation: Avicenna's Metaphysical Account," in Burrell *et al*, 80.

13. For Aquinas, as we will see, the most proper meaning of "*creatio ex nihilo*" does not refer to the fact that the world began in time, and for this reason he argues that even an eternal world does not contradict the doctrine of creation *ex nihilo*, though he admits that he accepts the temporal beginning of the universe on the basis of revelation. See *Aquinas on Creation*, 83–6.

14. Aquinas, *On Being and Essence*, trans. Armand A. Maurer (Toronto: Pontifical Institute of Medieval Studies, 1968).

15. *SCG* 1.22: "[T]he essence and the being are therefore related as potency and act." Appropriating the Aristotelian distinction between potency and act, Aquinas understands essence as potentiality to be actualized in existence. In this sense, existence is on a higher ontological level than essence.

16. I borrow the terms "essentialist" and "existentialist" from Fredrick Copleston, who, in comparing the metaphysics of Aquinas to that of Aristotle, notes that there are two aspects of metaphysics and writes that "if we like to call this first aspect the 'essentialist' aspect and the second the 'existentialist' aspect . . . we can say that it is in emphasizing the existentialist aspect that Aquinas goes beyond Aristotle." Copleston, *Aquinas*, 82–3.

17. Burrell, "Aquinas and Islamic and Jewish Thinkers," 70.

18. Aristotle, *Physics* I.7, trans. Robin Waterfield (Oxford: Oxford University Press, 1996).

19. Copleston, *Aquinas*, 83.

20. Aristotle's account of the four-cause-theory can be found in *Physics* II.3.

21. Aristotle, *Physics* I.7.

22. Ibid, I.4.

23. In *ST* 1.44. 2, Aquinas offers his own interpretation of the history of philosophy.

24. *Aquinas on Creation*, 74.

25. *ST* 1.45.1, emphases added.

26. Ibid.

27. *Aquinas on Creation*, 74.

28. *ST* 1.46.1.

29. The implications for science-theology dialogue will be discussed in the conclusion. For a detailed treatment of the topic, see Yonghua Ge, "Aquinas on Creation and Its Implications for Modern Science-Religion Dialogues," *Crux* 53, no. 2 (2017): 11–8.

30. *Aquinas on Creation*, 74–5; emphases added.

31. Aquinas, *On the Power of God*, trans. English Dominican Fathers (Westminster, MD: Newman, 1952), 5.1.

32. Baldner and Carroll, "Analysis," *Aquinas on Creation*, 62. One aspect that cannot be shown by reason is that the world is temporally finite. But, for Aquinas, it seems that the temporal beginning of the universe is not an essential part of the metaphysical doctrine of *creatio ex nihilo*.

33. *Republic* X, 596 a6–7.

34. Quoted in Hubler, "*Creatio ex nihilo*," 180.

35. *An Exposition of the* On the hebdomads *of Boethius*, trans. Janice L. Schultz and Edward A. Synan (Washington, D.C.: Catholic University of America Press, 2001), 19, emphases added.

36. Aristotle, *Metaphysics* I, 9, 991 *a* 20.

37. *ST* 1.44.1, emphases added. Note that Aquinas's Aristotle is a modified Aristotle, by virtue of Muslim translators and commentators.

38. Note that "participationem" is translated as "sharing" in the Blackfriar's edition. To make the idea clearer, I have translated it literally as "participation."

39. For the following discussion, I consulted Wippel, *Metaphysical Thought of Aquinas*, 65–131.

40. See *Physics* I, 2 and *Metaphysics* XII, which contain a summary of the arguments of Parmenides and Melissus.

41. Aquinas disagrees, however, with Aristotle on the number of first principles. While Aristotle posits multiple first principles, Aquinas argues that there is only one first principle.

42. Aquinas, *In I Phys.*, lect.3, pp.13–14, nn.20–21. Likewise, he points out the term "one" is not univocal either; it can mean different things. Ibid., lect.3, pp.14–15, nn.22–24.

43. Te Velde, *Aquinas on God*, 95.

44. For Aquinas's proof that there is only one first principle, see *Aquinas on Creation*, 71–4.

45. Gilson, *Being and Some Philosophers*, 52.

46. This is not to say that Augustine is the only source of inspiration for Aquinas. In fact, Aristotle has written on the convertibility of one and being in *Metaphysics*, on which Aquinas has commented. In addition, Boethius has stated clearly that one and being are convertible in *The Theological Tractates*, ed. Steward (Cambridge, MA, 1973), 94.

47. *ST* 1.13.11.

48. In *ST* 1.13.11, Aquinas points out that the names of God are used "because of the perfections that flow from God to creatures, and of these the primary one is existence itself, from which we get the name 'He who is.'"

49. For the historical development of these transcendental concepts, see Jan A. Aertsen, *Medieval Philosophy and the Transcendentals: The Case of Thomas Aquinas* (Leiden: Brill, 1996), 159–242.

50. *Metaphysics* IV 1003b 22–25. For a detailed analysis of this topic, see E. Halper, "Aristotle on the Convertibility of One and Being," *The New Scholasticism* 59 (1985): 213–27.

51. Aertsen, *Medieval Philosophy and Transcendentals*, 205.

52. *Metaphysics* X, 1.

53. Aquinas, *In IV Metaph.*, lect. 2, 555.

54. Aertsen, *Medieval Philosophy and Transcendentals*, 207.

55. *ST* 1.11.1, emphasis added. Note that in the Blackfriars edition *ens* is translated as "existing." However, I prefer to translate *ens* as "being" instead of "existing," for from the text itself it's not clear that *ens* refers specifically to the act of existing.

56. *In I Sent.* 24.1.3 ad 3.

57. Ibid.

58. *ST* 1.11.1. Note that, among simple beings, Aquinas recognizes different levels of simplicity. As we will see, even though angels are called "simple beings," God alone has absolute simplicity.

59. *ST* 1.11.3.

60. For the development of divine simplicity, see Jeffery E. Brower, "Simplicity and Aseity" *Oxford Handbook of Philosophical Theology*, ed. Thomas R. Flint and Michael Rea (New York: Oxford University Press, 2011).

61. Thomas Gilby, "Appendix 12: Simplicity and Unity," *ST* vol.2, p. 214.

62. It is true that Aquinas calls immaterial, separate things such as angels "simple" beings. But, as we will show, even these so-called simple beings are not strictly, absolutely simple as God is, for there is still a distinction between their essence and existence, while in God the two are identical. In this sense, God alone has unqualified simplicity.

63. Preface to *ST* vol.2.

64. Ibid.

65. *ST* 1.3.3.

66. *ST* 1.3.4.

67. Ibid.

68. Of course, there are plenty of criticisms of Augustine's idea of divine simplicity, but since Aquinas's concept is a development from the former and arguably the more sophisticated version, by responding to critics of Aquinas, I will have addressed Augustine's critics as well.

69. See, for instance, Alvin Plantinga, *Does God Have a Nature?* (Milwaukee, WI: Marquette University Press, 1980). For a comprehensive and sophisticated attack on Aquinas's notion of divine simplicity, see Christopher Hughes, *A Complex Theory of a Simple God* (Ithaca, NY: Cornell University Press, 1989).

70. For example, Stephan Mckenna, the translator of Augustine's *De Trinitate*, comments: "[T]o Augustine it seemed better to begin with the unity of the divine nature, since this is a truth which is demonstrated by reason. . . . The logic of this arrangement is today commonly recognized and in the textbooks of dogma the treatise *De Deo Uno* precedes that of *De Deo Trino*" ("Introduction" to Augustine, *The Trinity* [Washington D.C.: Catholic University of America Press, 1963]). The critique is also directed at Aquinas. Karl Rahner, for instance, complains about Aquinas's separation between *De Deo Uno* and *De Deo Trino* in that "it looks as if everything which matters to us in God has already been said in the treatise *On the One God*" (*The Trinity*, trans. Joseph Donceel [London: Burns and Oates, 1970]).

71. Plantinga argues that if we adopt divine simplicity, which identifies God with his property, "then he isn't a person but a mere abstract object; he has no knowledge, awareness, power, love or life" (*Does God Have a Nature*, 47).

72. Jenson, "Decision Tree," 8-16. As Jenson recalls, from his early days on, Gunton had regarded Aquinas as the father of classical theism, the main fault of which lies in the idea of divine simplicity.

73. *ST* 1.11.3.

74. *Ibid.*

75. *ST* 1.4.1.

76. *Ibid.*

77. *ST* 1.4.2.

78. Stump, "God's Simplicity," emphasis added.

79. This view, as Ayres points out, is based on older scholarship and has been challenged by recent scholarship: "We have noted that older scholarship tended to associate the doctrine of simplicity with 'Hellenization'. However, more recent scholarship tends to look at it as part of the set of concepts that Christians used to deal with problems and tensions involved in reading Scripture as a coherent whole." Lewis Ayres and Andrew Radde-Gallwitz, "Doctrine of God," *The Oxford Handbook of Early Christian Studies*, ed. Susan A. Harvey and David G. Hunter (New York: Oxford University Press, 2008), 875.

80. For the biblical foundations of *creatio ex nihilo*, see Janet M. Soskice, "*Creatio ex nihilo*: Its Jewish and Christian Foundations," 24–39.

81. Of course, Aquinas does not immediately embark on a treatment of God as the cause of creatures, which happens later, but it should be argued that his notion of divine simplicity is rooted in the truth of creation, which, as we have seen, is the hidden key in his entire system. It is in this sense that Aquinas begins his discussion of divine nature with the truth of creation.

82. In the Latin text, Aquinas uses the word "Simplex" to describe the totally simple nature of God.

83. Gilby, "Appendix 12," 214.

84. *ST* 1.4.2.

85. Ibid.

Chapter 5

Multiplicity in Aquinas's Participatory Ontology

One of the key concerns of Reformed theologians about RO's participatory ontology, as we have seen, is its reliance on Platonism and its subsequent tendency to undermine the goodness of creation. The concern is justified to some extent, for the straightforwardly Platonic tradition indeed has a low view of matter and multiplicity. The Reformed objection to RO reminds us that we need a participatory ontology that avoids the Platonic tendency in disparaging matter and multiplicity. In chapter 2, we argued that Augustine had made significant contributions in this direction. By distinguishing between multiplicity and non-simplicity and defending the goodness of materiality against the Platonists, Augustine took an important step in Christianizing participatory ontology. Augustine's work, as we will see in this chapter, is furthered by Aquinas, who, with his metaphysic of participation, provides an even more sophisticated account of multiplicity that avoids the pitfalls of Platonism and affirms the goodness of plurality. In Aquinas, we will find a more Christianized version of participatory ontology.

THE NATURE OF MULTIPLICITY
IN AQUINAS'S THOUGHT

In the Platonic tradition, especially in Plotinus, multiplicity is seen as an imperfection, since it is the negation of the One, which alone is perfection. In his exposition of the nature of "the One," Plotinus explains that "this name, The One, contains really no more than the *negation* of plurality: under the same pressure the Pythagoreans found their indication in the symbol 'Apollo' (α = not; πολλων = of many) with its *repudiation* of the multiple."[1] This understanding is consistent with Aristotle's definitions of "the many" as that which is divided or divisible and of "the one" as that which is undivided or indivisible.[2] Since undividedness is the opposite of dividedness, the one is the opposite of the many. In mainstream Greek philosophy, therefore, the many is understood as the opposite of the one. If unity alone is associated with goodness or perfection, then multiplicity is necessarily defective—the elevation of the one inevitably entails the degradation of the many.

In chapter 2, we saw that Augustine did not fully accept this logic but reached the idea—though still vaguely formed—that unity is not the negation of multiplicity but of division. Now, with a better command of analytic skills, Aquinas is able to bring this insight into a sharper focus, arguing explicitly that multiplicity is not identical to division and hence not the opposite of unity. Unity is not the negation of multiplicity but of division. This view is clearly articulated in *Summa theologiae*: "'One' does not exclude the 'many' but the division which can be thought of prior to one or many."[3] In his understanding of multiplicity, therefore, Aquinas departs from both Plotinus and Aristotle.

Aquinas rejects a straight opposition between the one and the many, because he believes that such opposition inevitably leads to a vicious cycle in definitions. On the one hand, if one is defined as the negation of many, it rests on the definition of the many. On the other hand, the notion of the many is also defined in terms of unity, because the many is made up of unities, which is essentially "defining in cycles."[4] To avoid this dilemma, Aquinas clarifies that unity is not the direct negation of multiplicity but of division. He repeatedly emphasizes that multiplicity is not the same thing as division. So, while embracing Aristotle's insight concerning division, he rejects the identification between multiplicity and division, which is evident in his account of the generation of primary notions in the human mind:

> The first object of the intellect is being; the second is the negation of being. From these two there follows thirdly the understanding of division (since from the fact that we understand that this thing is and that it is not that thing we realize that these two are divided); and it follows fourthly that the intellect apprehends the idea of unity, in that it understands that this thing is not divided in itself; and fifthly the intellect apprehends number, in that it understands this as distinct from that and each as one in itself. For however much things are conceived as distinct from one another, there is no idea of number unless each be conceived as one.[5]

There have been controversies over the interpretation of this passage, especially over the exact meaning of the second notion—non-being, but for our purpose it is sufficient to point out that for Aquinas the second and third notions—non-being and division of being—are inseparable.[6] In fact, in a similar passage in *Summa theologiae*, he leaves out the second notion, because in his view it is immediately linked to the third, namely division.[7] As such, only four primary notions are listed: "So that the first idea to arise in the mind is being, then that this being is not that being and so we grasp division, thirdly unity and fourthly the many."[8] Roughly speaking, the order of the primary notions is: being, division, unity, and multiplicity. Whether the number of notions is four or five, it does not change the fact that division is not the same as multiplicity and unity is not the direct opposite of multiplicity. But what exactly is multiplicity?

Definition and Nature of Multiplicity

To understand Aquinas's concept of multiplicity, which is one of the most complex issues in his metaphysics, we need to first discuss the distinction between two kinds of division. Although Aquinas does not make it explicit, it is clear from the preceding discussion that there are two different kinds of division.[9] The first is *internal division*. As Aquinas observes, "the intellect apprehends the idea of unity, in that it understands that this thing is not divided in itself." The notion of unity is formed when we realize that something has no internal division, because if it were internally divided, it would not exist as one thing. Unity can thus be defined as the absence of internal division. The second is *external division*, which is the basis for multiplicity. As Aquinas puts it, "from the fact that we understand that this thing is and that it is not that thing, we realize that these two are divided." For instance, when we see that this apple is separated from that apple and that apples are separated from oranges, we say that the two apples are divided and that apples are divided from oranges.[10] This kind of division is external and differs from internal division, whereby things are divided in themselves and cease to exist. Although this apple is divided from that apple, each apple is undivided in itself. So external division presupposes the internal unity of things that are externally divided.

Once we accept the distinction between the two kinds of division—internal and external[11]—it becomes clear that multiplicity is a result of *external* division between individual things that are internally undivided. If unity, the fourth primary notion, is the negation of *internal* division, then multiplicity, which is the fifth notion, assumes unity but adds *external* division to it. In this sense, multiplicity falls between the two kinds of division; it denies internal division but requires external division. In a sense, we may define multiplicity as "the external division of things that are internally undivided." Both unity and division are thus essential for the notion of multiplicity. But to better understand Aquinas's concept of multiplicity, we need to further unpack the relationship between the three concepts: unity, division, and multiplicity.

First, unity is foundational to multiplicity in that "unity enters the definition of the many."[12] "[T]he many implies something composed of unities."
As such, "when we speak of 'many things', the 'many' here refers to things
in question with the implication that none of them is divided."[13] Before the
concept of multiplicity arises in the mind, we must first have individual
things that are internally undivided, for if they were internally divided, they
would not exist as the building blocks for multiplicity.[14] Internal unity is thus
fundamental to multiplicity. On this understanding, there is no such thing as
absolute multiplicity: "the many as such cannot be said to exist, except insofar as they have a certain unity. Thus, Dionysius says that no *manifold exists
without being somehow one.*"[15]

Back in chapter 1, we discussed about the convertibility between unity and
being. If unity is interchangeable with being, then absolute multiplicity that
is completely devoid of unity has no being either—it simply cannot exist.
Thus, unity needs to be part of multiplicity. This understanding is anchored
in Aquinas' metaphysic of creation and reflects the truth of creation—since
all things receive existence from God, multiplicity must contain being and
as such unity. Augustine already understood this insight, but Aquinas now
articulates it in more precise philosophical terms.

Second, division—not internal but external—forms the other essential part
of multiplicity. Because external division is based on difference, which is a
type of negation, between things, multiplicity involves a double-negation.
The first is the negation of internal division; the second is the negation that
separates one thing from another. Aquinas clearly explains this idea in a passage in *On the Power of God*: "Accordingly, while one adds to being one
negation inasmuch as a thing is undivided in itself; plurality adds *two* nega-
tions, inasmuch as a certain thing is undivided, and distinct from another; i.e.
one of them is not the other."[16]

Unity alone does not define multiplicity. We must add the external division
of individual things to the notion of multiplicity. In a sense, multiplicity is a
special kind of division—it simultaneously *is* and is *not* division. In comparison to thinkers before him who wrote about multiplicity, Aquinas is remarkable for clarifying the relation between multiplicity and division. On the one
hand, *contra* Plotinus and Aristotle, he asserts that multiplicity is *not* division
in an unqualified, absolute sense, because it consists of things that are unified
in themselves. On the other hand, *contra* Parmenides and Melissus, he affirms
the reality of external division and diversity. This concept of multiplicity
accepts the reality of both unity and diversity and paves the way for a promising solution for the problem of the One and the Many.

For Aquinas, one of main reasons why unity and multiplicity are not
directly opposed is that they are associated with two different kinds of division—unity has to do with *internal* division, while multiplicity has to do with

external division. If there were only one kind of division, unity would indeed be the negation of multiplicity. But because there are two kinds of division, unity is no longer in opposition to multiplicity—the One and the Many are no longer mutually exclusive. Aquinas expresses this understanding clearly in *Summa theologiae.* "'One' does not exclude the 'many' but the division which can be thought of prior to one or many. And 'many' does not exclude unity but division between realities forming the whole."[17] He then concludes that "there is nothing to stop things from being divided from one point of view and undivided from another . . . and they will then be from one point of view one, and from another many."[18] On this view, the elevation of the One is no longer necessarily coupled with the degradation of the Many—they can be affirmed at once. Things can be both *one* and *many*. Astonishingly, Aquinas extends the same principle to the very being of God, claiming that God is simultaneously one and many. In his attempt to harmonize between the absolute unity of God and the plurality of Triune Persons, he has to expand the concept of multiplicity, suggesting that multiplicity is not univocal. Indeed, there are at least three types of multiplicity in Aquinas's thought.

Three Types of Multiplicity

We have already discussed that there are two kinds of division—internal and external—and that multiplicity is associated with the latter. Within external division, however, there are two sub-types of division: material division and formal division. Subsequently, there are two different kinds of multiplicity, as is explained by Aquinas in the passage below:

> To clear the matter up, bear in mind that all plurality is the consequence of some division. Now there are two kinds of division. One, *material division*, which comes about by division of a continuum; from this number results, which is a kind of quantity. The other is *formal division*, which comes about by the opposition or diversity of forms; from this results that kind of plurality which is in none of the categories but is one of the transcendentals, in the sense that being itself is diversified by the "one" and the "many". And only this kind of "many" applies to spiritual realities.[19]

The two types of division mentioned above are clearly external divisions. As a result, we now have three types of division: internal division, material division, and formal division. Multiplicity is associated only with the last two kinds of division. Of these two, material division applies to corporeal things only. Things are divided as they are separated by physical boundaries and as such they cannot form a continuum.[20] Based on this kind of division, we have the notion of multiplicity associated with number and quantity. Such multiplicity can be called quantitative multiplicity, as we can count things that are divided, as in the example of "five loaves of bread." The other kind of division, namely formal division, is not based on quantitative division but differences between forms. For instance, a human being is divided from a cat due to the difference between two species. Multiplicity corresponding to formal division can be called formal multiplicity, which, as Aquinas suggests, is a "transcendental," a notion that is not restricted to certain types of being but applicable to all categories and as such transcends categories. Normal transcendentals include *being*, *one*, *true*, and *good*, but Aquinas remarkably names "many" as one of the transcendentals. Recall Gunton's critique of Aquinas's disregard for multiplicity: "Unity, but not plurality, is the transcendental."[21] But *contra* Gunton, here Aquinas explicitly places "plurality" among the transcendentals.

Of material realities, we can predicate both quantitative multiplicity and formal multiplicity. Of spiritual things, however, we can only predicate formal multiplicity, as quantitative multiplicity does not apply to them. They cannot be numbered quantitatively, because they are immaterial and as such cannot be distinguished from each other through material differences. As Aquinas puts it, "among immortal things we see but *one* individual to a species, one being enough to perpetuate the species."[22] Multiplicity in spiritual things, therefore, differs in kind from material multiplicity, as it is based on formal division instead of material division. In comparison to material multiplicity, Aquinas believes that formal multiplicity is more fundamental, just as form is more fundamental than matter.[23] But beyond these two kinds, Aquinas even introduces a further type of multiplicity, which does not come from material division or formal division but from relational *distinction*. This kind of multiplicity, as we will see, applies to God alone, as it is a way to account for the plurality of Persons in the Trinity.

One of the most challenging tasks of Christian theologians is to explain how the simplicity of God is consistent with the plurality of the Trinity. Aquinas addresses this question in a number of places, not the least of which is *De Potentia* 9.8, where he denies *diversity* in God, but admits a *distinction* between the Persons. As usual, he first lists all the counterarguments that suggest there are differences between the Persons in the Trinity. The fourth argument is of special interest, as it touches on two key concepts: division and diversity. The argument is as follows: "Number results from division, as stated above. Now where there is *division* there must be *diversity*. Therefore in God, since there is number, there must be diversity."[24]

In response, Aquinas suggests that "careless use of terms leads to heresy" and so "in speaking of God we must choose our words so as to avoid any occasion of error." Regarding the relationship between the unity and trinity of God, he lists two types of heresy: "the error of Arius, who denied the unity of the essence, and asserted the *difference* between the essence of the Father and that of the Son; and the error of Sabellius, who denied the *distinction* of the Persons." As Aquinas believes that heresy originates in confusion of terms, he seeks to expose the fallacy of heretics by clarifying terms and concepts. Arius's error arises from an idea of diversity "which is incompatible with the unity of essence" and division "which is incompatible with divine simplicity." Sabellius's fallacy comes from an idea of unity that "excludes real distinction of the Persons," against which Aquinas affirms the distinction between the Persons. His solution consists of the rejection of some terms and the defense of others:

> Accordingly against diversity we acknowledge unity of essence; against division, simplicity; against inequality, equality; against difference, likeness; not one only but several Persons; distinction against identity; order against confusion.[25]

Aquinas rejects "difference" and "division" but accepts "distinction" as an appropriate term for describing God. For while difference and division introduce real diversity to the divine nature, distinction is needed to distinguish between the Persons. As such, he meticulously explains that the term "distinction" is not identical to "difference" or "diversity." Distinction does not indicate a difference in essence and "some things are described as distinct in respect of a mere relation or even logically." We can say that there is distinction in the Godhead, since there are three distinct relations among the Persons. But there is no difference or diversity in God, since "diversity refers more to an essential division." As a result, we can simultaneously affirm that God is one and that there are three Persons. The first part of the sentence denies difference or diversity in God's nature, while the second protects the distinction between the Persons. Based on this clarification, Aquinas then proceeds to make a response to the objections. His reply to the fourth objection is particularly instructive: "Though properly speaking there is no *division* in God, there is relative *distinction*, and this suffices to make a number of Persons."[26]

At times, Aquinas uses division (especially formal division) and distinction interchangeably. For instance, in *ST* 1.47.2, when discussing whether inequality comes from God, he chooses to use distinction: "There is a double *distinctio* in things, one formal, between things different in kinds, the other material, between things different only merely numerically."[27] What Aquinas means by "distinction" is in fact "division" and so he does not always clearly distinguish between division and distinction. But when treating the Trinity, he stresses that the two notions are fundamentally different and that we must reject division but preserve distinction, because division is unsuitable for describing divine nature—it compromises divine simplicity. The distinction between the three divine Persons cannot be formal division, otherwise that the Persons would differ essentially from one another. To protect the mystery of God, Aquinas has to be meticulous in his word choices.[28] But when discussing the relation between distinction and division, he also stretches the notion of multiplicity, which allows him to use the term for God:

> Since "one" is a transcendental, it has a wider range of meaning than "substance" and "relation"; so, too, has "many". Hence when used of God both terms can stand for both substance and relation according to the context.[29]

We discussed about two kinds of multiplicity—material and formal. Beyond the two, Aquinas now introduces a further type of multiplicity that is not associated with division but with *relational distinction*. It is with this type of multiplicity that we can predicate of God. When speaking of God, however, we must be reminded that this kind of multiplicity differs fundamentally from the kinds of multiplicity we use for creatures. God's multiplicity is unique in itself. As Aquinas reminds us, terms used for God differ profoundly from their regular usage:

> I say then that in speaking of God we do not predicate the unity and plurality which belong to the genus of quantity, but one that is convertible with being and corresponding plurality. Wherefore one and many predicate in God that which they signify: but they add nothing besides distinction and indistinction.[30]

In summary, there are at least three types of multiplicity in Aquinas's thought. The first type is quantitative multiplicity, which results from material division; the second, formal multiplicity, which is based on formal division, whereby one species is distinguished essentially from another; the last, divine multiplicity, which is based on relational distinctions between the three Persons in the Trinity. Only this kind of multiplicity can be said about God. When we speak of multiplicity, we must clarify what kind of multiplicity we talk about, for multiplicity can mean different things. Aquinas reminds us that reality is neither monistic nor purely pluralistic but consists of both unity and multiplicity. Maintaining this picture of reality is not easy: one needs to be ready to face serious challenges, not the least of which is the question of the ultimate origin of multiplicity. Specifically, how does creaturely multiplicity derive from the One, who is simple? This is the question we will address next.

THE DERIVATION OF THE MANY FROM THE ONE

In the history of philosophy, one of the most vexing questions within the problem of the One and the Many is: how does the Many come from the

One?[31] To a certain extent, Plotinus's entire philosophical endeavor is to find a good answer to that question. As we have seen, his solution is unsatisfactory in certain respects. In particular, assigning the origin of multiplicity to the Absolute Evil proves problematic and clashes with the Christian teaching that all things, including matter, come from God. But to maintain the Christian position, one is faced with a similar challenge: how can God, who is simple, be the source of multiplicity? Aquinas seeks to solve the problem in two stages. First, he asks *whether* God is the ultimate origin of multiplicity, and then explains *how* God in his simplicity can have multiplicity.

God as the Origin of Multiplicity

Aquinas devotes the whole question of *ST* 1.47.1 to the question whether multiplicity is from God. According to him, there are two main fallacious views on this matter. First is the position of pre-Socratic natural philosophers, such as Democritus, who regarded matter as the ultimate source of distinction in things:

> Some ascribed it to matter, either alone or in combination with an agent. Democritus, for instance, and the early natural philosophers, recognizing only the material cause in things, set down diversity to matter alone and treated it as a chance result of matter in motion.[32]

Aquinas counters the materialists' position by arguing that matter itself is created by God and as such the ultimate source of distinction is God. Furthermore, since matter is for the sake of form, formal distinction is more fundamental than material distinction and it is mistaken to assign matter as the source of all distinctions.

The second fallacy comes from those who do not attribute distinction of things to God but to secondary agents. Such is the position of Avicenna:

> Avicenna, for instance, taught that by understanding himself God produced the first intelligence, into which the composition of potentiality and actuality necessarily enters, since it is not its own existence. . . . Then this first intelligence by knowing the first cause produced the second intelligence; then by knowing itself as being in potentiality, produced the body of the heavens, from which motion arises.[33]

In response to Avicenna, Aquinas argues that because all things are created by God, God alone is ultimate cause of all things, including multiplicity. He further critiques that Avicenna subjects the world to chance and destroys the unity of all things in God. After refuting the fallacies, he then presents his own position:

> Instead we should state that distinctiveness and plurality of things is because the first agent, who is God, intended them. For he brought things into existence so that his goodness might be communicated to creatures and re-enacted through them. And because one single creature was not enough, he produced many and diverse, so that what was wanting in one expression of divine goodness might be supplied by another, for goodness, which in God is single and all together, in creatures is multiple and scattered. . . . And because divine wisdom is the cause of variety of things, Moses tells us of God's word—the Word indeed which is the concept of his wisdom.[34]

A few important points can be made about this passage. First, the foundation of the argument is the doctrine of creation. Since all things are immediately created by God out of nothing, nothing apart from God can account for the distinction in things—God must be the sole source of plurality. Second, the idea of goodness is essential for understanding the purpose of creation. Because God is perfect, he is not obligated to produce anything other than himself. The only motivation for him to create is to communicate his own goodness or good will to things other than himself. Since the act of creation is God's communication of his goodness, created multiplicity is intrinsically good. Diversity or multiplicity in the creation is thus not an unfortunate deviation from the One, but the intended product of God's love. This view of multiplicity is a far cry from that of Plotinus. Third, Aquinas's view of creation is deeply Trinitarian. Following Augustine, he usually associates God's goodness with the Holy Spirit. So, he makes it clear that the Spirit is the purpose or goal of creation. But he also points out that "the cause of variety of things" is the Divine Wisdom or Word, which is nothing but Christ.[35] Creation is thus not a result of the solitary One, but a loving product of the Trinitarian God.

Finally, and perhaps most significantly, Aquinas provides a crucial clue as to why God creates multiple creatures, a clue that has been largely neglected in Thomistic scholarship. Scholars have debated on how created multiplicity should be understood in terms of participation, but none has examined its connection to Christology.[36] However, for Aquinas, Christology provides the key to understanding the multiplicity in creation. In the preceding text, he expresses it explicitly that divine wisdom is the cause of variety of things. But divine wisdom is nothing but Christ and so Aquinas makes it clear that Christ is the origin of multiplicity in creation. Specifically, created multiplicity is rooted in the ontological gap between the Son and the creatures.

As we have seen, Aquinas suggests that the purpose for creation is such that the goodness of God can be manifested through creatures. However, because of the infinite ontological difference between God and creatures, no single creature can have the full "expression of divine goodness," which is possible only through Christ, the perfect image of God. In order that his goodness can be more adequately manifested in the creation, God chooses to create multiple things so that what is lacking in one can be supplemented by others. In other words, because each creature is a severely limited manifestation of divine goodness, the totality of creation in great multiplicity and diversity can reflect God's goodness more fully. As Aquinas puts it, "the whole universe less incompletely than one alone shares and represents his goodness."[37]

By contrast, as the perfect image of God, Christ is the full representation of God. Since there is no ontological difference between the Son and the Father, Christ alone can fully manifest God. As such, there can only be one Son, for "the Uncreated Image, the full image of God, is single."[38] There is no need for multiple Sons, since the Son, being ontologically identical to God, is capable of perfectly manifesting divine goodness. "No single creature, however, is a complete reproduction of the first exemplar, which is the divine essence, though a multitude is less adequate."[39] When we compare the perfect image of God in the Son with the inadequate expression of God in creation, it becomes clear that multiplicity is a necessary condition for creaturely mode of existence. Because of the ontological divide, that which is absolutely unified in God inevitably becomes diverse and divided when it is manifested in creation. Creation is necessarily multiple because it falls short of the perfect image of God. All creatures exist by participation in Christ, who alone is the perfect expression of divine goodness.

But the question remains: how does God's absolute simplicity cause multiplicity in creation? For it is one thing to claim that God *is* the origin of multiplicity; it is another to explain *how* God, who contains neither formal nor material multiplicity, can produce formal and material multiplicity in creation. To answer this question, Aquinas again resorts to Christ, the Wisdom of God, who is "the cause of variety of things." We must note that when Aquinas speaks of multiplicity in creation, he primarily has formal multiplicity in mind, because formal multiplicity is more fundamental than material multiplicity.[40] It is more essential to explain how formal plurality of things can be caused by God.

God as the Cause of Multiplicity

In *ST* 1.47.1, Aquinas first presents three arguments against the possibility of God's causing plurality in creatures, the first being: because a unity only engenders a unity and the unity of God is supreme, his effect must also be one. The second argument is that an effect necessarily resembles the exemplar, and because God, being the exemplar of his effects, is one, his effects must also be one. The third is that things are oriented toward their end, and because the end of creation is God, who is one, creation must also be one. In essence, these arguments correspond to three causes of creation, namely efficient, exemplary, and final causes. To refute them, Aquinas chooses to clarify the unique relationship between God, the cause, and creatures, the effects.

In response to the first objection, which is based on efficient causality, he argues that there are two different kinds of causal agents: natural and voluntary. The opponent's argument, he suggests, is true for natural agents, but not for voluntary ones:

> A merely natural agent operates through the form by which it is what it is, and for each thing this is one; which is why it produces but one sort of thing. Whereas a *voluntary* agent which acts through *will*, and God is such as we have seen, acts through a form as held in his mind. Since, therefore, it is not against God's singleness and simplicity that he should *understand* many things, as we have also seen, the truth remains that although he is the One he can also make the many.[41]

A natural nonvoluntary agent produces effects through its essential form and as such only produces effects that are essentially the same as itself. An illustration is that a dog only produces a dog. One may object: a dog can produce multiple dogs and therefore a natural agent may also produce multiple effects. But this objection fails to recognize, as we already clarified, that Aquinas has formal—not material or quantitative—multiplicity in mind when he speaks of multiplicity in creation. It is true that one dog can produce several dogs, but there is no formal division between dogs and there is no formal multiplicity in the produced dogs. Formal multiplicity would arise if a dog produced a cat. The conclusion that one natural agent can produce one effect thus still holds.

In contrast, a voluntary agent, such as an artist, does not produce things through her essential form but through a form in her mind, and as such can produce effects that are formally multiple or diverse. Just as an artist can produce various kinds of artwork, such as paintings and sculptures, a single voluntary agent can produce multiple effects. Aquinas thus refutes the objection by stressing that God is a voluntary agent. His answer to the objection is particularly important. In effect, he is arguing that God's creation is not by necessity, but entirely free through his will.[42] Only a free and voluntary agent can produce things that differ essentially from the agent itself but nonetheless are good in themselves. Unlike in Plotinus, where difference is a deviation from the Good, difference in this framework is essentially good, as is intended by the Mind and the Will of God, which is the divine goodness. In Aquinas, the Trinitarian mode of creation makes it possible for God, who is simple, to produce a multiplicity of creation that is essentially good.

Responding to the second objection, which is based on exemplary causality, Aquinas contrasts the multiplicity of creatures to the singularity of Christ and thereby brings out the concept of divine ideas.

> The objection is valid of a full copy of its exemplar; multiplication in that case is only numerical repetition. Hence the uncreated Image, the full image of God is single. No single creature, however, is a complete reproduction of the first exemplar, which is the divine essence, though a multitude of things is less inadequate. Note, therefore, that if you take ideas as exemplars, the plurality of things corresponds to a plurality of ideas in the divine mind.[43]

Again, it is easy to misinterpret the first part of the argument, namely the oneness of the full image of God. It seems that "the full image of God" is not necessarily single, for it is possible to have multiple full copies of an exemplar. For instance, there is nothing to stop us from making two or three perfect copies of a model car. But this again is to confuse between quantitative and formal multiplicities. Quantitative multiplicity applies only to corporeal things, not to immaterial realities such as God. When Aquinas asserts that the full image of God is single, he is not speaking of a numerical singularity but a formal one. There is only one full image of God, because the full image of God is essentially indistinguishable from God himself. By contrast, no creature can be a full image of God and it is thus possible to have multiple creatures. Of course, God could create only one kind of creature, since he is not forced to create a multitude. He creates more than one kind of creature nevertheless, for he chooses to do so through his good will. Due to the infinite distinction between God and creation, it is possible for God to create multiple creatures that are different from himself and from each other. The ontological difference between God and creation provides the foundation for formal multiplicity in creation. What remains to be answered is how this possibility is carried out by God, who has no formal multiplicity. Aquinas's answer to this question lies in his theory of divine ideas.

Aquinas's Theory of Divine Ideas

The theory of divine ideas is a subject of much controversy. On the one hand, it is suggested that Aquinas would agree with Augustine, for whom "to deny the divine Ideas is to deny the Son of God."[44] Indeed, Aquinas follows Augustine closely in his defense of divine ideas.[45] On the other hand, some modern Thomists have argued that the doctrine of "divine ideas" is simply "a useless fiction."[46] Controversies around divine ideas in fact do not begin with Aquinas—they have existed since Plato first proposed the theory of Ideas as part of his ontology of participation, which was repeatedly criticized by his student—Aristotle.[47] In order to find an unchanging basis for the ever-changing world, Plato suggests that sensible things are copies of Ideas, which alone are "the really real."[48] Unlike Parmenides, Plato does not wish to deny the reality of plurality[49] and as such posits a plurality of Ideas. But where are the Ideas and how do they exist? The "ultimate status and ground of the world of ideas," as Clarke observes, seems "veiled in obscurity for Plato."[50] In Plotinus, the multiplicity of Ideas is placed in the Mind below the One, which is devoid of multiplicity and even knowledge, since knowledge entails multiplicity.[51] The solution of Plotinus, in which the Ideas are placed outside of the One, however, is unacceptable for Christian thinkers. To retain the Platonic tradition, Christian thinkers such as Augustine engage in a profound transformation of the theory of Ideas. Part of their solution is to place the Ideas in God's mind such that God "may personally know and love his creatures."[52] But the question remains: if the multiplicity of Ideas is real in God, how can the multiplicity of divine ideas be consistent with divine simplicity. This question is left largely unresolved by Augustine.[53]

Aquinas embraces the tradition of divine ideas, but in accepting the Augustinian heritage, he takes up the challenges associated with it and seeks to answer how divine simplicity is consistent with the plurality of ideas. With his strength in analytical reasoning, he provides a rigorous answer to the question:

> That this is not inconsistent with the divine simplicity is easy to see if we bear in mind that the idea of a work is in the mind of the agent as *that which* is known, not as the knowledge-likeness *by which* there is knowledge, the latter being the form which makes the intellect actually knowing. Thus the form of a house in the mind of the architect is something understood by him, to the likeness of which he produces the form of a house in the matter. It is not contradictory to its simplicity of the divine intellect to know many things; but it would be contrary to its simplicity were the divine intellect informed by a plurality of knowledge-likeness. Hence many Ideas in the divine mind are objects of God's knowledge.[54]

The key to Aquinas's answer is the distinction he makes between the object of knowledge and the species by which something is known. A divine idea is an object of God's knowledge, *that* which is known by God, not the species *by* which God knows things. For instance, God knows the species of humanity, which is an *object* of his knowledge, but not the species by which God knows humanity, which is God's own essence. So, while there is one species by which God knows things, there can be multiple ideas that are known by God. But to understand this argument adequately, we must understand Aquinas's theory of knowledge, especially his theory about God's knowledge of created things. For our purpose, I will only offer a brief discussion below.[55]

First, Aquinas distinguishes between knowing and non-knowing subjects in that "the latter have nothing but their own form, whereas a knowing subject is one whose nature it is to have in addition the form of something else; for the likeness of the thing known is in the knower."[56] To know something is to have its intelligible form or likeness in the knower's mind. When the form of a sensible thing is impressed upon the mind, one gains the knowledge of that thing. The human mind, which was in the condition of potentiality, now becomes actualized when it is informed by the intelligible likeness of something.[57] Hence, for us to have knowledge of a thing, its intelligible species must exist in our mind, since it is by the species or its likeness that we know the thing. "[I]t is not the substance of the thing" that exists in the knower but only "its likeness," as is stated inAristotle's quote,"the stone is not in the soul but its likeness."[58] Aquinas claims that God knows things in a similar fashion—he knows them through their intelligible likenesses in his mind.

In contrast to creaturely minds, however, God's mind can never be in potentiality but is always in absolute actuality—that is, he always knows all things. God cannot be informed by any species or likeness external to him. Rather, he knows all things by the species or likeness that is identical to his essence. There is only one species by which God has knowledge and it is nothing other than his own essence.[59] Not only does God know himself through his essence; he knows things other than himself only by his essence, which "contains the likeness of things."[60] God does not need to go outside of himself to know things; he knows them in himself. The unity of God's essence is not the negation of multiplicity but the infinite source of all forms and perfections.

[A]ll that makes for perfection in any creature is to be found first in God, and is contained in an eminent degree. . . . In fact, every form giving a thing its own specific characteristics is a perfection. And thus all things are to be found first in God, not only as regards to what they have in common but also as regards to what they all have as *distinct* from each other. Therefore since God contains all perfections, the essence of God stands to all the essences of things not as what is common to what is special to each, in the way that the unit stands to numbers or the centre to the lines, but as the complete *actuality* stands to incomplete actualities; as one might say, as man stands to animal, or as the number six, a perfect number, to imperfect numbers contained within it.[61]

Central to the argument is the concept of actuality, namely that what is imperfectly actualized is contained in what is perfectly actualized. For instance, in comparison to a boy, a full-grown man is more actualized. Not only does he possess all the perfections the boy possesses, such as strength and intelligence, but he possesses the perfections more fully. Likewise, because God is the Creator of all things, he contains eminently all the perfections which are possessed partially by creatures. God's simplicity is not a common denominator of created perfections but the infinite source of all that *is*. Divine simplicity is thus not exclusive but inclusive of creaturely multiplicity. Since God is the Creator of all, whatever exists in creation, including multiplicity, must preexist supremely in God. In other words, created multiplicity participates in God's simple essence. The plurality of creation corresponds to the multiplicity of ways in which creatures participate in God, but it is the infinite richness of God's essence that allows such participation:

> Therefore, since the essence of God contains all that makes for perfection in the essence of every other thing, and more besides, God can know all things in himself with a knowledge of what is proper to each. For the nature proper to each thing consists in its *participation* in the divine perfection in some degree. But God would not know himself perfectly if he did not know all the ways in which his perfection can be *participated* by other things; nor would he know perfectly the nature of existence if he did not know all the degrees of existence. Hence it is clear that God knows all things in what is proper to each and makes them different from one another.[62]

The ontological gap between God and creation is infinite and so the number of ways in which God can be participated in by creatures is also infinite. It is this infinite possibility that serves as the foundation for creaturely multiplicity. But because God knows all the ways in which his essence can be participated in by creatures, he must have all the possibilities in his mind. His knowledge of each possibility, namely each way in which his essence can be participated in by a creature, is what is called a "divine idea." The multiplicity of ways in which God can be participated in by creatures corresponds to the multiplicity of divine ideas.

But we need to stress that an idea is the form of a thing that exists apart from the thing itself. To be more accurate, an idea is the likeness of the form of a thing and is intelligible in nature. So, when we say that God's essence contains all the created forms, we do not mean that all creaturely forms exist substantially in God, but that the intelligible likenesses of all the forms exist in God's mind, which we call divine ideas. A divine idea is thus an *object* of God's knowledge—*that* which God knows—and differs from the divine essence, *by* which God knows. In a sense, divine ideas can be considered as

God's speculative thought, which does not correspond to any *reality* in God's mind.[63] As such, the multiplicity of divine ideas does not make God's essence multiple. To further explain how this is possible, Aquinas writes:

> God knows his essence perfectly; he knows it therefore in all the ways in which it is knowable. Now the divine essence can be known not only as it is in itself, but as it can be participated in some degrees of likeness by creatures. On the other hand every creature has its own nature insofar as it participates in some way the likeness of the divine essence. In this way then God, in knowing his essence as imitable in this particular way by this particular creature, knows his essence as the nature and Idea proper to that creature; and similarly in other cases. It is clear then that God knows many natures proper to many things; and these natures are many Ideas.[64]

Each divine idea, then, corresponds to a possible mode in which God's essence can be imitated or participated in by creatures. An idea exists only in the intellectual order, but not in the order of reality. An idea in God's mind is thus not identical to a form that actually exists in a creature. As Clarke puts it, divine ideas are simply the "signifying signs of things (*intentiones rerum*), not things themselves; their being is *esse intentionale* not *esse naturale* or *reale.*"[65] This understanding of divine ideas is in fact a far cry from that of Plato, who insisted that only ideas are "the really real." But in departing from this Platonic view, Aquinas is not alone among the Christian thinkers of his time. In fact, there is a consensus among the leading thinkers, including Bonaventure, who is otherwise strongly sympathetic to Platonism, that the ultra-Platonic realism must be laid aside. For instance, Bonaventure clearly expresses this view in *On Spiritual Creatures*:

> God knows things through their eternal "reasons". . . . But these eternal intelligibilities are not the true essences and quiddities of things, since they are not other than the Creator, whereas creature and Creator necessarily have different essences. And therefore it is necessary that they be exemplary Forms and hence *similitudes representativae* of things themselves. Consequently these are intelligibilities whereby things that are are made known, because knowledge, precisely as knowledge, signifies assimilation and expression between knower and known. And therefore we must assert, as the holy doctors say and reason shows, that God knows things through their similitude.[66]

In a sense, a divine idea is a possibility or potentiality of creatures which does not yet exist in reality unless given the act of existence by God. This view is consistent with Aquinas's theory of existence as the actuality of essence, whereby essence becomes real only when it is actualized by existence. In designating divine ideas as objects of God's knowledge, therefore, Aquinas makes a decisive distinction between the order of intellect and that of reality—the former can have relative independence from the latter. Logical possibility is not the same as real possibility. A divine idea is like a logical possibility, a possible mode in which God can be participated in by creatures. But differences between possible modes are not real differences in God's simple essence. Ultimately, it is through deontologizing divine ideas that Aquinas is able to reconcile between the simplicity of God with the plurality of divine ideas. In doing so, he makes a profound shift in the metaphysics of participation.

In conclusion, as we have argued, Aquinas is deeply concerned with the question of the One and the Many and has worked hard to provide a sufficient ontological foundation for the reality of multiplicity. His affirmation of the dignity of multiplicity is evident by the fact that he places "the many" among the transcendentals. With a careful distinction between various types of multiplicity, he asserts that there is even plurality in God himself, although this plurality differs fundamentally from created plurality. Aquinas's metaphysics of participation is thus a triumphant celebration of multiplicity. *Contra* Greek philosophers who relegate the origin of multiplicity to matter, chance, or deviation from the One, Aquinas firmly asserts that God alone, as the Creator of all that is, is the author of diversity and plurality.

Hence, in Aquinas's thought, multiplicity is essentially good, because it is creatively produced by God in his Wisdom. The reality and goodness of multiplicity is anchored in the goodness of the Word, through whom all things are brought into existence. In other words, the intrinsic goodness of created multiplicity reflects the goodness of Christ, and to diminish the dignity of plurality is to downplay Christ's power and wisdom. It is therefore this Christological anchorage that undergirds Aquinas's affirmation of the integrity of multiplicity. Christology in connection to *creatio ex nihilo* thus plays a fundamental role in Aquinas's participatory ontology and solution to the problem of the One and the Many. It is ultimately Christ—within the metaphysical framework of creation—that brings the radically transcendent One into a radically immanent relationship with the Many, which takes us to the next chapter.

NOTES

1. *Enneads* V, 5.6, emphases added.
2. *Metaphysics* X, 3.
3. *ST* 1.30.3.
4. *ST* 1.11.2.

5. Aquinas, *On the Power of God*, trans. The English Dominican Fathers (London: Burns Oates & Washbourne, 1934), 9.7 ad 15. In this edition, the third notion—*divisio*—is translated as "distinction," but I choose to translate it more literally as "division."

6. Aertsen, *Medieval Philosophy and Transcendentals*, 221–3; John F. Wippel, "Thomas Aquinas on the Distinction and Derivation of the Many from the One: A Dialectic between Being and Nonbeing," *The Review of Metaphysics* 30 (1985): 563–90.

7. *ST* 1.11.2 ad 4: "Now division arises in the mind simply negating being."

8. Ibid.

9. Although Aquinas does not clearly distinguish these two kinds of division, he does distinguish between *extrinsic* multitude and *intrinsic* multitude. See *Power of God* 3.16 ad3.

10. In terms of its meaning, "external division" is close to "distinction" between things, and that is why certain translators of *De potentia* have chosen to translate the Latin world "*divisio*" in the abovementioned passage on primary notions as "distinction" instead of "division" (see *Power of God*, 9.7 ad 15, the English Dominican Fathers edition). But, as we will see, in his treatment of the Trinity, Aquinas introduces a subtle and yet profound difference between the two concepts: division and distinction (see *Power of God*, 9.8 ad 4).

11. Although Aquinas himself does not make this distinction explicit, it is definitely there in his writings and helps us clarify why unity is not the negation of multiplicity.

12. *ST* 1.11.2.

13. *ST* 1.30.3.

14. The idea that unities are building blocks for multiplicity is clearly illustrated by the following analogy: "The many is composed of unities, like the house from things [that are] not houses." *ST* 1.11.2.

15. *ST* 1.11.1.

16. *Power of God*, 9.7.

17. *ST* 1.30.3.

18. *ST* 1.11.1.

19. *ST* 1.30.3, emphases added.

20. On the nature of continuum, we can consult Aristotle's discussion in *Physics*, V.

21. Gunton, *One, Three and Many*, 138.

22. *ST* 1.47.2.

23. Ibid.

24. Aquinas, *Power of God*, 9.8.

25. Ibid.

26. Ibid.

27. *ST* 1.47.2.

28. He could have been more consistent with his word choice if he reserved "distinction" for God and used "division" in other occasions.

29. *Power of God*, 9.7.

30. Ibid.

31. In *Enneads* 5.1.6, Plotinus writes:

The mind demands the existence of these Beings, but it is still in trouble over the problem endlessly debated by the most ancient philosophers: from such a unity as we have declared The One to be, how does anything at all come into substantial existence, any multiplicity, dyad, or number? Why has the Primal not remained self-governed so that there be none of this profusion of the manifold we observe in existence and yet are compelled to trace to that absolute unity?

32. *ST* 1.47.2.

33. Ibid.

34. Ibid.

35. In *ST* 1.27.2, Aquinas states clearly that "the Word itself proceeding is called 'Son'."

36. See Te Velde, *Participation and Substantiality*, Chapter 6; Wippel, *Metaphysical Thought*, 94–131; Gregory Doolan, *Aquinas on the Divine Ideas as Exemplar Causes* (Washington, DC: Catholic University of America Press, 2008): 194–243.

37. *ST* 1.47.1.

38. Ibid.

39. Ibid.

40. *ST* 1.47.2: "Now since matter is for the sake of form, distinction by number subserves that by form. . . . This shows that formal distinction is more capital than material distinction."

41. *ST* 1.47.1 ad 1, emphases added.

42. In *Power of God* 3.15, Aquinas writes explicitly: "I answer that without any doubt we must hold that God by the decree of his will and by no natural necessity brought creatures into being."

43. *ST* 1.47.1.

44. Albert the Great, *In* 1 *Sent.* d. 35, E, a. 7, 4th authority, quoted by Thomas Gilby, Introduction to Thomas Aquinas, *Summae Theologiae*, vol. 4, xxii.

45. *ST* 1.15.1. Aquinas explicitly quotes Augustine to refute the opposing arguments that there are no divine ideas.

46. See Gilby, Introduction to *Summae Theologiae*, vol. 4, xxii.

47. In *Metaphysics* I, 9, Aristotle writes harshly: "To say that they are patterns and the other things share in them is to use empty words and poetical metaphors."

48. See *Phaedo* 100C. For a detail discussion of Plato's theory of Ideas, see Collingwood, *Idea of Nature*, 66–72.

49. See Socrates' debate with Parmenides in Plato, *Parmenides*.

50. Norris W. Clarke, "The Problem of the Reality and Multiplicity of Divine Ideas," *Neoplatonism and Christian Thought,* ed. Dominic J. O'Meara (Albany, NY: State University of New York, 1982), 110.

51. *Enneads* V. 1.

52. Clarke, "Reality and Multiplicity of Divine Ideas," 113.

53. Ibid., 115.

54. *ST* 1.15.2.

55. For an introduction to Thomas's theory of knowledge, see Scott MacDonald, "Theory of Knowledge," *Cambridge Companion to Aquinas*, 160–95.

56. *ST* 1.14.1.

57. *ST* 1.14.2: "We have actual sensation or actual knowledge because our intellect or our senses are informed by the species or likeness of the sensible or intelligible object."

58. *ST* 1.14.5 ad 2.

59. Ibid.

60. *ST* 1.14.5.

61. *ST* 1.14.6. The number six is perfect because it is the sum of its constituent factors (6 = 1 + 2 + 3). Man is more perfect than animal, because man, a primary substance, *contains* all that is in animal, which is a secondary substance. For more clarification on the relation of man to animal, see Aristotle, *Categories* V 2a 11–27.

62. *ST* 1.14.6, emphases added.

63. In *ST* 1.14.6 ad 2, Aquinas draws an analogy between divine ideas and the intelligible forms of house in an architect:

Thus the architect, when he knows the form of a house in the matter, is said to know the house; but when he knows the form of a house as an object of his own *speculative* thought, in knowing that he knows it, knows the idea or intelligible nature of the house. (emphasis added)

In *ST* 1.14.6 ad 4, he makes it explicit that while "the relations which multiply Ideas" are in God, "they are not *real* relations, like those which distinguish the divine Persons, but relations understood by God" (emphasis added).

64. *ST* 1.14.6.

65. Clarke, "Reality and Multiplicity of Divine Ideas," 122–3.

66. Bonaventure, *De spiritualibus creaturis* a. 8, ad 10 and a. 9, ad 2 (quoted in Ibid, 122).

Chapter 6

Transcendence and Immanence in Aquinas's Participatory Ontology

An essential aspect of the Platonic theory of participation was to explain how various things in the sensible world relate to the Forms. Christian thinkers adopted the theory to account for the relation between God and creation. They did not accept the concept of participation as it is, but were able to transform it in the light of the doctrine of creation. Augustine, as we discussed in the first three chapters, played an important role in this process. By providing a vision of God that is at once transcendent and immanent, he made an important contribution toward a solution to the dialectic of transcendence and immanence. One of the full implications of *creatio ex nihilo,* namely God's radical immanence in the world, however, was not fleshed out in Augustine, as reflected in his insufficient attention to the religious relevance of the material world. In this chapter, we will discuss how Aquinas extends the implications of God's transcendence and immanence more fully, which enables him to affirm unequivocally the integrity of material creatures. We will first look at the idea of relation in his metaphysic of creation and then discuss his treatment of transcendence and immanence. Finally, we will show how his conception of God's transcendence and immanence undergirds his affirmation of the goodness and existential stability of creatures.

RELATIONSHIP IN AQUINAS'S
METAPHYSIC OF CREATION

Participation is essentially about relationship and it thus would seem natural that Aquinas's participatory ontology should provide an adequate account for relation. However, since his concept of participation is essentially connected to the doctrine of creation, and since for many the doctrine of creation does not seem to explicitly support a participatory relation between God and creatures, it is necessary to examine the concept of relation in Aquinas's metaphysic of creation.

In fact, for Aquinas, the heart of his metaphysic of creation is relationship, as he emphasizes repeatedly that creation is not a change but a *relation*. In one of his earliest treatments on creation, *Commentary on the Sentences*, he clearly distinguishes creation from a change. In a change, as he puts it, "a subject which is a complete being is presupposed. Hence, the causality of the generator or of the alterer does not extend to everything which is found in the thing." In contrast, "the causality of the Creator . . . extends to everything that is in the thing."[1] Creation is absolutely out of nothing and is thus not a temporal event but "a certain *relation* of having being from another following upon the divine operation."[2] In this sense, the fact that creation is essentially a relation is contained in the very definition of creation.

In addition, as we have discussed, Aquinas argues that *creatio ex nihilo* not only means that creation has no material cause—that there is no presupposed matter out of which God creates—but that non-being is prior to being in the creature. This priority is not temporal but ontological in that "if the created thing is left to itself, it would not exist, because it only has its being from the causality of the higher cause."[3] Hence, at the heart of "*ex nihilo*" is the reality that creatures cannot exist on their own but must continually depend upon God for their existence. Creation is essentially the ongoing relation of ontological dependence on God. For this reason, creation and providence are the same operation:

> Even as the air as long as it is lit is illuminated by the sun, so may we say with Augustine (*Gen. ad lit.* viii, I2) that the creature, as long as it is in being, is made by God. But this is only a distinction of words, inasmuch as creation may be understood with newness of existence or without.[4]

In his middle works,[5] Aquinas makes it even more explicit that creation is not a change but a relation that is real in the creature. In *De Potentia* 3.2, after listing the objections, he writes:

> On the contrary, according to the Philosopher in his work on the *Categories,* there are six kinds of movement or change: but none of them is creation, as may be seen by taking them one by one. Therefore creation is not a change.[6]

Having demonstrated that creation is not a change, he states that creation is "nothing but a relation of the creature to the Creator together with a beginning of existence."[7] Again, it is clear that at the heart of creation is the creature's dependent relation to the Creator.

In *Summa theologiae*, one of his mature works, Aquinas again succinctly and yet clearly states the idea that creation is essentially a relation:

> Creation puts a reality into a created thing only as a *relation*. For to be created is not to be produced through a motion or mutation which works on something that already exists, as is the case with limited causality that produces some sorts of being. Not, however, with the production of existence entire by the universal cause of all beings, which is God. Hence in creating he produces a thing without motion in the making. Take away motion from the acting-on acted-upon situation and only relation remains. . . . Hence creation is left just as a *relation* to the creature as the origin of its existence.[8]

For Aquinas, then, a creature's being is essentially a being-in-relation-to-God. A creature is never a being-in-itself but always a being in relation to God. As Burrell puts it, "the very existence (*esse*) of a creature is an *esse-ad*, an existence which is itself a relation to its source."[9] Because relation is nothing but "being with reference to another"[10] and to explain one thing in terms of "its reference to another" is at the heart of participation, it is natural for Aquinas to conceive "'creation' in terms of participation."[11] For him, creation and participation speak of the same—the profound *relatedness* of creatures to God. It is thus clear that Aquinas's metaphysic of creation provides a more-than-sufficient foundation for relationality.

But to affirm the relation between God and creation, we immediately face the crucial question of transcendence and immanence. A dialectic existed, as we have seen, between transcendence and immanence in Greek philosophy. But Christian thinkers, especially Augustine, were able to bring transcendence and immanence into harmony, showing that a transcendent God can be immanent to creatures. Building upon the work of Augustine, Aquinas further clarifies the coherence between God's transcendence and immanence in relation to creation.

TRANSCENDENCE AND IMMANENCE IN AQUINAS'S THOUGHT

The Transcendence of God

Like simplicity, the concept of transcendence is fundamental to Aquinas's treatment of God's nature. In *Summa theologiae*, after explaining the nature of theology, he proceeds to investigate "the nature of God," particularly the way in which God exists.[12] Here, he decides to employ the negative way. Because we cannot know what God is, but only what he is not; we must therefore consider the ways in which God does *not* exist . . . [and] rule out from him everything inappropriate, such as compositeness, change and the like.[13]

We cannot speak of God positively because the mode of God's existence is entirely different from that of creatures. In other words, God transcends creaturely categories.

As discussed earlier, in Augustine's exposition of God's transcendence, God is differentiated from various levels of creatures—first from material things and then from spiritual things such as the human mind—until we arrive at the understanding that God is transcendent because he is the Creator of all things. In a similar fashion, in his discussion of God's nature (*ST* 1.3), Aquinas seeks to distinguish God from all levels of creatures: first, God is not a body (*ST* 1.3.1); then, he is not a composite of matter and form (*ST* 1.3.2); finally, he is not merely a nonmaterial thing but the One whose nature is to exist (*ST* 1.3.3-4). Aquinas closely follows Augustine on the negative approach to treating God's transcendence. But with the help of Aristotle's philosophy, Aquinas now gives God's transcendence a more precise metaphysical articulation—the identification between essence and existence—which is at the core of his understanding of divine simplicity.[14] For Aquinas, divine simplicity is the summit of transcendence and most decisively distinguishes God from creatures: "The very fact that God's existence itself subsists without being acquired by anything, and as such is limitless, distinguishes it from everything else and sets other things aside from it."[15] God is simple because his existence is not determined by any essence that differs from his existence. The simplicity of God means that his existence is limitless—hence transcendent.[16]

To say that God is limitless, however, Aquinas must redefine the term against the backdrop of a long tradition that associates limitlessness with imperfection. In Plato's thought, for instance, limitlessness is always linked with matter, which is to be limited and hence perfected by a form.[17] But apart from material limitlessness, Aquinas argues, there is another type of limitlessness, which is not an imperfection but the summit of perfection:

> Now there is both a sense in which matter is limited by form, and a sense in which form is limited by matter. Form limits matter because before assuming form matter is potential of many forms, but afterwards is determined by the one assumed. Matter limits form because a form as such may be shared by many things, but when acquired by matter becomes determinately the form of this thing. Now a form in limiting matter perfects it, so that material limitlessness is imperfect in character: a sort of matter without form. Matter however does not perfect a form but rather restricts its full scope so that the limitlessness of a form undetermined by matter is perfect in character.[18]

Aquinas makes it clear that because form stands to matter as perfection stands to imperfection, while the limitlessness of matter is an imperfection, the limitlessness of form is a perfection. God's limitlessness is the limitlessness of form and as such is supreme perfection. With such clarification, Aquinas transforms the Greek concept of limitlessness, making it suitable for describing the nature of God.

Aquinas's discussion of limitlessness does not stop here. For God is not the only being that is not limited by matter, since other immaterial beings such as angels are not limited by matter either. To distinguish God's limitlessness from other kinds of limitlessness, he resorts to his definition of existence as the act of all perfections. For him, the relation of existence to essence is equivalent to the relation of form to matter. Just as form is limited by matter, existence is limited by an essence that differs from it. So, although the forms of non-corporeal things other than God are not limited by matter, their existence is limited by essence and as such they do not have absolute limitlessness:

> [I]f there exist created forms not assumed by matter but subsisting themselves, as some people say is the case with angels, then such forms will be in a certain respect unlimited, inasmuch as they are not contained or restricted by matter. Since such subsistent created forms however acquire their existence, and are not identical with it, that existence itself is of necessity contained and restricted by some specifying nature. Such a form then cannot be in all respects unlimited.[19]

In contrast, because essence and existence are completely identical in God, his existence is not limited by his essence and as such he has absolute limitlessness. This limitlessness is not only the limitlessness of form but also that of existence—the Form of all forms. Since "God is existence itself subsistent . . . he himself is both limitless and perfect."[20] God's transcendence is thus most clearly manifested in the limitlessness of his existence. An implication of this conclusion is that God's existence is not restricted by time or space and as such he is present in all things—in other words, God is immanent to all creatures. "And it is because he is boundless and unlimited that God is said to exist everywhere in everything."[21] Aquinas makes it clear that God is immanent because he is limitless in existence. God's transcendence undergirds his immanence.

The Immanence of God

For Augustine, the immanence of God means that he exists *in* creatures—God is most intimate to creatures, for nothing would exist if God were not sustaining their innermost being.[22] It is clear that God's immanence is anchored in the fact that he is the Creator of all things. This insight is most affirmatively embraced by Aquinas, who devotes a whole question in *Summa theologiae* to God's existence *in* things. In the first article, he explicitly asserts that "God exists in everything" (*Deus est in omnibus rebus*). In order not to confuse God's immanence with any pantheistic views, he explains that "God exists in everything; not indeed as part of their substance or as an accident, but as an agent is present to that in which its action is taking place."[23] Like Augustine, Aquinas's understanding of God's immanence thus rests on the truth of creation: God is present to creatures as a cause is present to its effects. Aquinas then goes on to explain why and how a creative agent must be immediately present to its effects:

> For unless it acts through intermediaries every agent must be connected with that upon which it acts, and be in causal contact with it: compare Aristotle's proof that for one thing to move another the two must be in contact.[24]

Essentially, Aquinas's argument is that God is present to all things because he creates without intermediaries—he directly creates all things—which is a rejection of Plotinus's and Avicenna's position. Since God is the immediate creator of all things, he is immediately present to his effects. In addition, to distinguish God's causality of creation from other kinds of causality, Aquinas points out that God's immediate presence to all things is not a onetime event but a continuous reality:

> God is causing this effect in things not just when they begin to exist, but all the time they are maintained in existence, just as the sun is lighting up the atmosphere all the time the atmosphere remains lit. During the whole period of a thing's existence, therefore, God must be present to its existence, and present in a way in keeping with the way in which the thing possesses its existence. Now existence is more intimately and profoundly interior to things than anything else, for everything as we said is potential when compared to existence. So God must exist and exist intimately in things.[25]

From this passage, we can see that Aquinas's discussion of God's immanence is profoundly anchored in the doctrine of creation. To say that God is present to creatures not only initially but continually is simply to reaffirm the implications of *creatio ex nihilo*, namely that God must exist most intimately in things to sustain their existence and that creatures must wholly depend on God for the entire duration of their existence.

Such insights, as we have seen, have already been obtained by Augustine. But Aquinas is able to place these insights upon more rigorous philosophical grounds. For instance, to prove that God must be present to creatures, he employs Aristotle's principle of direct contact between the mover and the moved object. His exposition of creatures' dependence on God is based on his metaphysic of creation. In a sense, we can say that if Augustine's discussion of God's immanence is largely intuitive, Aquinas's treatment is clearly more philosophical. Whereas Augustine writes: "My God, I would have no being, I would have any existence, unless you were *in* me. Or rather, I would have no being if I were not *in* you,"[26] Aquinas reasons that because "God must be present to" creatures and "existence is more intimately and profoundly interior to things than anything else," God must "exist most intimately in things."[27] In so doing, Aquinas is essentially giving the biblical teaching of God's immanence a metaphysical articulation.

Aquinas's ability to provide philosophical precision to biblical doctrines is also evident in his distinction between three types of immanence. He states that "God is said to exist in two ways": the first relates to the fact that God is the creator (the way of nature); the second concerns God's special presence in "reasoning creatures" (the way of grace).[28] Within the first kind of immanence, there are still three modes in which God exists *in* creatures.

1. The first is immanence by *power*. To illustrate, he uses an analogy: "in virtue of his power a king can be said to exist throughout his kingdom, though not everywhere present."[29] This is the lowest level of immanence, for presence by power does not require physical presence and as such even things other than God, such as a king, can be immanent in this way. At a minimal level, God is immanent by power in all things because he creates and sustains all things by his providence. For Aquinas, to affirm the immanence by power is to refute Manicheans who hold that "immaterial and imperishable things are subject to God's power, but visible and perishable things to some contrary power." But the Christian position maintains that "we must say that God exists by power in everything."[30]
2. The second is immanence by *presence*.

   > Again, in the virtue of its presence, a thing exists in everything within its field of view, so that everything in a house is said to be present even to a person not existing substantially in every part of that house.[31]

   Like the first kind, this immanence does not require physical presence. Nonetheless, it is more advanced than the first kind, because it involves intentional care or providence. God is present to creatures not only by power but also by knowledge, for he knows every detail of every creature. This type of immanence must be affirmed of God because he not only initiates the creation of things but also provides continuous care over them. By affirming such immanence, Aquinas seeks to refute those who "believed everything to be subjected to God's power, but yet withdrew things here below from his providence."[32] While he does not specify the name of the opponent, we can assume that he has Aristotle in mind,[33] since the Aristotelian god only thinks of his own thought and is not concerned with lower things. Despite the respect for "the Philosopher," he decisively departs from Aristotle on this point, stressing that "we must say that God exists by presence in everything."[34] Such a departure is necessitated by the doctrine of creation, which emphasizes that God is not aloof to creatures but intimately knows and sustains all creatures with care.

3. Most significantly, Aquinas affirms God's immanence by *substance* (*per essentiam*) in all things. As he puts it, "A thing exists in substance in the place where its substance is." To claim that "God exists in all things by substance," he does not mean that God is present in things by *their* substance "as though he belonged to" a creaturely substance. Rather, he means that God exists by his *own* substance, which "exists in everything as causing their existence."[35] In essence, to say that God is present in things by substance is to affirm that the Creator of all must be profoundly intimate to all things. Should God withdraw his presence, all creatures would fall into nothing. Immanence by substance discloses the fact that God creates without mediation and exists at the foundation of all creatures. By affirming God's immanence by substance, Aquinas criticizes those who "said that God's providence oversees everything, but nonetheless asserted that God did not create everything without intermediaries."[36] His main target of criticism here is Avicenna, who, following Plotinus, claims that God only produces the first creature below him, which then produces a being below it, and hence the chain of being.[37] In such a framework, God does not directly create lower things and as such cannot be present to them by his substance. By contrast, the Christian position teaches that God immediately creates all levels of being and is immediately present to them all.

Having explained these three types of immanence, Aquinas concludes that God's immanence must be understood in all three modes:

> Thus God exists in everything by power inasmuch as everything is subject to his power, by presence inasmuch as everything is naked and open to his gaze, by substance inasmuch as he exists in everything causing their existence.[38]

Of the three kinds of immanence, the last kind is the most fundamental and can be seen as the foundation for the first two. God is present in things by power and by providence only because he directly brings them into existence and is substantially present in their innermost being. But, as we have seen,

God's immanence by substance is a logical consequence of the metaphysic of creation and so God's immanence is ultimately grounded in *creatio ex nihilo*. Indeed, it is on this foundation that Aquinas develops a most sophisticated account of transcendence and immanence, which not only overcomes the Greek dialectic but also goes beyond Augustine's work. For, as we discussed, although Augustine' worldview is grounded in *creatio ex nihilo*, its deepest implications have not been fully instantiated in his vision of reality, as is evident in his suspicion of scientific investigations and reluctance in giving full substantiality and stability to creatures. These inadequacies are now overcome by Aquinas, whose sophisticated metaphysic of creation finally enables him to flesh out the implications of *creatio ex nihilo*—especially God's radical transcendence and immanence more fully. There are at least two areas in which Aquinas takes a step further than Augustine: the first concerning the substantial goodness and stability of creation; the second, the reliability of the material world as a source for the knowledge of God.

THE IMPLICATIONS OF RADICAL TRANSCENDENCE

Participation and Substantial Goodness

In Plato's theory of participation, the intelligible realm is "really real," while the sensible world is a shadowy copy, and it is questionable whether material things have any substantial reality. Such a straightforwardly Platonic worldview is, of course, unacceptable for Christians, who confess that the material world as God's good creation is substantially real. It is for this reason that Augustine, though influenced by Platonism, ultimately clashes with the Platonists over the goodness of matter. Against the Platonists who see matter as the source of corruption, Augustine stresses that matter is intrinsically good. This view of matter is certainly an advance over Platonism. In another aspect, as we pointed out in chapter 3, Augustine's progress from Platonism does not seem far enough. He seems to share the Platonic understanding that because creatures participate in the goodness of God, they do not have their own goodness. Things are good insofar as they are related to God, the source of goodness, but they have no goodness that belongs to themselves. Following Augustine, contemporary proponents of participatory theology also seem reluctant in attributing intrinsic and substantial goodness to creatures. For instance, Boersma asserts that "the goodness of the created order is always predicated on its participatory status: that is, its goodness is *not its own*."[39] Such a statement seems to suggest that the fact that creatures participate in God means that they have no goodness of their own. Participation and substantial goodness are mutually exclusive.

This tension is in fact as old as the conflict between Plato and Aristotle. In order to explain why things are good, Plato claims that things are good because they reflect the Idea of the Good. In other words, things are good because they participate in the Good, which is external to them. For Aristotle, however, things are good not because they participate in external Forms, but because they have substantial goodness within. Hence, one of the hardest questions in history arises: are things good by participation or by substance? The sixth-century Christian philosopher Boethius revisits the question, as he writes: "One must inquire as to the way in which they [creatures] might be good: whether by participation or by substance."[40] On the one hand, he assumes that creatures cannot be good by substance because God alone is substantially good. On the other hand, following the Augustinian tradition that identifies goodness with being,[41] he acknowledges that all created substances are good insofar as they exist. These two conclusions lead to a conundrum—how can things be good both by participation and by substance? In raising this question, Boethius shares the Augustinian assumption that since creatures participate in God, they "do not have goodness as their own essence."[42]

In comparison to Augustine and Boethius, Aquinas makes an important breakthrough in this respect. He specifically tackles this question in *Summa theologiae* 1.6.4. First, he presents two seemingly contradictory statements: the first is that creatures are good by participation in God's goodness; the second is that "things are good inasmuch as they exist . . . . So things are good, not by God's goodness, but by their own."[43] Hence the conflict between Plato and Aristotle. In response, Aquinas seeks to reconcile Plato's concept of participation with Aristotle's theory of substantial forms. To begin with, he reasons that "there is nothing to stop things being named by reference to others, if the name is a relative term, as when things are said to be 'in place' by reference to place, or 'measured' by reference to measure." For instance, Augustine is named "Augustine of Hippo," because Hippo is where he served as a bishop. However, it is controversial whether we can name things in the same fashion when the name is "non-relative," which is in fact the core disagreement between Plato and Aristotle:

> Plato believed that the forms of things exist separately, and that individual things are named after these separate Forms which they participate in some way: Socrates, for example, is called a "man" by reference to some separate Idea of man. . . . Aristotle repeatedly proves [that] . . . this opinion which postulates separate, self-subsistent Ideas of natural things appears to be absurd.[44]

While Plato claims that things are what they are because they participate in a Form that is separate, Aristotle teaches that things are what they are because of substantial forms *within*. Aquinas agrees with Aristotle on this point. Nonetheless, he asserts that it is "absolutely true" for Plato to posit the existence of "some first thing called God, good by nature. . . . And with this opinion Aristotle also is in agreement."[45] For Aquinas, it is thus in the transcendent God that the two conflicting theories—Plato's participation and Aristotle's substantial forms—become unified:

> One may therefore call things good and existent by reference to this first thing, existent and good by nature, inasmuch as they somehow participate and resemble it.... And in this sense all things are said to be good by divine good-ness, which is the pattern, source and goal of all goodness. Nevertheless the resemblance to divine goodness which leads us to call the thing good is *inherent* in the thing itself, *belonging to it* as a form and therefore naming it. And there is one goodness in all things, and yet many.[46]

As Aquinas points out, we can simultaneously affirm that things are good by participation and by substance, because we no longer need to choose between them. Boethius's question thus proves to be misguided. Having substantial goodness does not mean that creatures are equal to God, but that creatures' goodness is not shadowy or external to them but real and intrinsic to themselves. Creatures are good "at heart," as they possess their *own* form of goodness.

By reinterpreting the theory of participation, Aquinas makes a significant move in the history of philosophy. Not only does he reconcile the conflict between Plato and Aristotle; he also moves the Christian-Platonic synthesis away from one of the defects of Platonism, namely the reluctance to credit full reality to sensible things. Although Augustine, as we have seen, defends the goodness of matter against the Platonists, he basically shares the Platonic view of the world as shadowy and fleeting, as is reflected in his interpreta-tion of *creatio ex nihilo*. By "nothing," Augustine often means formlessness or mutability and the fact that creatures were made from nothing means that they have a tendency of falling back into nothing.[47] It can be argued that this aspect of Augustine's thought retains a Platonic residue that has not been Christianized. With his metaphysic of creation, however, Aquinas is able to remove this residue by recognizing that, in participating in the truly transcen-dent God, creatures are not shadowy copies of Forms but substantial things that have their own goodness. His insistence on creatures' substantiality is rooted in God's radical transcendence.

Substantiality and Transcendence

A further exposition of the relationship between creatures' inherent form and participation in God can be found in *De veritate*:

If, therefore, the first goodness is the effective cause of all goods, it must *imprint* its likeness upon the things produced; and so each thing will be called good by reason of an *inherent* form because of the likeness of the highest good *implanted* in it, and also because of the first goodness taken as the *exemplar* and *effective* cause of all created goodness.[48]

On the one hand, the creature is good by participation insofar as it receives the Form of goodness from God—the first cause. On the other hand, the creature truly has its own inherent form, since its form is a *real* effect of the cause—it has real existence that is distinguishable from the cause. This can be explained by the analogy of a seal. When a seal is pressed on a piece of clay, an image is formed in the clay. The image is like the seal but not the seal itself. Hence, although produced by the seal, the image on the clay is nonetheless real in itself. In a similar way, the created form of goodness is "implanted" by God in the creature in the likeness of the divine Form, but the created form has a *separate* reality and is intrinsic to the creature.

In fact, Aquinas's defense of creatures' substantial goodness is inseparable from his stress on God's transcendence—the complete ontological difference between God and creatures. While it is well-known that Aquinas is a strong defender of the goodness of creation,[49] it is often overlooked that his defense of the goodness of creation is intimately connected to his rejection of pantheism. It can be argued that, to insist on creatures' inherent form of goodness, Aquinas is more interested in upholding the ontological distinction between God and creation, hence rejecting pantheism, than in merely defending "the goodness of creation" as such. In other words, the substantial goodness of creation is necessitated by the fact that God is truly transcendent.

In Aquinas's view, a benchmark of orthodoxy is the *real difference* between divine essence and created essence. But for this difference to be real, each side of the difference—God and the creature—must be *real* in itself. For if the creature did not have its own separate essence or form, the real difference between God and creation would collapse, which would lead to pantheism. For Aquinas, therefore, the existence of intrinsic goodness in the creature is a logical consequence of the real difference between God and the creature. In emphasizing that the creature has its intrinsic goodness, Aquinas's goal is to maintain the essential difference between God and creation, thereby denying any mingling of God's essence with created ones. In other words, he defends the intrinsic goodness of creation in order to protect God's transcendence—the ontological difference between God and creation.

It is in fact for this reason that Aquinas uses "exemplary cause" instead of "formal cause" when discussing God's causality in creation. He refuses to call God the "formal cause" of creation, which would imply that creatures somehow possess the "form" of God—a hint of pantheism.[50] He is therefore emphatic that God is not the formal but *exemplary* cause of creation and that the created form is only a remote *likeness* of the divine Form. As the exemplar of created goodness, the divine goodness cannot be a form "in such a way that by it the creature can be said to be good formally as by an intrinsic form."[51] The essence of the creature must be defined by its *own intrinsic* form—not by the divine Form. Thus, apart from the divine Form, there must exist a form of goodness that is proper to the creature. If the created form of goodness were unreal, the distinction between God and creation would collapse—nothing but God would "really" exist and creatures would be divine. Hence, in order to maintain God's transcendence, it is essential for Aquinas to assert that "all things are good by a created goodness formally as by an *inherent* form, but by the uncreated goodness as by an *exemplary* form."[52]

As shall be clear by now, Aquinas's theology of participation as a metaphysical expression of creation by no means undermines the substantial goodness of creation. Created out of nothing, all creatures must exist by participation and totally depend on God, but it does not make them unreal or insubstantial. "[S]uch derived or participated things are no less real than Aristotelian substances, since now there is no other way to be except to participate in the *ipsum esse* of the Creator."[53] It is thus the radical implications of God's transcendence that enable Aquinas to see that participation in God does not diminish but sustains the substantiality of creatures. Only a truly transcendent God allows creatures to participate in him while maintaining their substantiality. God's transcendence does not allow a contrastive relation between God and creation. As Thomas Gilby observes,

> One of St Thomas's original contributions to religious thought is to have developed the truth that creatures wholly dependent on God are also *real in themselves*. Bodily things are first substances in their very particularity and individuality, not as examples of a type or as shadows, flickering and transient, cast by some external world of separate Ideas.[54]

THE IMPLICATIONS OF RADICAL IMMANENCE

Existential Stability of Creatures

In our discussion of Augustine, we noted that a key theme in his thought is "mutability."[55] As MacDonald puts it, "The attribute that Augustine links most closely to true being is *immutability*. He very often discusses them together, and he takes them to be mutually entailing."[56] The higher the being of something is, the more immutable it is. Consequently, being in its highest sense must be absolutely immutable. "That which truly *is* is that which unchangeably abides."[57] God, the Supreme Being, is thus necessarily "incorruptible, immune from injury, and unchangeable."[58] By contrast, all creatures, whose being is from nothing, are inherently mutable and tend to fall back to nothing. On this interpretation, *creatio ex nihilo* means that creatures are naturally changeable and unstable. In Augustine's thought, "the tendency which created nature displays to fall short of the good, its incompleteness, its instability and fragility, the difficulty it experiences in holding on to existence, is an inherent part of its nature."[59] The doctrine of *creatio ex nihilo* above all reveals the ontological instability and *precariousness* of creatures. They must completely depend on God because their existence is unstable and insecure in itself.

As we have seen, both of these insights on creation—creatures' natural nothingness and radical dependence upon God—are embraced and further developed by Aquinas. Like Augustine, Aquinas suggests that *ex nihilo* means that non-being is prior to being in all creatures and as such they must continuously depend on God for their existence. Despite their continuity, there is a subtle and yet profound difference between their concepts of "nothingness." For Augustine, the fact that creatures were made out of nothing means that they have an inherent tendency to fall back to nothing. This understanding, however, is plainly rejected by Aquinas, who argues that God "gives being in such a way that the tendency of the given being is not to lapse into non-being but precisely to remain in being."[60] He expresses this view explicitly in *Summa theologiae*:

> The natures of creatures manifest that no creatures are degenerating into nothing, either because they are immaterial beings, in which there is *no potency to non-being*, or because they are material beings, and these remain in existence, at least in their matter, which is incorruptible.[61]

Aquinas maintains that creatures do not tend to fall back to non-being, even though they were brought into existence from nothing. First, he suggests that incorporeal things, such as angels, exist permanently and have no tendency to fall into nonexistence. Secondly, he claims that corporeal things, insofar as they are matter, do not perish either. No doubt, he admits that corporeal things are perishable, but he would argue that when they perish, it is not that matter itself ceases to exist but that the unity of matter with form or the cohesion of various parts breaks down. But matter or the material substrate of these things is nonperishable.[62] This position in fact is remarkably close to the principle of conservation of matter in classical physics. It seems that before the scientific law of conservation was discovered, Aquinas had already laid a theological foundation.

What is significant is that for Aquinas there is no conflict between the conservation of matter and creatures' radical contingency. The doctrine of creation stresses that God does not create out of necessity but freely, which means that the existence of creatures is not necessary but completely dependent on God's will. Should God choose not to create, nothing would exist. This contingency of creation seems incompatible with the law of conversation in physics. For this reason, Wolfhart Pannenberg raises theological questions for scientists whether the conservation of matter can be consistent with the contingency of creation.[63] But Aquinas would not raise such questions, because he has no trouble in simultaneously affirming the substantial stability or nonperishability of matter and its complete dependence upon God. Unlike Pannenberg, Aquinas does not see the contingency of creation as a negation of its ontological stability. Just as creatures' substantiality is compatible with their participation in God, the contingency of their existence is likewise compatible with their existential stability.

In many ways, this insight marks a profound difference between Aquinas's interpretation of *creatio ex nihilo* and that of Augustine. For Augustine, the fact that all creatures were made out of nothing and wholly depend on God means that their existence is inherently mutable and unstable. For Aquinas, however, while *creatio ex nihilo* does mean that creatures are absolutely dependent on God, it does not mean that their existence is unstable or precarious. Dependence upon God does not diminish creatures' existential stability. On the contrary, they are ontologically stable *because* they depend on God.

In fact, behind such confidence in creatures' substantiality is the conviction about God's true immanence in creation. For Aquinas, the fact that God is truly immanent means that his sustaining power permeates creatures' existence such that they do not tend to fall into nonexistence. In other words, creatures do not tend to fall into non-being, because their existence, the innermost of their being, is intimately sustained by God. Aquinas writes the following:

> Since the form of the thing is within the thing, since [form] is far more important as it is prior and more universal, and since God is properly the cause in all things of universal being, which is the most intimate reality in things, it follows that God operates intimately in all things.[64]

Hence, in Aquinas's thought, although it is true that creatures would be absolutely nothing if God withdrew his presence, the fact that God is indeed intimately present within them means that they do not simply fall into nothing. In this sense, his assertion that creatures do not have potency to non-being rests on his profound confidence on God's radical immanence in things. Conversely, the only reason why creatures would have the tendency to fall into nothing, as Augustine assumes, would be that God's power and presence did not truly exist at the innermost of creation. It is true that rational creatures with free will may choose to abandon God and move into non-being, but they need not have a *natural* tendency to move toward nothing. Otherwise, there would be a defect in their nature, which would be an imperfection of God. It can therefore be argued that Augustine's view of creatures' natural instability is indicative of an inconsistency in his understanding of God's immanence in creation. But this inconsistency is overcome by Aquinas, as he is able to fully flesh out the profound implications of God's radical immanence in his vision of reality. Compared to Augustine's world, which seems precarious and fleeting, Aquinas's world is much more solid and substantial. This openness and trust toward the physical world rests on a confidence in God's true immanence in creation.

Trustworthiness of the Material World

As we saw in chapter 2, Augustine's view of matter differs from that of Platonism, as he repeatedly debates with the Platonists on the goodness of matter. His defense of the goodness of matter is essentially a defense of the doctrine of creation and the goodness of the Creator. Toward the end of chapter 3, however, we suggested that Augustine seems to have been unable to fully extend the implications of *creatio ex nihilo* into his worldview, as is reflected in his distrust of the material world as a reliable source for the knowledge of God. The best route for Augustine to know God is through immaterial things, as is characteristic of the Platonic tradition. It can be argued that while Augustine departs from Platonism on the *ontological* value of matter, he is still in agreement with the latter on matter's *epistemological* relevance. Epistemologically, Augustine is arguably still Platonic.

By contrast, Aquinas's approach to knowledge—even the knowledge of God—is decisively Aristotelian. In comparison to Augustine, Aquinas has a considerably more open and affirmative attitude toward the world as a source of knowledge. How do we account for this difference? An apparent explanation is that the Aristotelian corpus, which had been unavailable to Augustine, became accessible to Aquinas, who then embraced Aristotelianism as his default epistemological position. Although there may be elements of truth to it, this explanation is, however, too simplistic. It not only overlooks the complexity in the medieval reception of Aristotle but also downplays Aquinas's critical thinking ability. When first introduced to the West, Aristotle's philosophy was not universally accepted, and many Christian thinkers sought to condemn it. In addition, Aquinas's adoption of Aristotelianism was not by default but through deliberation. It can be argued that one of the key reasons why Aquinas chooses Aristotelianism as an epistemological approach is because it allows him to affirm the empirical world as a reliable starting point for the knowledge of God. The world is reliable is because God is truly immanent in the world. For if God is equally immanent in material things and spiritual things, the latter are not nearer to God than the former. Nor are the latter necessarily a privileged route for knowing God. Hence, it can be argued that it is his profound awareness of God's immanence in all of creation that ultimately undergirds Aquinas's adoption of Aristotelianism—his trust and confidence in the material world. For Aquinas, the material world is of deep religious relevance because God is truly present in it, and as Gerard Hopkins puts it, the world is "charged with the grandeur of God."[65]

Such a sacramental view of the cosmos, as we have discussed, is not prominent in Augustine. Although he speaks of God's all-pervasive power in everything,[66] Augustine seems to fall short of a sacramental ontology. He shows a dubious attitude toward scientific investigations of the world, which he believes can distract us from pursuing God.[67] By contrast, in Aquinas we can find a true sacramental ontology. His profound sense of God's immanence allows him to see God's holiness penetrating all levels of creation, including the material world. The whole cosmos thus becomes a sacrament for God. In this vision, all domains of creation become relevant to religion and for this reason Aquinas incorporates all domains of learning, such as philosophy and metaphysics, in his theology. For him, although theology is a unique science, it touches upon all areas of knowledge. As Gilby observes, "theology, as conceived by St Thomas, is not sectarian nor even fanatical in the loftiest sense; it is open to the arts and sciences and can see its own proper implications in them all."[68] No secular learning is thus irrelevant to theology. Just as God's immanence permeates the cosmos, theology penetrates into all areas of learning, including the scientific investigation of the world. In his emphasis on God's immanence and the relatedness of all studies to theology, Aquinas may have well paved the way for the development of modern science long before the Reformation, which has been seen as the theological trigger for the rise of modern natural science.[69]

For instance, British philosopher Michael Foster argued that the un-Greek elements in early modern philosophy of nature provided the foundation for modern science and that the source of the un-Greek elements is Christian theology, especially the implications of the doctrine of creation. These implications, however, were restricted within the domain of theology until the Reformation removed the boundary between the sacred and the secular.

[A]s the Reformation in the practical sphere had the effect of extending the application of Christian principles of conduct beyond the religious to the secular life, so in the theoretical sphere it carried out the implications of Christian doctrines beyond the sacred into the profane sciences.[70]

In essence, Foster's argument is that the Reformation facilitated the rise of modern science by fleshing out the theological implications of the doctrine of creation into scientific investigations of nature. This approach was contrasted with medieval thought, which in his view did not extend the implications of creation to secular studies. While Foster makes a significant point about the impact of *creatio ex nihilo* on science, his assessment of medieval thought is questionable. As discussed above, Aquinas has already extended the implications of *creatio ex nihilo* to other areas of learning such as philosophy and metaphysics. Although he is not a scientist in the modern sense, Aquinas has developed a philosophy of nature that is consistent with the doctrine of creation. His theology has definitely seeped out of the boundary of religion, penetrating into other domains of knowledge. In Aquinas, there is

> no breach between the sacred and the profane, or between godly and worldly leaning. He himself never adopts such a position in depth, and avoids the various manifestations of sectarianism it involves in theological thought. His hostility to the 'double-truth theory' goes very deep, and it extends to any fragmentation into disparate and unrelated objects of knowledge.[71]

For Aquinas, therefore, although nature has its own integrity, it is never separate from grace. Rather, nature is deeply infused by grace, since God is truly immanent in the creation. There is no profane domain that is independent of the sacred. God's profound presence in everything makes all things religiously relevant. In this sense, the study of nature is by no means irrelevant to religion. If the world really participates in God and God is really present in the natural world, then, scientific investigation can be deeply relevant to theology. As Aquinas himself puts it, "this sort of mediation on the divine works is indeed necessary for instruction of faith."[72] Aquinas endorses the study of nature because he believes that studying creation enables us to obtain a glimpse of God's wisdom that exists in all things:

> Now, God brought things into being by His wisdom; wherefore the Psalm (103:24) declares: "Thou hast made all things in wisdom." Hence, from reflection upon God's works we are able to infer His wisdom, since, by a certain communication of His likeness, it is spread abroad in the things He has made. For it is written: "He poured her out," namely, wisdom, "upon all His works" (Eccli. 1:10).[73]

Aquinas states that God's wisdom is "spread abroad *in*" creatures, which suggests that God's wisdom is not external to creatures but deeply *within* them, because God exists in the innermost of creatures. Because all things are created by God through his wisdom, they have an intelligible structure that manifests the divine wisdom. In a sense, creatures are placed between two minds, "the Divine and the human,"[74] and have the ability to communicate the divine truths to us:

> Things can be known by us because God has creatively thought them; *as* creatively thought by God, things have not only their *own* nature ("for themselves alone"); but *as* creatively thought by God, things have also a reality "for us." Things have their intelligibility, their inner clarity and lucidity, and the power to reveal themselves, because God has creatively thought them. This is why they are essentially intelligible.[75]

For this reason, Aquinas affirms the significance of studying nature for the Christian faith,[76] which remarkably resembles the attitudes of later Christian thinkers toward science. John Calvin, for instance, asserts that "this study is not to be probated, nor this science to be condemned" for "this art unfolds the admirable wisdom of God."[77] Likewise, Johannes Kepler views science as "thinking God's thoughts after him."[78] Hence, contrary to Foster's position, it can be argued that Aquinas has already made significant theological preparations for the rise of modern science. By further extending the implications of *creatio ex nihilo*, especially God's radical immanence in the world, he recognizes that the study of nature has deep religious meaning and must not be despised but cherished.

This view of nature, as we can see, is an advance over that of Augustine. Of course, Augustine also speaks of obtaining knowledge of God through visible things. But for him, the value of visible things rests on the fact that they direct our gaze *away from* them and *toward* God. While Aquinas and modern philosophers of nature agree that visible things direct us to God, they would argue that we need not move away from visible things in order to move toward God. Rather, it is possible for us to gaze upon God by looking *at* or *within* visible things, because God is truly immanent in all things. In comparison to Augustine, Aquinas shows a remarkable trust and confidence in the material world because he is convinced of God's profound immanence in the world. Rudi te Velde sums it well:

> Thomas's theological vision is stamped by an attitude of trust and open acceptance of the natural world. . . . The Christian belief in creation motivates him to strongly oppose the Gnostic temptation to devalue material reality as something from which we should be saved. What seems to me the most characteristic of Thomas's view of creation is his conviction that any devaluation of the world of creatures means, in fact, derogation of the power of the Creator himself.[79]

Ultimately, it is by allowing the implications of *creatio ex nihilo* to penetrate more deeply in his worldview that Aquinas finally overcomes some of inadequacies in Augustine's thought. In so doing, Aquinas also brings the process of Christianizing participation closer to completion. Indeed, by transforming the theory of participation more thoroughly in the light of the doctrine of creation, Aquinas makes participation more suitable for describing the relation between God and creation. In this framework, God is simultaneously transcendent and immanent to all creatures, and although creatures completely depend on God for their existence, they are real and substantial in themselves. This participatory ontology is perhaps what modern proponents of participatory ontology, such as RO and Boersma, have been seeking. For such a theology of participation not only anchors created reality in a participatory relation to God, but also allows creation to maintain its own goodness and integrity. Adopting this participatory ontology can not only fulfill their needs but also help them to avoid the criticisms, because this participatory ontology is anchored more robustly in the doctrine of creation than in Platonism. Indeed, as a metaphysical expression of *creatio ex nihilo*, this more distinctively Christian version of participatory ontology has profound implications for postmodern theological and philosophical discussions.

NOTES

1. *Aquinas on Creation*, 74.

2. Ibid., 77, emphasis added.

3. Ibid., 74–5.

4. *De Potentia* 3.3 ad 6,

5. For instance *De Potentia* 3.2–3 and *ST* 1.45.3. *De Potentia* is believed to be composed in either 1259–61 or 1265–67. Thomas Gilby, introduction to *Power of God*, ix.

6. *De Potentia* 3.2. This seems to suggest that Aristotle does not have a teaching on creation.

7. Ibid., 3.3.

8. *ST* 1.45.3, emphases added.

9. David B. Burrell, "The Act of Creation," in Burrell et al., *Creation and the God of Abraham*, 51.

10. *ST* 1.45.3.

11. Te Velde, *Participation and Substantiality*, ix.

12. Preface to *ST* 1.2.

13. Preface to *ST* 1.3.

14. No doubt, for Augustine, divine simplicity is also a definitive mark of God's transcendence, but his notion (that God is what he has) is less refined than that of Aquinas, which more clearly stresses the existential dimension.

15. *ST* 1.7.1 ad 3.

16. *ST* 1.7. To be clear, the Latin title of the question is "*de infinitate Dei*," which can be translated as "On the infinity of God." But since *finis* means boundary or limit,

it is reasonable to translate *infinitas* as "limitless," which indeed is the essence of transcendence, as *transcendo* means to surpass or go beyond [limits].

17. Norris W. Clarke, "The Limitation of Act by Potency in St. Thomas: Aristotelianism or Neoplatonism?" *The New Scholasticism* 24 (1952): 165–94.

18. *ST* 1.7.1.

19. *ST* 1.7.2.

20. *ST* 1.7.1.

21. Preface to *ST* 1.7.

22. *Confessions,* 1.2.2.

23. *ST* 1.8.2.

24. Ibid.

25. *ST* 1.8.2.

26. *Confessions,* 1.2.2, emphasis added.

27. *ST* 1.8.2.

28. *ST* 1.8.3. Here, Aquinas speaks of Christ, in whom a special union between God and humanity is established.

29. *ST* 1.8.3.

30. Ibid.

31. Ibid.

32. Ibid.

33. He explicitly attributes this position to Aristotle and Averroes in *I Sent.* 39.2.2. See *ST* 1.8.3, footnote c.

34. *ST* 1.8.3.

35. *ST* 1.8.3.

36. Ibid.

37. See *Power of God* 3.16.

38. Ibid.

39. Boersma, *Heavenly Participation,* 31, emphases added.

40. Quoted in Aquinas, *Exposition*, 31.

41. It is a general consensus of the Platonist-Christian tradition. In *ST* 1.5.1, Aquinas quotes Augustine that "inasmuch as we exist, we are good" and argues extensively that "to be good is really the same thing as to exist."

42. Te Velde, *Participation and Substantiality*, 16.

43. As a *Magister in Sacra Pagina*, Aquinas cannot fail to heed to Genesis 1, which claims all creatures to be "good."

44. *ST* 1.6.4.

45. It has to be noted that the Aristotle Aquinas received had already been mediated by Muslim philosophers, which led Aquinas to believe that Aristotle would agree on the existence of the Good as the first cause of all things.

46. *ST* 1.6.4, emphases added.

47. See a detailed discussion of this topic in Yonghua Ge, "The Role of *creatio ex nihilo* in Augustine's Confessions," *Sino-Christian Studies* no. 22 (2016): 41–64.

48. Aquinas, *Truth,* vol. 3, Questions XXI-XXIX, trans. Robert W. Schmidt (Indianapolis, IN: Hackett, 1994), 21.4, emphases added. A detailed exposition of this passage is given by Te Velde in *Participation and Substantiality*, 23–34, but he

does not mention the fact that Aquinas's treatment of the harmony of participation and substantiality is driven by his rejection of pantheism, which I believe is the key to understanding his argument.

49. See Te Velde, *Aquinas on God*, 123.

50. *ST* 1.44.2.

51. Aquinas, *Truth*, 21.4.

52. Ibid., emphases added.

53. Burrell, "Act of Creation," 43.

54. Thomas Gilby, introduction to *Summa theologiae*, vol. 8: *Creation, Variety and Evil*, xxiii, emphases added.

55. Trapé, *Patrology*, 408.

56. Scott MacDonald, "The Divine Nature," in *Cambridge Companion to Augustine*, ed. Eleonore Stump and Norman Kretzmann (Cambridge: Cambridge University Press, 2001), 84.

57. *Confessions* 7.11.17.

58. *Confessions* 7.1.17.

59. Harrison, *Rethinking Augustine*, 91.

60. Baldner and Carroll, Analysis of *Aquinas on Creation*, 48.

61. *ST* 1.2.104.4, emphases added.

62. In *Power of God* 5.3, Aquinas asserts that "in the whole of created nature, there is no potency through which it is possible for something to tend into nothing."

63. Frank J. Tipler, "The Omega Point as Eschaton: Answers to Pannenberg Questions for Scientists," *Zygon* 6 (1989): 217–53.

64. *ST* 1.105.5.

65. Quoted in Boersma, "Heavenly Participation," 21.

66. See *City of God*, 5.11; 12.26.

67. See *Literal Meaning of Genesis*, 5.16.34.

68. Thomas Gilby, introduction to vol. 8 of *ST*, xix.

69. M. B. Foster, "The Christian Doctrine of Creation and the Rise of Modern Science," *Mind* 43 (1934): 446–68.

70. Ibid., 453.

71. Gilby, introduction to vol. 8 of *ST*, xxi.

72. *SCG* 2.2.1.

73. *SCG* 2.2.2.

74. Pieper, *Silence of St. Thomas*, 53–4.

75. Ibid., 55–6.

76. "It is therefore evident that the consideration of creatures has its part to play in building the Christian faith." *SCG* 2.2.6.

77. Quoted in *The Book of the Cosmos: Imagining the Universe from Heraclitus to Hawking*, ed. Dennis R. Danielson (Cambridge, MA: Perseus, 2000), 123–4.

78. Collin Russell, *Cross-Currents: Interactions between Science and Faith* (Leicester, England: Inter-Varsity, 1985), 76.

79. Te Velde, *Aquinas on God*, 123.

Conclusion

The relationship between God and creation lies at the heart of many contemporary theological controversies and movements, not the least of which is the resurgence of participatory ontology, as represented by RO and Boersma. While a laudable undertaking to combat secularism and restore a theocentric worldview, their theology of participation is, however, subject to the criticism that it relies too heavily on Platonism and tends to undermine the goodness of creation. With regard to the One and the Many, critics argue that the concept of participation elevates the One at the expense of the Many. The reason for this weakness, as we have suggested, is their insufficient engagement with the Christian doctrine of creation in their development of participatory ontology. The Platonic tradition, as we have shown, has indeed a tendency to disparage materiality and multiplicity. But this defect has been overcome by the doctrine of *creatio ex nihilo*, which affirms the goodness of creation and plurality. Thus, for participatory ontology to be used in the Christian context, it needs to be transformed in the light of the doctrine of creation. Augustine and Aquinas, as we have seen, made significant contributions to the Christianizing process of participation. For both thinkers, the ultimate foundation of participatory ontology is not Platonism but the doctrine of creation. For this reason, RO and Boersma should adopt the more distinctively Christian version of participation, as is found in Augustine and especially in Aquinas, whose concept of participation, as a metaphysical expression of creation, finally overcomes the weaknesses of Platonism. This participatory theology will help us to see that participation does not need to be "an unsalvageable Platonic heritage" but can be a truly Christian concept that is anchored in the doctrine of creation. Aquinas's participatory ontology can help contemporary theologies of participation to find their true home.

Because of its intrinsic link to creation, retrieving Aquinas's concept of participation can also make a unique contribution to contemporary science-religion debates. While *creatio ex nihilo* was "central to the theology of the early and medieval Church," its implications have been "strangely over-looked by the modern science and religion dialogue."[1] Contemporary litera-ture on science and religion hardly touches on the theological implications of the doctrine. At the heart of the science-theology dialogue, however, is God's relation with creation, which cannot be properly understood without *creatio ex nihilo*. As a metaphysical expression of creation, Aquinas's idea of participation discloses a picture of an absolutely transcendent God, who is nonetheless profoundly immanent to creation. Such a view of God's relation with creation can help science-theology dialogues keep the balance between transcendence and immanence.

Much of the modern science-theology debate, however, oscillates between two poles. On the one hand, under the influence of the mechanistic world-view, God is increasingly pushed out of the world, which has become the exclusive domain of science. As a result, God's immanence is almost lost. To save room for God, Christians either find faults with science, arguing that God is needed to explain the phenomena, or allocate God's action to domains where science has no certainty. An example of the first kind is the Intelligent Design Movement. It argues that the theory of evolution fails to explain the irreducible complexity in biology, which can only be accounted for by design.[2] An example of the second type is the proposal that God acts in a noninterventionist fashion via the indeterminacy of quantum physics.[3] In order to save room for God in the world, however, both approaches neglect the fact that God does not merely act in areas where science has no determi-nacy but in all domains of creation, because he is truly immanent in all things.

On the other hand, Christians who are eager to find "scientific" evidence for God are quick to contend that new developments in science provide proof for God. For instance, many have claimed that the Big Bang theory is the scientific evidence for God's creation. However, to identify God's operation with a scientific theory is to undermine God's transcendence, since God's action cannot be pinpointed by any scientific description of the world. God indeed acts in natural processes, but his action cannot be identified with natu-ral causality—it transcends the latter. In his participatory ontology, Aquinas distinguishes between two kinds of causality—first and secondary causalities. First causality is proper to God and secondary causality is associated with nat-ural laws. God's first causality acts in all things through secondary causality but cannot be identified with any secondary cause. To identify divine action with any natural process is to bring God down to purely immanent domains and diminish his transcendence. Aquinas's participatory ontology reminds us that because God is transcendent, divine action cannot be identified with any scientific theory, and that because God is immanent, he acts in all things through the secondary causality of natural processes.

As a unique vision of reality, Aquinas's theology of participatory is also vital for a postmodern worldview reconstruction. Affirming both unity and plurality, participatory ontology provides a middle ground between monism and pluralism, proving to be superior to alternative worldviews.

Indeed, Aquinas's participatory ontology helps us to see the deficiencies of radical postmodern pluralism or individualism. With its revolt against all totalizing schemes and its exclusive emphasis on difference, pluralism offers no ground for unity. In that system, the Many triumphs but the One disappears—it is a Many without the One. For this reason, the postmodern world, as Gunton points out, is characterized by deep-seated fragmentation. But, as Aquinas shows, plurality cannot exist without unity and absolute plurality only leads to nihilism, which lies at the heart of the crisis of modernity. The irony is that "the much vaulted pluralism of modern secular cultures conceals an underlying tendency to deny plurality and individuality."[4] In contrast, while participatory ontology affirms the integrity of the Many, it does not reject the One but grounds plurality in unity.

More importantly, with a transcendent source of unity, a participatory ontology rooted in the doctrine of creation defends the irreducible richness of reality against modern schemes of monism, where "the Many" is annihilated by "the One." Finding the ultimate source of all things has been the motivation for philosophical and scientific investigations.[5] With the advancement of science, this quest has become more acute in modern physics. One of Einstein's dreams was to unify all the fundamental forces—strong, weak, gravitational, and electromagnetic—into a single force, a task that continues to inspire theoretical physicists. As Barrow points out, the grand ambition of modern science is to find "a unified Theory of Everything," which offers the ultimate explanation to all of reality.[6] More recently, this vision has been explicitly voiced by Stephan Hawking and his collaborator in *The Grand Design: New Answers to the Ultimate Questions of Life*, which claims that there is no need for God, since the fundamental laws of physics can explain the origin of all things.[7] A quick glance at the title (note the words "grand" and "ultimate") reveals that the project is a quest for the Ultimate One. We cannot help but ask: can "the One"—a scientific theory—truly account for all of reality? We can reasonably doubt that *one* scientific law is capable of accounting for all of reality, because a scientific law is not transcendent enough—it is only part of the universe. To explain all things in terms of part of the universe inevitably reduces the richness and diversity of reality. Such scientism elevates the One at the cost of the Many.

Likewise, various versions of reductionist physicalism, which reduce all things to matter, also fail in this respect.[8] In essence, reductionist materialism is an attempt to reduce the Many—all of reality—into the immanent One, which is nothing but matter. In this system, everything—including the mind, emotion, poetry, and art—is reduced to *one* principle—matter, and anything that cannot be reduced into matter, for instance, God or soul, is automatically considered nonexistent, since it is presumed that only matter exists. In this framework, the Many completely vanishes and only the One—matter—exists. The Many is eliminated by the all-devouring One, which leads to the worst kind of monism. It is worse than scientism, since "the One" in scientism, namely the scientific law, still contains some degree of transcendence, while matter—"the One" in reductionist physicalism—is wholly immanent without any degree of transcendence. It is the complete lack of transcendence that makes "the One" the most suppressive. Under this tyrannical One, the world becomes utterly flattened and diversity utterly destroyed, which points to a most bleak vision of reality.[9] In terms of the One and the Many, reductionist physicalism is arguably the worst type of metaphysical system.[10] It is curious that in postmodernity extreme forms of pluralism and monism should coexist.

By contrast, as we have shown, only the truly transcendent One, as in Aquinas's metaphysics of participation, can give unity to all things and yet maintain the reality of individual things in their intrinsic diversity and particularity. For only a transcendent One—the Creator of all that *is*—does not compete with the plurality of things. Only in this system can unity be achieved without plurality being diminished. To solve the modern problematic of the One and the Many, therefore, we need to find the truly transcendent One. What is most remarkable about the transcendent One, as we find in Aquinas's metaphysics of participation, is that the One is also most intimate in all things. The One is not distant from us but closer to us than we are to ourselves. In Aquinas's participatory ontology, the most profound vision of simultaneous transcendence and immanence of the One in relation to the Many is Christ, in whom God becomes perfectly united with humanity.[11] Although it would be another book, it can be argued that the ultimate Christian answer to the question of the One and the Many is the Incarnation—the absolutely transcendent One became truly immanent in the Many.

NOTES

1. Preface to *Creation and the God of Abraham*.
2. See, for instance, Michael J. Behe, *Darwin's Black Box: The Biochemical Challenge to Evolution* (New York: Simon and Schuster, 2016).
3. For instance, Robert J. Russell, Philip Clayton, Kirk Wegter-McNelly, and John Polkinghorne, ed., *Quantum Mechanics: Scientific Perspectives on Divine*

Action (Vatican City and Berkeley, CA: Vatican Observatory and Center for Theology and the Natural Sciences, 2002).

4. Gunton, *One, Three and Many*, 30.

5. Louis-Marie Régis, *St. Thomas and Epistemology*, The 1946 Aquinas Lecture (Milwaukee: Marquette University Press, 1946), 40–1.

6. John D. Barrow, *Theories of Everything: The Quest for Ultimate Explanations* (Oxford: Clarendon Press, 1991), 30.

7. Stephan Hawking and Leonard Mlodinow, *The Grand Design: New Answers to the Ultimate Questions of Life* (London: Bantam, 2010).

8. SeeHart, *Experience of God*, 48–9; Thomas Nagel, *Mind and Cosmos: Why the Materialist Neo-Darwinian Concept of Nature Is Almost Certainly Wrong* (New York: Oxford University Press, 2012); Lynne Rudder Baker, *Saving Belief: A Critique of Physicalism* (Princeton: Princeton University Press, 1987); Mario De Caro and David Macarther, ed. *Naturalism in Question* (Cambridge, MA: Harvard University Press, 2004).

9. For a trenchant critique of such a vision in reductionist materialism, see Conor Cunningham, "Trying My very Best to Believe in Darwin, Or, the Supernaturalistic Fallacy: From Is to Nought," in Conor Cunningham and Peter M. Candler, Jr., eds., *Belief and Metaphysics* (London: SCM, 2007), 100–40.

10. In his account of the history of philosophy, Aquinas regards materialism of the early Greek philosophy, which recognized only the material cause, as the most primitive stage of philosophy. In a way, reductionist materialism is a return to that primitive phase.

11. *ST* 1.8.3 ad 4: "There is, however, another unique way in which God exists in a man, by being one with him."

Bibliography

Acar, Rahim. "Creation: Avicenna's Metaphysical Account." In *Creation and the God of Abraham*, edited by David B. Burrell, Carlo Cogliati, Janet M. Soskice and William R. Stoeger, 77–90. Cambridge: Cambridge University Press, 2010.

Aertsen, Jan A. "Aquinas's Philosophy in Its Historical Context." In *The Cambridge Companion to Aquinas*, edited by Norman Kretzmann and Eleonore Stump, 12–37. Cambridge: Cambridge University Press, 1993.

———. *Medieval Philosophy and the Transcendentals: The Case of Thomas Aquinas*. Leiden: Brill, 1996.

———. "The Convertibility of Being and Good in St Thomas Aquinas." *The New Scholasticism* 59 (1985): 449–70.

Allen, Diogenes and Eric O. Springsted. *Philosophy for Understanding Theology*. 2nd ed. Louisville, KY: Westminster John Knox, 2007.

Anderson, James F. *St. Augustine and Being: A Metaphysical Essay*. Hague: M. Nijhoff, 1965.

Annice, M. "Historical Sketch of the Theory of Participation." *The New Scholasticism* 26 (1952): 49–79.

Anton, John P. *Aristotle's Theory of Contrariety*. London: Routledge, 1957.

Aquinas, Thomas. *Summa contra Gentiles*. Translated by Anton C. Pegis, James F. Anderson, Vernon J. Bourke and Charles J. O'Neil. 4 vols. Notre Dame: University of Notre Dame Press, 1975–1977.

———. *Summa Theologiae*. Latin text and English translation, Introduction, Notes, Appendices and Glossaries. Cambridge, UK: Blackfriars, 1964–1975.

———. *An Exposition of the* On the hebdomads *of Boethius*. Translated by Janice L. Schultz and Edward A. Synan. Washington, DC: Catholic University of America Press, 2001.

———. *Aquinas on Creation: Writings on the "Sentences" of Peter Lombard 2.1.1*. Translated by Steven E. Baldner and William E. Carroll. Toronto: Pontifical Institute of Medieval Studies, 1997.

————. *Commentary on the Metaphysics of Aristotle.* Translated by John P. Rowan. Chicago, IL: Regnery, 1961.

————. *Compendium of Theology.* Translated by Richard J. Regan. Oxford: Oxford University Press, 2009.

————. *On Essence and Being.* Translated by Armand A. Maurer. Toronto: Pontifical Institute of Medieval Studies, 1968.

————. *On the Power of God = Quæstiones disputatæ de potentia Dei.* Translated by English Dominican Fathers. 3 vols. Westminster, MD: Newman, 1952.

————. *The Division and Methods of the Sciences.* Translated by Armand Maurer. 4th ed. Toronto: Pontifical Institute of Medieval Studies, 1986.

————. *Truth.* Translated by Robert W. Schmidt. 3 vols. Indianapolis, IN: Hackett, 1994.

————. *Nature and Grace: Selections from the* Summa Theologica *of Thomas Aquinas.* Translated and edited by A. M. Fairweather. London: SCM, 1954.

Aristotle, *Metaphysics.* Translated and edited by W. David Ross. 2 vols. New York: Oxford University Press, 1924.

————. *Physics.* Translated by Robin Waterfield. Oxford: Oxford University Press, 1996.

————. *The Categories*; *On Interpretation*, with an English translation by Harold P. Cooke; *Posterior Analytics*, with an English translation by Hugh Tredennick. Loeb Classical Library. Cambridge, MA: Harvard University Press, 1962.

Armstrong, A. H. *The Architecture of the Intelligible Universe in the Philosophy of Plotinus.* Cambridge: Cambridge University Press, 1940.

————. *St. Augustine and Christian Platonism.* The Saint Augustine Lecture 1966. Villanova: Villanova University Press, 1967.

Augustine. *Confessions.* Translated by Henry Chadwick. Oxford: Oxford University Press, 1991.

————. *The Literal Meaning of Genesis.* Translated by John H. Taylor. 2 vols. New York: Newman Press, 1982.

————. *The City of God against the Pagans.* Translated and edited by R.W. Dyson. Cambridge: Cambridge University Press, 2001.

————. *The Trinity.* The Fathers of the Church 45. Translated by Stephen J. Mckenna. Washington, DC: The Catholic University of America, 1970.

————. *Against the Academicians*; *The Teacher.* Translated by Peter King. Indianapolis, IN: Hackett, 1995.

————. *The Enchiridion on Faith, Hope and Love.* Translated by J. B. Shaw. Washington, DC: Regnery, 1996.

————. *Homilies on the Gospel of John; Homilies on the First Epistle of John; Soliloquies.* Nicene and Post-Nicene Fathers, 1st series, vol. 7. Edited by Philip Schaff. Peabody, MA: Hendrickson, 2004.

————. *On Genesis: Two Books on Genesis against the Manichees; On the Literal Interpretation of Genesis, an Unfinished Book.* Translated by Roland J. Teske. Washington, DC: Catholic University of America Press, 1991.

————. *Augustine: Early Writings.* Translated and edited by J. H. Burleigh. Philadelphia: Westminster, 2000.

―――. *The Manichean Debate*. Translated by Roland Teske. Edited by Boniface Ramsey. Hyde Park, NY: New City Press, 2006.

―――. *Teaching Christianity*. Translated by Edmund Hill. Edited by John E. Rotelle. Hyde Park, NY: New City Press, 2006.

―――. *Responses to Miscellaneous Questions*. Translated by Boniface Ramsey. Hyde Park, NY: New City Press, 2008.

Ayres, Lewis. *Augustine and the Trinity*. Cambridge: Cambridge University Press, 2010.

―――. *Nicaea and Its Legacy: An Approach to Fourth-Century Trinitarian Theology*. Oxford: Oxford University Press, 2004.

―――. "The Fundamental Grammar of Augustine's Trinitarianism." In *Augustine and His Critics*, edited by Robert Dodaro and George Lawless. London: Routledge, 2000: 51–76.

―――. "'Remember That You Are Catholic' (serm. 52.2): Augustine on the Unity of the Triune God." *Journal of Early Christian Studies* 8, no. 1 (2000): 39–82.

――― and Andrew Radde-Gallwitz. "Doctrine of God." In *The Oxford Handbook of Early Christian Studies*, edited by Susan A. Harvey and David G. Hunter, 864–85. New York: Oxford University Press, 2008.

Baker, Lynne R. *Saving Belief: A Critique of Physicalism*. Princeton: Princeton University Press, 1987.

Barnes, Michel R. "Re-reading Augustine's Theology of Trinity." In *The Trinity: An Interdisciplinary Symposium on the Trinity*, edited by Stephen T. Davis, D. Kendall and Gerald O'Collins, 145–76. New York: Oxford University Press, 1999.

―――. "Augustine in Contemporary Trinitarian Theology." *Theological Studies* 56 (1995): 237–50.

Barrow, John D. *Theories of Everything: The Quest for Ultimate Explanation*. Oxford: Clarendon, 1991.

Barth, Karl. *Church Dogmatics* II/1. Translated by G. W. Bromiley and T. F. Torrance. London: T&T Clark, 2009.

Bartholomew, Craig. "The Healing of Modernity: A Trinitarian Remedy? A Critical Dialogue with Colin Gunton's *The One, the Three and the Many: God, Creation and the Culture of Modernity*." *European Journal of Theology* 6, no. 2 (1997): 111–30.

Bigger, Charles P. *Participation: A Platonic Inquiry*. Baton Rouge: Louisiana State University Press, 1968.

Blond, Philip, ed. *Post-secular Philosophy: Between Philosophy and Theology*. London: Routledge, 1998.

Boersma, Gerald P. "The Context of Augustine's Early Theology of the *Imago Dei*." PhD diss., University of Durham, 2013.

Boersma, Hans. *Heavenly Participation: The Weaving of a Sacramental Tapestry*. Grand Rapids, MI: Eerdmans, 2011.

―――. *Nouvelle Théologie and Sacramental Ontology: A Return to Mystery*. Oxford: Oxford University Press, 2009.

Boethius, *The Consolation of Philosophy*. Translated by Peter Walsh. Oxford: Oxford University Press, 1999.

————. *The Theological Tractates*, with an English translation by H. F. Steward and E. K. Rand; *The Consolation of Philosophy*, with an English translation by H. F. Steward. Loeb Classical Library. Cambridge, MA: Harvard University Press, 1973.

Boff, Leonardo. *Trinity and Society*. Translated by Paul Burns. Maryknoll, NY: Orbis, 1988.

Boland, Vivian. *Ideas in God according to Saint Thomas Aquinas*. Studies in the History of Christian Thought 69. Leiden: Brill, 1996.

Bonner, Gerald. "Augustine's Concept of Deification." *Journal of Theological Studies* 37, no. 2 (1986): 369–86.

Bourke, Vernon. *Augustine's View of Reality*. The Saint Augustine Lecture 1963. Villanova: Villanova University Press, 1964.

Bracken, Joseph. *The One in the Many: A Contemporary Reconstruction of the God-World Relations*. Grand Rapids, MI: Eerdmans, 2001.

Brunn, Emilie Z. *St. Augustine: Being and Nothingness*. Translated by Ruth Namad. NY: Paragon House, 1988.

Brower, Jeffery E. "Simplicity and Aseity." In *The Oxford Handbook of Philosophical Theology*, edited by Thomas R. Flint and Michael Rea, 105–28. New York: Oxford University Press, 2011.

Buber, Martin. *I and Thou*. Translated by Walter Kaufmann. Edinburgh: T&T Clark, 1971.

Burrell, David B. "The Act of Creation." In *Creation and the God of Abraham*, edited by David B. Burrell, Carlo Cogliati, Janet M. Soskice and William R. Stoeger, 40–52. Cambridge: Cambridge University Press, 2010.

————. "Aquinas and Islamic and Jewish Thinkers." In *The Cambridge Companion to Aquinas*, edited by Norman Kretzmann and Eleonore Stump, 60–84. Cambridge: Cambridge University Press, 1993.

————. *Freedom and Creation in Three Traditions*. Notre Dame: University of Notre Dame Press, 1993.

————. "Metaphysics of Creation." In *Belief and Metaphysics*, edited by Conor Cunningham and Peter M. Candler, Jr, 66–72. London: SCM, 2007.

————. *Knowing the Unknowable God: Ibn-Sina, Maimonides, Aquinas*. Notre Dame: University of Notre Dame Press, 1986.

————. Review of *On a Complex Theory of a Simple God*, by Christopher Hughes. *Journal of Religion* 72, no.1 (1992): 120–1.

Caro, Mario De and David Macarther, eds. *Naturalism in Question*. Cambridge, MA: Harvard University Press, 2004.

Christian, William A. "Augustine on the Creation of the World." *Harvard Theological Review* 47, no. 1 (1953): 1–25.

Clarke, W. Norris. *Explorations in Metaphysics: Being—God—Person*. Notre Dame, IN: University of Notre Dame Press, 1994.

————. *The One and the Many: A Contemporary Thomistic Metaphysics*. Notre Dame, IN: University of Notre Dame Press, 2001.

————. "The Problem of the Reality and Multiplicity of Divine Ideas in Christian Neoplatonism." In *Neoplatonism and Christian Thought*, edited by Dominic J. O'Meara, 109–27. Albany, NY: State University of New York Press, 1982.

Clayton, Philip. *God and Contemporary Science.* Edinburgh Studies in Constructive Theology. Edinburgh: Edinburgh University Press, 1997.

Coakley, Sarah. "'Person' in the 'Social' Doctrine of the Trinity: A Critique of Current Analytic Discussion." In *The Trinity: An Interdisciplinary Symposium on the Trinity*, edited by Stephen T. Davis, D. Kendall and Gerald O'Collins, 124–44. New York: Oxford University Press, 1999.

Collingwood, R. G. *The Idea of Nature.* Oxford: Clarendon, 1945.

Copan, Paul and William L. Craig. *Creation Out of Nothing: A Biblical, Philosophical and Scientific Exploration.* Grand Rapids, MI: Baker Academic, 2004.

Copleston, Fredrick C. *Aquinas.* Harmondsworth, UK: Penguin, 1955.

Cunningham, Conor. *Genealogy of Nihilism: Philosophies of Nothing and the Difference of Theology.* London: Routledge, 2002.

———. "Trying My very Best to Believe Darwin, or, The Supernaturalistic Fallacy: From Is to Naught." In *Belief and Metaphysics*, edited by Conor Cunningham and Peter M. Candler, 100–40. London: SCM, 2007.

Crouse, Robert. "*Paucis mutatis verbis*: St Augustine's Platonism." In *Augustine and His Critics*, edited by Robert Dodaro and George Lawless, 35–50. London: Routledge, 2000.

Cyril of Alexandria, *Commentary on the Gospel of John.* Translated by P. E. Pusey. Oxford: James Parker, 1874.

Danielson, Dennis R., ed. *The Book of the Cosmos: Imagining the Universe from Heraclitus to Hawking.* Cambridge, MA: Perseus, 2000.

Davis, Oliver. *A Theology of Compassion: Metaphysics of Difference and the Renewal of Tradition.* London: SCM, 2001.

Davison, Andrew P. "The Conceptualization of Finitude in Thomas Aquinas and John Duns Scotus." PhD diss., The University of Cambridge, 2013.

———. *Participation in God: A Study in Christian Doctrine and Metaphysics.* Cambridge: Cambridge University Press, 2019).

De Rijk, L. M. "Causation and Participation in Proclus: The Pivotal Role of Scope Distinction in his Metaphysics." In *On Proclus and his Influence in Medieval Philosophy*, edited by E. P. Bos and P. A. Meijr, 1–34. Leiden: Brill, 1992.

Dolezal, James E. *God without Parts: Divine Simplicity and the Metaphysics of God's Absoluteness.* Eugene, OR: Pickwick, 2011.

———. "Trinity, Simplicity and the Status of God's Personal Relations." *International Journal of Systematic Theology* 16, no. 1 (2014): 79–98.

Doolan, Gregory T. *Aquinas on the Divine Ideas as Exemplary Causes.* Washington DC: Catholic University of America Press, 2008.

Doyle, John J. "The Square of Opposition in Action." *The New Scholasticism* 35 (1961): 41–75.

Dupré, Louis. *Passage to Modernity: An Essay in the Hermeneutics of Nature and Culture.* New Haven: Yale University Press, 1993.

Dunham, Scott A. *Trinity and Creation in Augustine: An Ecological Analysis.* Albany, NY: State University of New York Press, 2008.

Elders, Leo J. *The Philosophical Theology of St. Thomas Aquinas.* Leiden: Brill, 1990.

————. *The Metaphysics of Being of St. Thomas Aquinas in a Historical Perspective.* Leiden: Brill, 1993.

Epperly, Bruce G. *Process Theology: A Guide for the Perplexed.* London: T&T Clarke, 2011.

Evans, George, R. *Augustine on Evil.* Cambridge: Cambridge University Press, 1982.

Fabro, Cornelio. *La Nozione Metafisica di Partecipazione Secondo S. Tommaso d'Aquino,* 2nd ed. Torino: Società Editrice Internazionale, 1950.

————. "Platonism, Neo-Platonism, and Thomism: Convergencies and Divergencies." *The New Scholasticism* 44 (1970): 69–100.

————. "The Intensive Hermeneutics of Thomistic Philosophy: The Notion of Participation." Translated by B. M. Bonansea. *The Review of Metaphysics* 27, no. 3 (1974): 449–91.

————. "The Overcoming of the Neoplatonic Triads of Being, Life and Intellect by Thomas Aquinas." In *Neoplatonism and Christian Thought,* edited by Dominic J. O'Meara, 97–108. Albany, NY: State University of New York Press, 1982.

Farmer, Tamsin J. "Revealing the Invisible: Gregory of Nyssa on the Gift of Revelation." *Modern Theology* 21, no. 1 (2005): 67–85.

Foster, Michael B. "The Christian Doctrine of Creation and the Rise of Modern Science." *Mind* 43 (1934): 446–68.

————. "Christian Theology and Modern Science of Nature I." *Mind* 44 (1935): 439–66.

————. "Christian Theology and Modern Science of Nature II." *Mind* 45 (1936): 1–27.

Fredriksen, Paula. "Beyond the Body/Soul Dichotomy: Augustine on Paul against the Manichees and the Pelagians." *Recherches augustiniennes* 23 (1988): 87–114.

Gay, Craig M. *The Way of the (Modern) Word: Or, Why It's Tempting to Live as if God Doesn't Exist.* Grand Rapids, MI: Eerdmans, 1998.

Ge, Yonghua. "The One and the Many: Revisiting an Old Philosophical Question in the Light of Theologies of Creation and Participation." *The Heythrop Journal* 57, no. 1 (2016): 109–21.

————. "Augustine on Participation and 'the One'." *Sino-Christian Studies* no. 30 (2020): 125–50 (in Chinese).

————. "Did Augustine Really Denigrate Multiplicity and Matter? Rethinking Gunton's Accusation." *Sino-Christian Studies* no. 23 (2017): 81–106 (in Chinese).

————. "The Role of *creation ex nihilo* in Augustine's *Confessions.*" *Sino-Christian Studies* 22 (2016): 41–64.

Geiger, L.-B. *La participation dans la philosophie de saint Thomas d'Aquin,* 2nd ed. Paris: Vrin, 1953.

Gilson, Etienne. *Being and Some Philosophers,* 2nd ed. Toronto: Pontifical Institute of Medieval Studies, 1952.

————. *Reason and Revelation in the Middle Ages.* New York: Scribner, 1950.

————. *The Christian Philosophy of St Augustine.* Translated by L. Lynch. New York: Random House, 1960.

————. *The Unity of Philosophical Experience.* New York: Scribner, 1950.

————. *God and Philosophy.* New Haven, CT: Yale University Press, 2002.

Gerson, Lloyd. ed. *The Cambridge Companion to Plotinus*. Cambridge: Cambridge University Press, 1996.

———. "Plotinus's Metaphysics: Emanation or Creation?" *The Review of Metaphysics* 46, no. 3 (1993): 559–74.

Goris, Harm, Herwi Rikhof, and Henk Schoot, eds. *Divine Transcendence and Immanence in the Works of Thomas Aquinas: A Collection of Studies Presented at the Third Conference of the Thomas Instituut te Utrecht, December 15-17, 2005.* Leuven: Peeters, 2009.

Green, Bradley G. "The Postmodern Augustine? Gunton and the Failure of Augustine." *International Journal of Systematic Theology* 9, no.3 (2007): 328–41.

———. *Colin Gunton and the Failure of Augustine: The Theology of Colin Gunton in the light of Augustine*. Eugene, OR: Wipf and Stock, 2011.

———. "Colin Gunton and the Theological Origin of Modernity." In *The Theology of Colin Gunton*, edited by Lincoln Harvey, 165–81. London: T & T Clark, 2012.

Gregory of Nyssa. *From Glory to Glory*. Translated by Herbert Musurillo. Crestwood, New York: St. Vladimir's Seminary Press, 1995.

Grenz, Stanley J. *The Named God and the Question of Being: A Trinitarian Theo-ontology*. Louisville, KY: Westminster John Knox, 2011.

Gunton, Colin E. *The One, the Three and the Many: God, Creation and the Culture of Modernity*. Cambridge: Cambridge University Press, 1993.

———. "Augustine, the Trinity and the Theological Crisis of the West." *Scottish Journal of Theology* 43, no.1 (1990): 33–58.

———. "The Doctrine of Creation." In *The Cambridge Companion to Christian Doctrine*, edited by Colin E. Gunton, 141–88. Cambridge: Cambridge University Press, 1997.

Guthrie, W. K. C. *A History of Greek Philosophy*, Vol. 1, *The Earlier Presocratics and the Pythagoreans*. Cambridge: Cambridge University Press, 1971.

Halper, E. "Aristotle on the Convertibility of One and Being." *The New Scholasticism* 59 (1985): 213–27.

Harrison, Carol. *Rethinking Augustine's Early Theology: An Argument for Continuity*. Oxford: Oxford University Press, 2006.

———. "The Role of *creatio ex nihilo* in Augustine's *Confessions*." In *Le Confessions Di Agostino (402-2002): Bilancio e Prospective*, 415–19. Roma: Institutum Patristicum Augustinianu, 2003.

Harrison, Simon. *Augustine's Way into the Will: The Theological and Philosophical Significance of De libero aribitrio*. Oxford: Oxford University Press, 2006.

Hart, David B. *The Experience of God: Being, Consciousness, Bliss*. New Haven: Yale University Press. 2013.

———. "The Offering of Names: Metaphysics, Nihilism, and Analogy." In *Reason and the Reasons of Faith*, edited by Paul J. Griffiths and Reinhard Hütter, 255–91. London: T & T Clark, 2005.

———. *The Beauty of the Infinite: The Aesthetics of Christian Faith*. Grand Rapids, MI: Eerdmans, 2003.

Hassel, David J. Review of *Augustine and Christian Platonism*, by A. H. Armstrong. *The Modern Schoolman* 48 (1971): 275–6.

Hawking, Stephan and Leonard Mlodinow. *The Grand Design: New Answers to the Ultimate Questions of Life.* London: Bantam, 2010.

Heidegger, Martin. *The Question Concerning Technology and Other Essays.* Translated by William Loviit. New York: Harper & Row, 1977.

Henry, Paul. *The Path to Transcendence: From Philosophy to Mysticism in Saint Augustine.* Pittsburgh Theological Monograph Series 37. Translated by Francis F. Burch. Pittsburgh: Pickwick, 1981.

Höhne, David A. "The Spirit and Sonship: Colin Gunton's Theology of Particularity." PhD diss., The University of Cambridge, 2006.

Hua, Wei 花威. "Lun Aogusiding Yizhi Gainian de Yuanqi" 论奥古斯丁意志概念的缘起 [On the rise of Augustine's concept of *voluntas*]. *Sino-Christian Studies* 汉语基督教学术评论 15 (2013): 111–29.

Hubler, J. Noel. "*Creatio ex nihilo*: Matter, Creation and the Body in Classical and Christian Philosophy through Aquinas." PhD diss., University of Pennsylvania, 1995.

Hughes, Christopher. *A Complex Theory of a Simple God.* Ithaca, NY: Cornell University Press, 1989.

Hughes, John. "*Creatio ex nihilo* and Divine Ideas in Aquinas: How Fair is Bulgakov's Critique?." *Modern Theology* 29, no. 2 (2013): 124–37.

Husbands, Mark. "The Trinity is *Not* Our Social Program: Volf, Gregory of Nyssa and Barth." In *Trinitarian Theology for the Church: Scripture, Community, Worship*, edited by Daniel J. Treier and David Lauber, 120–41. Downers Grove, IL: IVP Academic, 2009.

Irwin, Terrence H. "Who Discovered the Will." *Philosophical Perspective* 6 (1992): 454–73.

James, William. *Pragmatism: A New Way for Some Old Ways of Thinking*; *The Meaning of Truth, a Sequel to Pragmatism.* Cambridge, MA: Harvard University Press, 1907, reprint 1987.

Jenson Robert. "A Decision Tree of Colin Gunton's Thinking." In *The Theology of Colin Gunton*, edited by Lincoln Harvey, 8–16. London: T & T Clark, 2012.

Jordon, Mark D. "Theology and Philosophy." In *The Cambridge Companion to Aquinas,* edited by Norman Kretzmann and Eleonore Stump, 232–51. Cambridge: Cambridge University Press, 1993.

Jüngel, Eberhard. *God's Being Is in Becoming: Trinitarian Being of God in the Theology of Karl Barth.* Translated by John Webster. Edinburgh: T&T Clark, 2001.

Kenny, Anthony. *A New History of Western Philosophy.* Oxford: Clarendon Press, 2010.

King, Andrew A. "St. Augustine's Doctrine of Participation as a Metaphysics of Persuasion." *Rhetoric Society Quarterly* 15, no. 3 (1985): 112–15.

Knowles, David. *The Evolution of Medieval Thought.* New York: Vintage, 1962.

Kress, D. A. "Augustine's Privation Account of Evil: A Defence." *Augustinian Studies* 20 (1989): 109–28.

Kretzmann, Norman. *The Metaphysics of Creation: Aquinas's Natural Theology in* Summa contra Gentiles *II.* Oxford: Clarendon; New York: Oxford University Press, 1999.

Lamont, John. "Aquinas on Divine Simplicity." *The Monist* 80, no. 4 (1997): 521–38.

Taylor, Charles. *A Secular Age*. Cambridge, MA: Harvard University Press, 2007.

Levinas, Emmanuel. *Totality and Infinity: An Essay on Exteriority*. Translated by Alphonso Lingis. Pittsburgh: Duquesne University Press, 1969.

Levine, Michael P. *Pantheism: A Non-theistic Concept of Deity*. London: Routledge, 1994.

Lindbeck, George. "Participation and Existence in the Interpretation of St. Thomas Aquinas." *Franciscan Studies* 17 (1957): 1–22, 107–25.

Little, Arthur. *The Platonic Heritage of Thomism*. Dublin: Golden Eagle, 1950.

Leftow, Brian. "Anti Social Trinitarianism." In *The Trinity: An Interdisciplinary Symposium on the Trinity*, edited by Stephen T. Davis, D. Kendall and Gerald O'Collins, 203–49. New York: Oxford University Press, 1999.

Lössl, Josef. "The One *(unum)* - A Guiding Concept in *De uera religion*: An Outline of the Text and the History of Its Interpretation." *Revue des Études Augustiniennes,* 40 (1994): 79–103.

Louth, Andrew. *The Origins of the Christian Mystical Tradition from Plato to Denys*. Oxford: Oxford University Press, 1981.

Lovejoy. Arthur. *The Great Chain of Being: A Study of the History of an Idea*. Cambridge, MA: Harvard University Press, 1936.

MacDonald, Scott. "The Divine Nature." In *The Cambridge Companion to Augustine*, edited by Eleonore Stump and Norman Kretzmann, 71–90. Cambridge: Cambridge University Press, 2001.

———, ed. *Being and Goodness: The Concept of Good in Metaphysics and Philosophical Theology*. Ithaca, NY: Cornell University Press, 1991.

Marion, Jean-Luc. *God without Being*, hors-texte, 2nd ed. Translated by Thomas A. Carlson. Chicago, IL: The University of Chicago Press, 1995.

Marrocco, Mary N. "Participation in the Divine Life in St. Augustine's *De Trinitate* and Selected Contemporary Homiletic Discourses." PhD diss., University of St. Michael's College, 2000.

May, Gerhard. *Creatio Ex Nihilo: The Doctrine of 'Creation out of Nothing' in Early Christian Thought*. Translated by A. S. Worrall. Edinburgh: T&T Clark, 1994.

Maximus the Confessor. *On the Cosmic Mystery of Christ: Selected Writings from St. Maximus the Confessor*. Translated by Paul M. Blowers and Robert L. Wilken. Crestwood, NY: St. Vladimir's Seminary Press, 2003.

McCormak, Bruce L. "The One, the Three and the Many: In Memory of Colin Gunton." *Cultural Encounters* 1, no. 1 (2005): 7–17.

McGrath, Alister E. *The Science of God: An Introduction to Scientific Theology*. New York: T&T Clarke, 2004.

McIntosh, Mark. "The Maker's Meaning: Divine Ideas and Salvation." *Theology* 28, no. 3 (2012): 365–84.

McMullin, Ernan. "Creation *ex nihilo*: Early History." In *Creation and the God of Abraham*, edited by David B. Burrell, Carlo Cogliati, Janet M. Soskice and William R. Stoeger, 11–23. Cambridge: Cambridge University Press, 2010.

McWhorter, Matthew R. "Aquinas's Theology of Creation in *Summa theologiae*: A Study and Defense of Selected Questions." PhD diss., Ave Maria University, 2011.

Meconi, David Vincent. "St. Augustine's Early Theory of Participation." *Augustinian Studies* 27 (1996): 81–98.

———. *The One Christ: St. Augustine's Theology of Deification*. Washington, DC: The Catholic University of America Press, 2013.

Milbank, John, and Catherine Pickstock. *Truth in Aquinas*, Radical Orthodoxy Series. London: Routledge, 2001.

Milbank, John, Catherine Pickstock, and Graham Ward, eds. *Radical Orthodoxy: A New Theology*. London: Routledge, 1999.

Milbank, John. *Theology and Social Theory: Beyond Secular Reason*. Oxford: Blackwell, 1990.

———. "Materialism and Transcendence." In *Theology and the Political: The New Debate*, edited by Creston Davis, John Milbank and Slavoj Žižek, 393–426. Durham, NC: Duke University Press, 2005.

Moltmann, Jürgen. *God in Creation: A New Theology of Creation and the Spirit of God*. Translated by Margaret Kohl. Minneapolis: Fortress, 1993.

———. *The Trinity and the Kingdom of God: The Doctrine of God*. Translated by Margaret Kohl. London: SCM, 1981.

Moser, Paul and J. D. Trout, eds. *Contemporary Materialism: A Reader*. London: Routledge, 1995.

Mullins, R. T. "Simply Impossible: A Case against Divine Simplicity." *Journal of Reformed Theology* 123, no. 7 (2013): 181–203.

Nagel, Thomas. *Mind and Cosmos: Why the Materialist Neo-Darwinian Concept of Nature is Almost Certainly Wrong*. New York: Oxford University Press, 2012.

Nausner, Bernhard. "The Failure of a Laudable Project: Gunton, the Trinity and Human Self-Understanding." *Scottish Journal of Theology* 62, no. 4 (1992): 403–20.

Norris, Richard A. *God and World in Early Christian Theology*. London: Adam & Charles Black, 1966.

O'Brien, David. *The Origin of Matter and the Origin of Evil in Plotinus's Criticism of the Gnostics*. Paris: Épiméthé Paris Presses Universitaires de, 1990.

O'Donnell, James J. *Augustine: Confessions III: Commentary on Book 8-13*. Oxford: Clarendon, 1992.

Oliver, Simon. *Philosophy, God and Motion*. London: Routledge, 2005.

O'Meara, John J. "The Neoplatonism of Saint Augustine." In *Neoplatonism and Christian Thought*, edited by Dominic J. O'Meara, 34–44. Albany, NY: State University of New York Press, 1982.

Ormerod, Neil. "Augustine and the Trinity: Whose Crisis?" *Pacifica* 16 (2003): 17–32.

O'Rourke, Fran. "Aquinas and Platonism." In *Contemplating Aquinas: On the Varieties of Interpretation*, edited by Fergus Kerr, 263–72. London: SCM, 2003.

Ortiz, Jared. "Creation in Saint Augustine's *Confessions*." PhD diss., The Catholic University of America, 2012.

O'Tool, Christopher J. *The Philosophy of Creation in the Writings of St. Augustine*. The Catholic University of America Philosophy Series. Washington, DC: Catholic University of America Press, 1944.

Owen, Joseph. "Aristotle and Aquinas." In *The Cambridge Companion to Aquinas*, edited by Norman Kretzmann and Eleonore Stump, 38–59. Cambridge: Cambridge University Press, 1993.

Pabst, Adrian. *Metaphysics: The Creation of Hierarchy*. Grand Rapids, MI: Eerdmanns, 2012.

Pannenberg, Wolfhart. *Systematic Theology*, vol.1. Translated by Geoffrey W. Bromiley. Grand Rapids, MI: Eerdmans, 1991.

Pegis, Acton C. *Saint Thomas and the Greeks*. The Aquinas Lecture 1939. Marquette: Marquette University Press, 1939.

———. "The Dilemma of Being and Unity." In *Essays in Thomism*, edited by R. Brennan, 158–9. New York: Sheed and Ward, 1942.

Perl, Eric. "Hierarchy and Participation in Dionysius the Areopagite and Greek Neoplatonism." *American Catholic Philosophical Quarterly* 73, no. 1 (1994): 15–30.

———. "The Presence of the Paradigm: Immanence and Transcendence in Plato's Theory of Forms." *The Review of Metaphysics* 53 (1999): 339–62.

Pickstock, Catherine. *After Writing: On the Liturgical Consummation of Philosophy*. London: Blackwell-Wiley, 1997.

Pieper, Josef. *The Silence of St. Thomas*. Translated by John Murray and Daniel O'Connor. South Bend, IN: St. Augustine's Press, 1999.

Pinnock, Clark H., Richard Rice, John Sander, William Hasker, and David Basinger. *The Openness of God: A Biblical Challenge to the Traditional Understanding of God*. Downers Grove, IL: IVP, 1994.

Plantinga, Alvin. *Does God Have a Nature?* Milwaukee, WI: Marquette University Press, 1980.

Plato, *Timaeus and Critias*. Translated by A. E. Taylor. London: Methuen, 1929.

———. *Cratylus; Parmenides; Greater Hippias; Lesser Hippias*, with an English Translation by H. N. Fowler. Loeb Classical Library. Cambridge, MA: Harvard University Press, 1926.

———. *The Republic of Plato*. Translated by F. M. Cornford. Oxford: Oxford University Press, 1972.

———. *Phaedo*. Translated by David Gallop. Oxford: Clarendon Press, 1975.

Plotinus. *The Enneads*. Translated by Stephen MacKenna. London: Faber and Faber, 1969.

———. *The Enneads*. Edited by Lloyd P. Gerson. Translated by George Boys-Stones, John M. Dillon, Lloyd P. Gerson, R. A. H. King, Andrew Smith and James Wilberding. Cambridge: Cambridge University Press, 2019.

Popper, Karl. *The Open Society and Its Enemies*, Vol. 1, *The Spell of Plato*. London: Routledge, 1962.

Rahner, Karl. *The Trinity*. Translated by Joseph Donceel. London: Burns and Oates, 1970.

Régis, Louis-Marie. *St. Thomas and Epistemology*. The Aquinas Lecture 1946. Milwaukee, IL: Marquette University Press, 1946.

Reno, R. R. "Review of *Radical Orthodoxy: A New Theology*." *Modern Theology* 15 (1999): 530.

Rice, Richard. *The Openness of God: The Relationship of Divine Foreknowledge and Human Free Will.* Hagerstown, MD: Review and Herald Pub. Association, 1980.

Rist, John. *Augustine: Ancient Thought Baptised.* Cambridge: Cambridge University Press, 1996.

———. *Plotinus: The Road to Reality.* Cambridge: Cambridge University Press, 1967.

———. *Platonism and Its Christian Heritage.* London: Variorum,1985.

———. "Plotinus and Augustine on Evil." In *Plotino ed il Neoplatonismo in Oriente e in Occidente.* Rome: Accademia Nazionale dei Lincei, 1974.

Rushdoony, Rousas J. "The One and the Many Problem – The Contribution of Van Til." In *Jerusalem and Athens: Critical Discussions on the Theology and Apologetics of Cornelius Van Til,* edited by R. Geehan, 339–48. Philipsburg, NJ: Presbyterian and Reformed, 1971.

Russell, Collin. *Cross-Currents: Interactions between Science and Faith.* Leicester, UK: IVP, 1985.

Russell, Norman. *The Doctrine of Deification in the Greek Patristic Tradition.* Oxford: Oxford University Press, 2006.

Schindler, David C. "What's the Difference? On the Metaphysics of Participation in a Christian Context." *The Saint Anselm Journal* 3, no. 1 (2005): 1–27.

Schleiermacher, Friedrich. *On Religion: Speeches to Its Cultured Despisers.* Translated by Richard Crouter. Cambridge: Cambridge University Press, 1996.

Schwartz, Regina M. *The Violence of Monotheism.* Chicago, IL: The University of Chicago Press, 1997.

Sinnige, TH. G. "Gnostic Influences in the Early Works of Plotinus and Augustine." In *Plotinus amid Gnostics and Christians,* edited by David T. Runia, 73–98. Amsterdam: Free University Press, 1984.

Smith, James K. A. *Introducing Radical Orthodoxy: Mapping a Post-secular Theology.* Grand Rapids, MI: Baker Academic, 2012.

Smith, James K., and James H. Olthuis, eds. *Radical Orthodoxy and the Reformed Tradition: Creation, Covenant, and Participation.* Grand Rapids, MI: Baker Academic, 2005.

Somma, Ianuarius D. "De naturali participatione divini luminis in mente humana secundum S. Augustinum et S. Thoman." *Gregorianum* 7 (1926): 321–38.

Sorabji, Richard. *Time, Creation and the Continuum: Theories in Antiquity and the Early Middle Ages.* London: Duckworth, 1983.

Soskice, Janet M. "*Creatio ex nihilo*: Jewish and Christian Foundations." In *Creation and the God of Abraham,* edited by David B. Burrell, Carlo Cogliati, Janet M. Soskice and William R. Stoeger, 24–39. Cambridge: Cambridge University Press, 2010.

———."Athens and Jerusalem, Alexandria and Edessa: Is There a Metaphysics of Scripture?" *International Journal of Systematic Theology* 8, no. 2 (2006): 149–62.

———. "Aquinas and Augustine on Creation and God as 'Eternal Being.'" *New Blackfriars* 95 (2014): 190–207.

———. "Augustine on Knowing God and Knowing the Self." In *Faithful Reading: New Essays in Theology in Honour of Fergus Kerr, O.P.*, edited by Thomas O'Loughlin, Karen Kilby and Simon Oliver, 61–74. London: T&T Clark, 2012.

———. "Naming God: A Study in Faith and Reason." In *Reason and the Reasons of Faith*, edited by Paul J. Griffiths and Reinhard Hütter, 241–54. London: T & T Clark, 2005.

Stokes, Michael C. *One and Many in Presocratic Philosophy*. Washington, DC: Center for Hellenistic Studies, distributed by Harvard University Press, 1971.

Sweeny, Leo. *Divine Infinity in Greek and Medieval Thought*. New York: Peter Lang, 1992.

Stump, Eleonore. "God's simplicity." In *The Oxford Handbook of Aquinas*, edited by Brian David and Eleonore Stump, 135–46. New York: Oxford University Press, 2012.

Tallon, H. J. "Does Thomas Neglect Multitude?" *The New Scholasticism* 37 (1963): 267–92.

Tanner, Kathryn. *God and Creation in Christian Theology: Tyranny or Empowerment?* Oxford: Basil Blackwell, 1998.

———. *Christ the Key*. Current Issues in Theology. Cambridge: Cambridge University Press, 2010.

Te Velde, Rudi. *Participation and Substantiality in Thomas Aquinas*. Leiden: Brill, 1995.

———. *Aquinas on God: The 'Divine Science' of the* Summa Theologiae. UK: Ashgate, 2006.

———. "Metaphysics and the Question of Creation: Thomas Aquinas, Duns Scotus and Us." In *Belief and Metaphysics*, edited by Conor Cunningham and Peter M. Candler, Jr, 73–99. London: SCM, 2007.

———. "Thomas Aquinas's Understanding of Prayer in the Light of the Doctrine of *Creatio ex nihilo.*" *Modern Theology* 29, no. 2 (2013): 49–61.

Teske, Roland. "The Image and Likeness of God in St. Augustine's *De Genesi ad litteram liber imperfectus.*" *Augustinianum* 30 (1990): 441–51.

Torchia, N. Joseph. *Creatio ex nihilo and the Theology of St. Augustine: The Anti-Manichaean Polemic and beyond*. New York: Peter Lang, 1999.

Torrance, Alan J. *Persons in Communion: An essay on Trinitarian Description and Human Participation with Special Reference to Volume One of Karl Barth's* Church Dogmatics. Edinburgh: T&T Clark, 1996.

Trapé, Agonstino. *Patrology*, vol. 4, edited by Angelo Di Berardino. Allen, TX: Christian Classics, 1986.

Turner, Denys. *Faith, Reason and the Existence of God*. Cambridge: Cambridge University Press, 2004.

Vorster, N. "A Critical Assessment of John Milbank's Christology." *Acta Theologica* 32, no. 2 (2012): 277–98.

Volf, Mirosalv. "'The Trinity is Our Social Program': The Doctrine of the Trinity and the Shape of Social Engagement." *Modern Theology* 14, no. 3 (1998): 403–23.

Wainwright, William J. "Augustine on God's Simplicity: A Reply." *The New Scholasticism* 53 (1979): 118–23.

Ward, Graham. *Cities of God*, Radical Orthodoxy Series. London: Routledge, 2001.

Webster, John. "'Love Is Also a Lover of Life': *Creatio ex nihilo* and Creaturely Goodness." *Modern Theology* 29, no. 2 (2013): 156–71.

———. "Systematic Theology after Barth: Jüngel, Jenson and Gunton." In *The Modern Theologians: An Introduction to Christian Theology since 1918*, 3rd ed., edited by David F. Ford and Rachel Muers, 249–64. London: Wiley-Blackwell, 2005.

Westphal, Merold. *Overcoming Onto-theology: Toward a Postmodern Christian Faith*. Washington, DC: Fordham University Press, 2011.

———. "Participation and Kenosis: A List for Schindler." *The Saint Anselm Journal* 3, no. 1 (2005): 28–37.

Williams, Rowan D. "Afterword: Making Differences." In *Balthasar at the End of Modernity*, edited by Lucy Gardner, *et al.* Edinburgh: T&T Clark, 1999: 173–9.

———. "'Good for Nothing'? Augustine on Creation." *Augustinian Studies* 25 (1994): 9–24.

———. "Insubstantial Evil." In *Augustine and His Critics*, edited by Robert Dodaro and George Lawless. London and New York: Routledge, 2000: 105–23.

Williams, Stephen N. *Revelation and Reconciliation: A Window on Modernity*. Cambridge: Cambridge University Press, 1995.

Wilken, Robert L. *The Spirit of Early Christian Thought: Seeking the Face of God*. New Haven: Yale University Press, 2003.

Wilson-Kastner, Patricia. "Grace as Participation in the Divine Life in the Theology of Augustine of Hippo." *Augustinian Studies* 7 (1976): 135–52.

Wippel, John F. *The Metaphysical Thought of Thomas Aquinas: From Finite Being to Uncreated Being*. Washington, DC: The Catholic University Press of America, 2000.

———. "Metaphysics." In *The Cambridge Companion to Aquinas*, edited by Norman Kretzmann and Eleonore Stump, 85–127. Cambridge: Cambridge University Press, 1993.

———. *Aquinas on the Divine Ideas*. Etienne Gilson Series 16. Toronto: Pontifical Institute of Medieval Studies, 1993.

———. "Thomas Aquinas on the Distinction and Derivation of the Many from the One: A Dialectic between Being and Nonbeing." *The Review of Metaphysics* 30 (1985): 563–90.

Wisse, Maarten. *Trinitarian Theology beyond Participation: Augustine's De Trinitate and Contemporary Theology*. London, UK: Continuum, 2011.

Young, Frances. "'Creatio Ex Nihilo': A Context for the Emergence of the Christian Doctrine of Creation." *Scottish Journal of Theology* 44, no. 2 (1991): 139–51.

Yu, Carver T. *Being and Relation: A Theological Critique of Western Dualism and Individualism*. Edinburgh: Scottish Academic, 1987.

Zizioulas, John D. *Being as Communion: Studies in the Person and the Church*. London: Darton, Longman and Todd, 1985.

Index

accident, 36, 48, 49, 61, 62, 97, 102, 108, 146
analogy of being, 3, 6, 54, 104
Aquinas, Thomas: on concept of participation, 9–11, 88, 96, 101–5, 109, 113, 135–36, 141–43, 149, 153, 160–66; on *creatio ex nihilo*, 10–12, 96–101, 111, 136, 142–45, 149, 154–55, 157, 163–64; on divine simplicity, 11, 97, 105, 108–13, 126, 132, 134, 144; on God's immanence, 11, 101, 145–49, 153–59, 165–66; on God's transcendence, 11, 101, 143–45, 149–53, 166; on metaphysic of creation, 9–11, 95–101, 104–5, 112, 122, 129, 141–43, 158; on multiplicity, 11, 119–36; on relation between God and creation, 11, 104, 141–43; relation to Platonism, 95–98, 102–5, 109–13, 119, 122, 127–36, 139, 144–53, 156, 163; on unity, 104–13
Arius, 124–25
Aristotle, 24, 32, 36, 48–50, 98, 101–6, 119–20, 122, 132, 142, 144, 146–48, 150–51, 156
Armstrong, A. H., 85
Athanasius, 18
Augustine: on concept of creation, 8, 9, 24–30, 45, 53, 57, 71, 77, 81, 156;

on concept of participation, 8–11, 17–24, 27–29, 38, 50, 52, 62, 71; on *creatio ex nihilo*, 11, 17, 24–27, 30, 38, 45, 48–54, 63, 67, 76, 84, 95–96, 149, 151–56; on divine simplicity, 10, 23, 29, 35–38, 47, 49, 95, 108; on God's immanence, 11, 71, 80–88, 147, 156; on God's transcendence, 11, 71, 73–81, 83–85; on immutability, 21–22, 26, 30, 36, 44n102, 47, 49, 68n17, 74, 76–77, 79, 153–54; on matter, 55–67; on multiplicity, 10–11, 37–38, 45–54, 71; relation to Platonism, 17–35, 37–38, 45, 47, 49–67, 71–82, 85–88, 95, 156; on unity, 10–11, 17, 29–38, 54, 71
Avicenna, 97, 127, 146, 148
Averroës, 97

Barrow, John D., 156
Barth, Karl, 2
being, 4, 26–29, 32–38, 49, 54, 72, 76, 79–83, 99–101, 104–7, 110–12, 120–24, 142, 148, 154–55
Being, the, 10, 26, 28–36, 38, 49, 54, 76, 78, 79, 84, 105, 110, 112, 154
Big Bang, the, 100, 164
Blond, Philip, 3

183

About the Author

Dr. **Yonghua Ge** is the Director of the Mandarin Program and Assistant Professor of Theology & Intercultural Philosophy at ACTS Seminaries of Trinity Western University. A native of China, he holds a PhD in Christian Theology and Philosophy of Religion from the University of Cambridge and did postdoctoral research in Jesus College, Cambridge University, and Regent College before coming to Trinity Western University. He has published in leading journals such as *Philosophy East and West, The Heythrop Journal, Tyndale Bulletin, Sino-Christian Studies*, and *Logos & Pneuma: Chinese Journal of Theology*, and is the author of *The Many and the One: Creation as Participation in Augustine and Aquinas*.